Dangerous Women

Clare Conville is a literary agent and discovered DBC Pierre on the Victoria line. She lives in London with her children and isn't very good at gardening.

Liz Hoggard is a columnist and interviewer who writes for the *Evening Standard*, *Observer* and *Independent*, and a variety of magazines. She lives in Peckham and her favourite words in the English language are 'restaurant' and 'taxi'.

Sarah-Jane Lovett has delivered The Bad Sex Awards, hosted numerous literary salons and performed her own poetry. She has appeared in French Absurdist plays, worked as a journalist and diarist on several newspapers and attended way too many parties. She has two children, lives in London and drives a black taxi.

Dangerous Women

The Guide to Modern Life

Clare Conville, Liz Hoggard
& Sarah-Jane Lovett

Weidenfeld & Nicolson

LONDON

First published in Great Britain in 2011
by Weidenfeld & Nicolson;
This hardback edition published in 2013
by Weidenfeld & Nicolson,
an imprint of Orion Books Ltd,
Orion House, 5 Upper Saint Martin's Lane,
London WC2H 9EA

An Hachette UK company

1 3 5 7 9 10 8 6 4 2

A CIP catalogue record for this book
is available from the British Library.

ISBN: 978 0 2978 6934 4

Typeset by Input Data Services Ltd, Bridgwater, Somerset

Printed and bound by CPI Group (UK) Ltd, Croydon CR0 4YY

The Orion Publishing Group's policy is to use papers that
are natural, renewable and recyclable products and
made from wood grown in sustainable forests. The logging
and manufacturing processes are expected to conform to
the environmental regulations of the country of origin.

www.orionbooks.co.uk

Dedicatees

For my beautiful children, Tom, Ted and Milly and
for DW Rowan Pelling and for Sue Armstrong
– CBC

To the friends I can call at 4 a.m.
(thank you, Marlene Dietrich),
this really is the best bit . . .
– LH

For Otis and Queenie Ingrams, forever
– SJL

'Now that our brain power cannot be
doubted our bodies have been requisitioned.
When a woman cannot feel comfortable in
her own body she has no home.'
– Jeanette Winterson

'What are days for?
Days are where we live.
They come, they wake us
Time and time over.
They are to be happy in:
Where can we live but days?'
– 'Days', Philip Larkin

'I am because you are.'
– African proverb

'If there's a book you
really want to read but
it hasn't been written yet,
then you must write it.'
– Toni Morrison

'If there is one person who is still not free, then I am not;
if there is one person who still suffers from insult and humiliation,
then I do.
Do you understand yet?'
– Ai Weiwei

❧

'Begin anywhere.'
– John Cage

'Introduction to the new edition'

'You are – your life and nothing else'
Jean-Paul Sartre

The idea to write *Dangerous Women: A Guide to Modern Life* arose out of many conversations. Liz, Sarah-Jane and I would meet as women do to chat, to talk about what became known as 'the stuff' and we gradually came to realise that while the topics we discussed were diverse, the themes remained constant. We also believed that many women of all ages were probably talking about the same things, at home, at school, at work, in bars with friends, mothers, sisters and cousins.

Some fifty years after a defining moment in women's emancipation: the legalisation of the 'The Pill', we realised that we were examining our own and other women's lives, perhaps in rather roundabout ways, but still asking some key questions:-

Had we fulfilled the dreams of the many women who had struggled to establish our basic human rights? Were we living 'good' lives? What would it be like to be born a girl in the 21st century as opposed to the 20th? Were we handling the choices we had been given, some would say blessed with, well enough? Why did we always feel so guilty so much of the time? What advice would we give to our daughters? And in case we were, in the words of Elizabeth II, at risk of 'taking ourselves too seriously' . . . were we having fun?

The 'stuff' eventually crystallised into a book of entries in alphabetical order which ranged from 'affairs', 'sloe gin' and 'pearls' to 'loneliness', 'making a will' and 'opening brown envelopes' and we also came up with the notion of cross-referencing so if you followed 'affairs' it would also take you not only to 'camiknickers' and 'contraception', but also to 'family therapy' and 'lawyers'. This helped us create narratives throughout the book which in turn allowed us to embrace conflicting viewpoints, tackle big themes; for instance, although cancer doesn't have its own entry, there are some seven related entries from 'hair loss', 'mummy boxes' to 'ward-wear', and reflect complex and often conflicting emotions and outcomes which we came to see, were a truer reflection of women's experience.

If we ever faltered for a second in what we were trying to do, it was when our brilliant American editor advised us to drop the use of the word 'feminist' in the US edition of the book: 'too academic', 'too boring'. So it is thrilling to see in the space of two years that word coming back in to general use and a generation of young women from around the world inspired by, among others, the story of Malala and the determination of the Pink Sari Revolution to begin once more to contextualise their experiences within a feminist framework. However, it is tragic that lives have also been lost and continue to be lost in this process.

Life can be painful. Alongside the entries we had what we felt were insightful and hopefully useful quotes from men as well as women, written in moments of deep joy and sometimes great despair. And while we have all experienced the often challenging nature of relationships between the sexes, both in the private and public spheres, we believe that women and men should enjoy their differences and reiterate their similarities. Indeed, we stole our motto 'Live as well as you dare' from a letter written in 1820 by Sydney Smith to Lady Georgina Morpeth in an effort to help her through a bout of severe depression. It's worth digging out the whole letter as it is compassionate, practical, supportive and loving; a blue print for friendship and love between men and women.

Since the book was published we have given readings and enjoyed discussions with women (and men) in bookshops, banks, churches, festivals, bars, tea rooms, hotels and community centres. We have been asked and in turn have asked countless questions about how, to borrow a phrase, 'to be a woman'. It would take hours if not days to piece together the complicated reply but if we were to keep it simple it would be to find self-worth and be *bien dans ta peau* ... happy in your skin. It was wonderful that so many people trusted us enough to share their experiences with us and joyous that the simple but profound African proverb that we had quoted at the beginning of the book, 'I am because you are', became our reality.

Clare Conville
July 2013

A

Abstract thought
'It would be so nice if something would make sense for a change.'
– Alice, from *Alice's Adventures in Wonderland*, LEWIS CARROLL

(v: Lateral thinking)

Accepting a compliment
Accepting a compliment can be extremely hard to do, particularly if you have grown up in an environment of criticism. In fact it is a skill that may take up to a lifetime to accomplish, but it's extremely important that you do.

The most cherished compliments often come out of context, and in unlikely places, and they can often leave the recipient feeling slightly lost for words. Poor compliment etiquette is when you 'deny' the compliment giver, i.e. you imply that the compliment given isn't actually true, because this means that he or she has to redouble his or her efforts and turns a charming, life-enhancing, generous gesture into slightly tedious, therapeutic reassurance.

The double-whammy is that you have also insulted the

giver a little. The underlying message being that they are somehow not intelligent enough, perceptive enough, or don't know enough about you to make this call.

So acknowledge the compliment gracefully, a simple but heartfelt 'Thank you' will suffice, and let the truth in about yourself too. Gradually, without becoming vain, you will develop self-acceptance and secret confidence.

(v: Secret confidence, Self-deprecation, Underbrag (The))

Accepting invitations

Whether it's a no or a yes to the opening of a biscuit tin it is extremely important that you respond, politely and in good time, to invitations. Our preferred method of reply is, of course, a handwritten letter but if this is just totally unrealistic, a text or email to the relevant person will do. If it was a private event such as a supper, a party or a trip to the theatre or something similar, don't forget to write a proper thank-you letter.

(v: Debt, Money matters)

Accepting responsibility

(v: Boundaries, Breaking the rules, Grasping the nettle, Money matters, Opening brown envelopes)

Adventure

'Adventure is worthwhile in itself.'
– AMELIA EARHART

What do you want to do? Where do you want to go? Until the twenty-first century, with a few notable exceptions – cf. *The Wilder Shores of Love* by Lesley Blanch – adventure was considered to be the province of men in topees. However, the combination of the vote, rising hemlines, two world wars, contraception, inspiring female athletes, the birth of television and sensationally effective extreme weather wear have opened up infinite vistas for all of us. So, without upsetting the whole domestic applecart, the time has come to be adventurous. A shortlist of near-to-home, gutsy, sports activities can help to focus the mind, challenge the body and blow away the cobwebs and the boom in Internet-based companies offering trekking, canoeing, archery, fencing, hiking, falconry, shooting, riding seems virtually limitless. If you fancy a greater challenge to mind, body and spirit, think about a camping expedition in the Kalahari, a riding holiday in Argentina, a bicycling trip through Cambodia and Vietnam, or charity work in Malawi.

(v: Comfort zone, Long-haul travel, Safety)

Advice (giving and receiving)

If somebody asks for your advice, give it thoughtfully and gracefully in the knowledge that they will, of course, ignore it. Ditto if you are asking for advice. Receive it thoughtfully and graciously before you ignore it. If you are on the receiving end of unasked-for advice, just ignore it. However, a father's advice to his daughter on her twenty-first birthday – 'However much you have to drink you must remember what you said and did in the morning. Never interfere in a great love affair and don't sleep with your secretary' – has stood her in good stead.

(v: Affairs, Insomnia, I don't)

Affairs

Should you or shouldn't you? The answer is that you shouldn't. But, as it is crucial to the excitement of having an affair to let all experience, wisdom and proffered advice go out of the window, you are probably going to go ahead anyway.

An affair can be thrilling: excitingly illicit, deeply passionate and often liberating on many levels – all the things that a long-term relationship isn't. However, affairs can also bring heartbreak, not just to the two people involved, but also to their respective partners, children and extended families.

If you are unable to practise self-restraint here are some guidelines:

1. Don't have an affair with your husband's best friend.
2. Be discreet.
3. Suspenders and stockings are always good.
4. Don't neglect your children.
5. Remember your friends, you may need them in due course.
6. However wonderful it is, remind yourself occasionally that most affairs have a lifetime of six months to two years.
7. Don't slag off your lover's partner, or join in when he does it. It's unfair and it's undignified.
8. If your lover is in a relationship and you are single, only you are allowed to set the rules.
9. If your lover tells you he wants to try and make his marriage work, have the good grace to let him try.
10. Occasionally put yourself through the shipwreck scenario, i.e. what are all the long-term options, both good and bad. Be honest with yourself.

11. If your lover's partner becomes seriously ill in any way, his job is to support her. You must put your relationship on hold.
12. Protect your heart.

(v: Camiknickers, Contraception, Creative corsetry, Family therapy, Grief, I don't, Lawyers, Loss, Money matters, Rejection, Teenagers)

(The) Afterlife

'There is a land of the living and a land of the dead and the bridge is love, the only survival, the only meaning.'
– THORNTON WILDER (1897–1975), *The Bridge of San Luis Ray* (1927)

Age

'Age is enlightenment at gunpoint.'
– ANNA HALPIN

'No woman should ever be quite accurate about her age. It looks so calculating.'
– OSCAR WILDE

'Age cannot wither her, nor custom stale
Her infinite variety.'
– *Antony and Cleopatra*, II. ii., WILLIAM SHAKESPEARE

'Ageing is the result of an accumulation of random molecular damage.'
– LEWIS WOLPERT

Ageless fashion

'Fashion fades, only style remains the same.'
– COCO CHANEL

It's called style. Some people have it and some people just don't.

(The) Age of bereavement

There is a moment in life when you find that you are attending more divorces and funerals than you are weddings and christenings. Losing a close friend or mentor or partner is acutely painful and with the death of both parents comes the final realisation that there is no road back. This milestone is complicated to deal with and you may feel alienated from your partner and/or children. After all, you are meant to be a grown-up, aren't you? It might be worth seeking professional help. Or talk to your friends. Many of your friends will be going through or have already gone through similar experiences. Allow yourself to mourn properly, focus on the good times. On bad days it really is important to use the coping tools of the mundane to get you through, i.e. airing the bedroom, making a fire, planting some geraniums in pots. It is also helpful to 'be the poet of your own life'. Keep a diary, write poetry, write letters. If you find it hard to concentrate, watch TV, listen to music and/or the radio. Sleep. See your mates. Remember that the darkest hour is before the dawn. Hope is essential. You will get through. *(v: BF, Mentors, Therapy)*

Agony
'One often learns more from ten days of agony than ten years of contentment.'
– MERLE SHAIN [journalist and writer]

Emotional agony, it's unmistakable and it can have physical symptoms such as lack of hunger, swift weight loss and feelings of acute stress, which are often accompanied by a racing, churning manic behaviour. We can take medication to overcome it. Or we may choose to live with emotional agony at least for a limited period of time. Therapists will argue that this acute pain, arising as it usually does out of separation from a loved one, through divorce or death, is a spiritual event that marks a moment of transformation. It is a journey into the underworld. The message from the gods is that if we can go through the fire we will find greater self-acceptance, self-knowledge and understanding as a result and return to the land of the living intact.
(*v: Age of bereavement, Ecstasy [not the drug], Persephone*)

A good man is hard to find
But not impossible.
(*v: Good husband material, Hope, Little black book, Top table*)

Alcohol
'*Wer nicht liebt Wein, Weib, Gesang,*
Der bleibt ein Narr sein Leben lang.'

'Who loves not wine, woman, and song
Remains a fool his whole life long.'
– Attributed to MARTIN LUTHER

(v: Bad habits, Booze, Champagne, Cocktails, Co-dependency, Dipsomania, Drunk-dialling, Grappa, How to make a gin Martini, Insomnia)

All about Eve
'She, as a veil, down to a slender waist
Her unadorned golden tresses wore
Dishevelled, but in wanton ringlets waved
As the vine curls her tendrils, which implied
Subjection, but required with gentle sway.
And by her, yielded, by him best received
Yielded with coy submission, modest pride,
And sweet, reluctant, amorous delay.'
– *Paradise Lost*, Book IV, JOHN MILTON

Allergies
For some reason it's hard to be sympathetic if somebody tells you that they can't eat Brazil nuts, nevertheless the fashion for allergies underlies a real twenty-first-century problem. We are too clean, our houses are too clean. And because of the current 'expert advice' on breastfeeding and weaning, our babies may not be getting a wide enough variety of foodstuffs and accompanying bacteria at a young enough age. Couple this with the extraordinarily successful worldwide campaign to eradicate killer diseases and the result is that we are developing incomplete immune systems in bodies that no longer have to fight external intruders (viral and bacterial) and are succumbing to a range of auto-immune diseases instead. It's tiresome but we need to be responsible and sympathetic to those who suffer from allergies and meet their dietary requirements without a murmur. If you suspect that you may be allergic to something, we

won't call you a moaning minny, just please go and get tested. The upside of all of this, for the less house-proud among us, is that there is a valid reason for not cleaning the kitchen floor more than once a week.

(v: Meds)

Allure

The essence of allure is to be in a private relationship with oneself. Allure is an ageless quality that combines sexuality with ancient wisdom, secret confidence, inner depth and the ability to remain still in a busy room. Contemporary ideas of beauty and the over-exposure of models and actresses in newspapers and magazines mean that it is rare to see a famous person who looks alluring. There are just too many light bulbs flashing in the background. The woman in the street, on the other hand, has every chance to develop these qualities.

(v: Elegance, Maturity, Secret confidence, Style)

(The) Almost date (and how to avoid it the second time round)

There was a time when if a man asked you out, you knew what his intentions were. But twenty-first-century dating is a minefield. Is he asking you out – or just out?

In the past, love was a formal contract. Today, romance is so laidback it's horizontal. Sometimes being laissez-faire can suit. It can give you time to get to know him without feeling pressured or rushed. However, if you are already very keen on him and/or very much in the dating zone or just somebody who likes knowing where they stand, here's a checklist from the writers of *He's Just Not That Into You*:

1. Expect a public excursion, a meal and some hand-holding.
2. Hopefully a message post-date to say he had a nice time.
3. Then some kind of further contact within three days.

Hanging out is not dating. If in doubt of his intentions, ask another man. As women, in our desire to be kind and supportive, we often do more harm than good by perpetuating our friends' mad romantic fantasies, i.e. checking out wedding dresses in shops or thinking up baby names, but there are times when we need tough love from the Dating Nazis and in turn your friends might need it from you too.

A trusted male friend will give it to you straight – and shoot down all the sex-cuses. Exhibit A: there is no such thing as mixed messages. If he's not calling you, you're not on his mind. Exhibit B: The dreaded 'It's not you, it's me' is a clue to run for the hills. Men are not complicated. If they like you, they phone. Full stop.

(v: Pep talk from a fiery redhead)

Aloneness (as opposed to loneliness)

'I've just done what I damn well wanted to, and I've made enough money to support myself, and ain't afraid of being alone.'

– KATHERINE HEPBURN

'The freedom of our age is that you can be alone. The price is that you might also have to feel lonely.'

– ALAIN DE BOTTON [Philosopher]

'Never less lonely than when completely alone.'
— CICERO

When you are busy, you aren't alone. Loneliness doesn't sit well with the upbeat image that we like to project to the outside world. People will admit to being depressed (intriguing and melancholy) or drinking too much (spontaneous and fun-loving), but we won't admit to being lonely because it makes us feel a failure.

In modern times there is ever increasing pressure for women to appear to be 'self-contained'. Any kind of neediness is frowned upon, but the truth is that loneliness can have a profound effect on our lives. Recent research has shown that it can damage the chemical and electrical responses in our immune systems that help prevent illness. Some studies argue that loneliness is a bigger killer than cancer or heart disease.

Our monkey ancestors lived in social groups and we have evolved into sociable human beings. The word 'lonely' wasn't used in the contemporary sense until the eighteenth century, partly because everyone lived so closely together that there was never a chance to be so. The Romantic poets changed the concept of loneliness with vivid intensity. Wordsworth's 'I Wandered Lonely as a Cloud', in our effort to express a new tension between the individual self and society.

If you are feeling lonely the first task is to identify whether this is something to be 'cured', or if it is something that needs to be 'managed'. It is also important to distinguish between aloneness, i.e. learning to enjoy a period of solitude whether it is chosen or enforced, and the real, grinding

loneliness that can make you feel like hell. Most important of all, don't beat yourself up for feeling lonely.
(v: Flow, Keep your diary full)

Alpha females
(v: Ambition, Top girls)

Ambition
Why is this still such a dirty word for women? For men ambition is a necessary and desirable part of their lives, but women so often play down their achievements for fear of being seen as egotistic or selfish – or worse still, a 'bitch'. Surely we all want our efforts and accomplishments acknowledged? It's perfectly acceptable to engage in competition. Ambition gets us up in the morning and it motivates us to keep going when things get rough. So why the double standard? When a male boss is cross at work we excuse him because he's a perfectionist. When a woman demands high standards, she's having a hissy fit. Remember, ambition is neutral: it's how you use it that defines whether you're operating in a healthy or an unhealthy way.
(v: Alpha females)

Ambivalence (about a lover)
Ambivalence about a lover usually signifies that there are big emotions at play, either positive or negative or both. If you are experiencing ambivalence about a partner, or aspects of your relationship, you need to get to the heart of the matter and be truthful about your feelings, pronto!
(v: Bachelors, Rejection)

Ambivalence (to an ex-lover)
The ultimate revenge for someone who has broken your heart.
(v: Rejection)

Amorality
We may argue that we live in an amoral age but every individual should have principles.
(v: Bachelors, Personal code of conduct)

Anal sex
Beloved of ex English public school boys, particularly Old Etonians, some women find they can work this into their repertoire. It's also an ancient, though not fail-safe, method of contraception. If it's not your cup of tea, don't get too het up about it. Simply apply the once in three rule and if you still don't like it you are allowed to say 'no'.

Androgyny
It's a look that has been around since the turn of the 20th century, most famously popularised by Yves Saint Laurent with his famous 'Le Smoking' in 1966. It can be great fun for women to play around with gender. A clean-cut, boyish tailored suit can look extremely striking on a woman (Tilda Swinton, Stella Tennant, Agyness Deyn). Mannish attire is no guarantee of sexuality (or lack of it). The androgynous person is simply a female or male who has a high degree of both feminine (expressive) and masculine (instrumental) traits. And a bloody great wardrobe viz David Bowie's.
(v: Suits, Think Like A Man, The Third Sex)

Angelou, Maya [icon]
'I've learned that people will forget what you said, people will forget what you did, but people will never forget how you made them feel.'

Anger
'I was angry with my friend:
I told my wrath, my wrath did end.
I was angry with my foe:
I told it not, my wrath did grow.'
— 'A Poison Tree', WILLIAM BLAKE

We could all benefit from cultivating an authentic voice for ourselves. We need to learn to express real feelings at work, with friends, in love, towards our children.

Of course, getting explosive in a situation isn't impressive. Rage has a childlike quality about it, so, while in the short term you may have a feeling of release, in the medium to long term nobody respects you for it.

No one wants to bottle resentment up. People become confused by your passivity and lose respect for you, cf. Lady Bertram in *Mansfield Park*. Dates slip through your hands and lazier friends take advantage.

Assertiveness is about recognising that you are entitled to certain things. So be confident in expressing your feelings or views while respecting that other people have them too. Get it right, and you'll be able to pole-vault over the whole anger thing altogether, while getting a little more of your own way some of the time, which, after all, is only fair but don't forget that righteous anger, if justified, can be extremely liberating too.
(v: Angry birds, Boxing, Flaming)

Angry birds

In the Eighties – as epitomised by Margaret Thatcher – there was a backlash against The Second Wave, i.e. the men-hating, hairy-legged feminists of the Seventies. Women put on suits instead and attempted to penetrate the corridors of power by other means. Feminism became a slightly passé concept: oh it's all alright now because women can get jobs and earn money. Notions of true equality got lost in the over-excitement about extended credit and to quote *Guardian* columnist Suzanne Moore: 'Postfeminism – as personified by the *Sex and the City* generation – basically confused sexual liberation with shopping'. However, the upside of the international economic meltdown is that revolution is, once again, in the air and a new generation of young feminists are finding a voice via the web or by direct action. So why not join them? It's never too late to become an angry bird.

(v: Demonstrations, Flaming, Lipstick, Mercy fuck)

Animal prints

The rules are: leopard-skin for fat days; zebra for bags, belts and shoes; snakeskin for cuffs and collars . . . We could write a sonnet to the sheer joy that is the animal print. Never out of fashion probably because they're never strictly in, animal prints always look chic even when they're retro.

No doubt our fascination is rooted in our primitive selves. We may atavistically associate animal prints with animal characteristics. In African tribal societies, the skin of a lion is worn to imbue a warrior with that particular animal's fabled characteristics.

There are sartorial rules, of course, especially if you don't want to look like a mini-me Rod Stewart. Keep it to one key piece (coat, shoes or scarf). Remember the only colour that really works with animal prints is black, although we would very occasionally make an exception for leopard-skin with a splash of red or pink.

And these days – unless you live in Outer Siberia – there is absolutely no excuse for buying the real thing. The new fakes are so fabulous they scream haute couture.

(v: Scarfology)

Annoying women who like football

There is an ever-increasing trend in women who pretend to like football in an effort to bond with their 'man'. This involves donning football strips, going to football games and drinking pints down the pub. It's irritating because it feels so forced. Eventually these women stop having to pretend to like football and actually do like football. This smacks of Pavlov's dog.

(v: Female sports presenters)

Apologising

If you have behaved badly you need to apologise. Whether you have been irritable to somebody at work, over-reacted to something a friend or partner has said, or shouted at your children just for the sake of it, however hard it feels and however resentful you feel about doing it (because of course it's always nicer to be right), you should make amends. They will feel better. You will feel better and although this may seem counter-intuitive, because some people will only respond to iron will, cf. Barack Obama/ Osama bin Laden, surely, ultimately people will love and respect you for doing it. It is particularly important that your children learn from you in this regard. As a

family therapist said: 'Everybody has rows, it's your ability to make a good peace that marks you out as a functioning person.'
(*v: Drawing a veil, Family therapy, It seemed like a good idea at the time*)

Armoury – the new cover-ups for arms
Even goddess Helen Mirren has made a fervent plea for sleeves on dresses. So insistent is she that she is even prepared to design the clothes herself, 'There are no dresses with sleeves and we need to bring back the sleeve: fine, see-through ones, long or short.'

So thank heaven for the the new fashion for cover-ups, shrugs, shawls, stoles and capes, wraps and lightweight pashminas that you throw on and layer up for day to evening. Shopping guru Mary Portas has even gone one step further and designed Armery – tights for the arms – where a stretchy high-denier hosiery tube allows you to slip your arms inside so you can discreetly conceal problem areas.

Shrugs are elegant and practical – you don't need to carry a coat in summer; and trust us, family photos no longer make you reel back in horror at the sight of your dimpled upper arms.
(*v: Arms, Boxing*)

Arms
The punctuation marks of our body: to hug, to hold, to stop, to seize, to embrace. The arms can be all things to all people and we express ourselves constantly through a huge variety of movements. They show excitement, fear and love. They carry and work for us. They hold food and our babies,

and are, very often, strangely ignored. A beautiful, well-toned arm is very sexy, and light work with weights and regular swimming will deliver results. However, if you do have a tendency to bingo wings, a forgiving cropped sleeve will do the trick.

To say nothing, of course, of the elegant and serene *port de bras* in ballet, meaning literally 'the carriage of the arms', where the aim is to be graceful, poised and seamless at all times. Love your arms.

(v: Boxing, Frocks, Pilates, Wild swimming)

(An) Arrangement

Who'd have known it? The arrangement is back in vogue. Does it mean many marriages that have hit the rocks could have trolleyed on if there had been a French-style/1940s 'arrangement' in place?

The definition of an arrangement is having a guy dangling around and then meeting him every few weeks for an elegant dinner or some seriously good sex (occasionally both). Think more Graham Greene than F. Scott Fitzgerald.

So, an arrangement means not getting hot under the collar, hysterically needy or sad. You are both just enjoying each other's company and having a good time. It's grown-up, very cool and you don't gossip about it or get demanding. It just is. Plus, it can continue for ages because there is no melodrama attached – that's a double plus.

(v: Affairs, Camiknickers, Cinq à sept)

(The) Art of make-up

Less is more where make-up is concerned, and it's great skin that counts. That said, a good concealer popped on the inner corner of the eyes and around the reddish area of the nose is an excellent idea. Eye liner inside the lashes defines the eye, as does a cat flick on the outside edge of the eye.

Lipstick – many wouldn't leave home without it. Keep key items of make-up in your handbag at all times and reapply. Foundation is good for parties where, if you're lucky, you might find yourself getting a bit hot and bothered. *(v: False eyelashes, Lipstick)*

Artisan mustard and cool condiments

Woman cannot live by salad alone. One of the quickest ways to pep up leaves is to add an interesting garnish. Spicy condiments such as Tabasco, chilli or wasabi make us feel full quicker (and raise your metabolic rate, the speed at which you burn calories).

Always spend as much as you can afford on fine black pepper and sea salt. Soy sauce adds kick (and Chinese dark soy sauce contains 10 times the antioxidants of red wine). In the past mustard was seen only as an accompaniment to a Sunday Roast (and certainly not for vegetarians) but now we're seeing all sorts of artisan offerings from Lapsang Souchong Mustard for barbecues or poached fish, to Bull Dog Mustard (not for the faint hearted).

And don't forget the first person to make mustard in the 18th century was a woman – Mrs Clemence. Her secret formula involved grinding the seeds in a mill and passing them through several processes similar to making flour from wheat, thus winning the patronage of King George I. Respect.

(v: Ballooning Weight, Champagne, I can't afford to buy cheap)

Astrology

Astrology ... a tricky one this. Especially, if like us, you love reading astrologers in newspapers and magazines, but wonder, quite simply, do they just rehash the same stuff, e.g. is Taurus interchangeable with Scorpio?

Of course, planetary action is always appealing, particularly when the likes of Dr Who are involved, and it naturally feels even more plausible if your astrological reading is super-positive. But, does it really help in the long run?

Perhaps closer to the truth is that we are all looking for a little bit of hope and positivity in our lives. So if you read for the forty-seventh time that 'today you might attend a party or group event with some friends', we suggest you look into the following alternatives instead:

(v: Chocolate, Comfort zone, Soothsayers)

At first I was afraid, I was petrified

If you suspect a obsessive-compulsive anxiety disorder (OCD) in yourself, or other people, you need to know that its main feature is that masses of time is spent on useless and futile tasks, i.e. washing your hands, checking that the oven is off or that the door is properly locked, in the vain and probably unconscious hope that they will help diminish worry or distress. They do not and they will not and, of course, the endless participation in repetitive and excessive anxieties begins to compound the problem because you are too busy cleaning the loo to face up to the reasons why you are anxious in the first place. If you are displaying any of these symptoms get help as soon as possible.

(v: Allergies)

Athill, Diana [icon]
'I'd been in love and thought I was going to end up happily married with children – a very simple wish, but I'd failed to make it and that was more spirit-weakening than I realised. When I got rid of it in my early forties by writing it out, it was like a new life. I felt like a new person and I've felt like that ever since.'

Aunts
Nowadays as the result of the extended family and the close ties between female friends (sometimes closer than those between sisters), anybody can be an 'aunt'. Aunts as evoked by P.G. Wodehouse and Roald Dahl are hopefully a thing of the past. Whether you are blood related or not, an aunt can have a special status in a woman's life. An aunt's role is necessarily fluid. From a mother's point of view, an aunt is probably a friend whom she can entirely trust, who shares her values and will take over, temporarily, if she needs help with childcare or the going gets tough. From a child's perspective, an aunt is somebody who is really good fun for adventures and treats and mini-breaks to Eurodisney. For an aunt, it is fun to be part of a family but not have to be there every day.
(v: Babies, Childfree, Godmothers, Teenagers)

Babies (your own or other people's)

'Hello, babies. Welcome to Earth. It's hot in the summer and cold in the winter. It's round and wet and crowded. At the outside, babies, you've got about a hundred years here. There's only one rule that I know of, babies – "God damn it, you've got to be kind"'.
– *God Bless You, Mr Rosewater*, KURT VONNEGUT

Babies are some of the most joyous and life-enhancing people you'll ever get to meet. If you haven't got one of your own try and make sure that you spend proper time with other people's. If you are a new godmother make the most of that connection – if an exhausted friend needs help, support and babysitting, offer! Babies may not be able to speak but they recognise familiar faces and babies and young children remember somebody who takes a genuine interest in them.

Baby bodies

There was a time when having a baby was seen as a milestone in the journey of life. It was also understood that having a baby would irrevocably change the shape of a

woman's body – this was both inevitable and OK. Sadly, celebrity magazines and even broadsheet newspapers are now saturated by images of people who have only given birth six weeks ago, yet whose bodies have miraculously snapped back to a size eight without apparent effort. They are really celebrated for looking like models, rather than new mothers who are subject to the natural changes of life. Yet what the headlines hide is the too-posh-to-push Caesarean operations done at 36 weeks to avoid gaining those last few pounds, post-birth crash dieting – which is incredibly bad for milk production – and an array of nannies, day and night, ensuring the mum gets her eight hours' sleep each night, while in daylight hours personal trainers and beauticians burnish these women back into a pre-baby shape. It's not fair, and it's not real, and we love Beyoncé because she said damn the diet and decided she was going to enjoy new motherhood. And all of us have a duty to convey this message to new or expectant mothers.
(v: Cosmetic surgery)

Baby dykes

'Girls, who are boys, who like boys to be girls, who do boys like they're girls, who do girls like they're boys.' Fashion has celebrated dyke chic, with boots and biker jackets, scrubbed faces and urchin crops. Certainly the new generation of early twenty-somethings no longer need to define themselves as straight or gay, and it's perfectly acceptable not only to be unsure, but to be neither. Diehard card-carrying feminists with dangly earrings may worry about the lack of sexual politics – but frankly it's a hell of a lot better than our teenage years when to be called a 'lesbo' in the school corridor induced a hot blush of shame.

One fine day how you dress will say nothing about who you take to bed (hurrah). And frankly no one will care, but in the meantime increasing sexual choice for women empowers everybody.

(v: Lesbian bed death)

Baby showers

An American import which started ten to fifteen years ago. Back in the day in the UK people were a bit superstitious about giving presents before a baby was born, in case something ghastly happened during childbirth, but thanks to expert prenatal care and birthing facilities those kind of fears have been largely assuaged.

The standard drill for a 'shower' is to arrive bearing a lovely gift for the incoming baby and probably a scented candle for the 'mamma to be' as well. In return you will be given a delicious tea and, if you are lucky, a cocktail into the bargain, but don't count on the latter. This kind of event can be hard for the unintentionally childfree, particularly if everybody else around them is about to give birth, but this may be the last time you spend time with your friend (and friends) before she becomes a mother and should be celebrated as such. Given that so many people have babies before they get married one could argue that the baby shower is the new hen night.

(v: Babies, Godmothers, Hen nights)

Bachelors (committed, toxic or otherwise)

Rather like 'war' what are they actually good for? The answer is that they have many uses but you must promise one thing, don't for even one nanosecond fantasise, contemplate or think that they will break the habit of a lifetime

and fall in love with you and want to marry you. You have been warned. Now to practical matters: it is very helpful to have a few bachelors in your little black book; they specialise in being charming and fun at dinner parties; they may, if it suits them (selfishness is a ubiquitous quality among this particular demographic), agree to escort you to a frightening social event; sometimes they can be a friend with benefits and that's good for your health if nothing else, and presumably because they don't have children of their own (or none they'll admit to), they are often extraordinarily sweet with other people's. This can occasionally begin to melt your heart but don't let it. Long-term bachelors can become very good friends indeed, but be realistic and be compassionate too, it may look as if they are having a lot of carefree fun but they are ploughing a lonely furrow.
(v: Boundaries, Complete wankers, Little black book, Narcissus)

Bad boys

'I want guitar heroes and boys who were raised on the streets by wolves. Atilla the Hun is my basic dream lover.'
– *Story Of My Life*, JAY MCINERNEY

(v: Caveman moment)

Bad habits

It's easy to spot other people's and very hard to own up to your own. Some bad habits are simply revolting, e.g. picking scabs off your legs or cutting your toenails in public places, and you will be judged accordingly. Others, such as interrupting other people while they are talking, are commonplace and they can really piss people off. Weirdly, the bad

habits that you find in others are sometimes the bad habits you can't see in yourself and it may take a friend or lover to point them out to you. Accept their comments gracefully.
(v: Affairs, Cocktails, Dipsomania)

Balcony holiday
You stay in and don't answer the phone and you do exactly what you want for two weeks. The advantages are that you will save a great deal of money and won't have to go through airport security; the disadvantages are that you have to stay indoors at all times and can't even leave the house to buy a packet of cigs.
(v: Money matters)

Ballooning weight
For health reasons, among many others, nip it in the bud while you can.
(v: Boxing, Carbohydrates, Climacteric, Comfort zone, Diets, Eat your greens, Trampolining, Waist, Wild swimming)

Ballroom dancing
Long to dance the tango but can't find a willing partner? Many hotels arrange afternoon 'tea dances' where, along-side tea and cucumber sandwiches, they provide good-looking dance partners for lessons and social dancing. Yes, you pay for the gent's ticket (and tea). No, they won't flirt/sleep with you (far too professional), but you will have a fabulous afternoon floating around the Palm Court on the arm of the charming Oleg doing the cha-cha-cha. We know of a few 'couples' who even went on to compete pro-fessionally together. It's especially good for people whose partners are too shy to hit the dance floor, or would frankly

rather spend an afternoon at the football. All ages and backgrounds are represented, from sweet old-timers to groovy young urbanites. And don't feel awkward about paying for a partner. Think like a man – they do it all the time.
(v: Ballooning weight, Flow, Think like a man)

Banana
The handbag essential. An instant energy boost, and rich in tryptophan – one of the 20 common amino acids that make up all proteins – which the body converts into serotonin, known to make you more relaxed and happy. And can we just applaud the brilliant no-waste packaging?
(v: Eat your greens, Fruit)

Bathhouses (the new democratic spas)
When you travel the world, some of the best, most memorable experiences can happen in a simple massage hut or bathhouse. Many cultures see a daily visit to a bathhouse as an essential way to de-stress or spend time with others.

For Finns the sauna is a place to relax in with friends and family, and it's a way of normalising the body – for young and old. The Japanese, by contrast, see bathing as ritual purification with water.

In Turkey, the essence of 'hammam' is forgetting the world outside, letting your mind and spirit wander free and just enjoying the feeling of purification. They are open to everyone regardless of their status; young and old, rich and poor, townsman or villager.

The uptight English are not renowned for communal bathing. We go swimming at pools and sports centres. But our puritan soul recoils at the idea of group recreation – or someone else soaping and scrubbing our bodies.

But now in the UK we're seeing a new breed of bath-houses, pop-up massage huts and Turkish spas or hammams. We should embrace them – looking after our-selves should be an everyday act not just a luxury.
(v: Bien dans ta peau, Ease, Flow, Wild Swimming)

Beach huts

Who doesn't want a beach hut? They are every grown-up girl's Wendy house. They went relatively unnoticed for years partly because of the fashion for 'abroad', but then suddenly airports became ghastly and everyone wanted to wander at Walberswick and skinny-dip at Salcombe, and the prices rocketed. If there is a beach hut in your family, it's worth keeping hold of it and tarting it up. Nowadays they are so sought-after that they are hard to buy. But once bought they can easily be shared with other people and everybody can chip in for the very basic running costs. It's an excellent excuse for you to get out of the city and you can while away many a summer's day overlooking the sea without sand in your sandwiches or flies in your gin. We haven't got a bad word to say about them.
(v: Bolt-hole, Infinite vistas, Separate Spaces)

Beauty

'I go to bed early. I meditate. I eat all the correct foods. I don't smoke or drink, and I believe with a passion in myself. You can only beat nature when you show the bitch who's boss.'
– MAE WEST

It is said that before the age of 40 you have the face that

God gives you and after 40 the face that you deserve. What is clear is that no amount of money or surgery can give you that inner glow that comes with the combination of self-acceptance, secret confidence and a general connection to the national grid of love and happiness. A dash of quiet spirituality doesn't go amiss either.
(v: Beauty industry, Bien dans ta peau, *Eat your greens, Facial acupuncture, Secret confidence)*

(The) Beauty industry

The global cosmetics, toiletries and fragrance industry is worth £6.2 billion and on average women in the UK spend £185,528 each on beauty products in their lifetime.

Anti-ageing is the holy grail of the beauty industry. It is the promise in the pot, the elixir of youth where the 'appearance of fine lines may diminish', albeit temporarily and with them a great deal of dosh. Often the domain of psychobabble and pseudo-science, it's a question of sorting the wheat from the chaff. Moisturising, massaging, exercising your face and controlling lymphatic drainage are key. Much of the beauty industry, ironically, is anti-women in that it trades on insecurities and low self-esteem.

Make sure your face is your fortune and not theirs.
(v: Facial acupuncture, Facial exercises)

Bee pollen

Gwyneth Paltrow and Olympic athletes swear by it. Some health experts claim if you were stranded on a desert island, bee pollen is all you would need to survive because it contains so many essential nutrients.

You can buy it in capsule form, but the most potent version comes in the tiny gold granules which you scatter on cereals or a smoothie for an energy boost. And it's extremely helpful with hay fever.

Dubbed nature's secret ingredient, bee pollen is a compound consisting of pollen that has been packed by worker honeybees – using their knees – into granules called pollen balls, with added honey or nectar.

Just don't overdo the dose (a teaspoon a day is enough) or you might give birth to a bee baby as in Roald Dahl's wicked short story 'Royal Jelly'.

(v: Allergies, Honey)

Beds

You want the best bed you can afford, the larger the better, especially if you have got kids. Preferably one with a mattress cobbled together by fairies with extra fluff and some stardust sprinkled on top, though do watch out for the odd, strategically placed pea. However, if you are partner- or child-free you can just make the most of your bed and spread out – you should sleep beautifully.

Ideally, beds should have fresh sheets weekly and be aired daily. We also really like the rather retro 'bolster', which is great for reading in bed. If cash is tight there are plenty of cheap options. Trawl the small ads for second-hand beds, although buy a new mattress to avoid bed-bugs. You can paint a wooden frame and create amazing valances with vintage fabric, or chintzy old curtains. Garage sales are usually piled high with cheap sheets, pillowcases and old curtains. It simply doesn't matter if it's not all 'matchy matchy'. Also, go online and search for heavy linen and, if you find any, snap it up. France is amazing for this, but stocks are dwindling so don't dally: hit the Lille antique markets with a fistful of Euros (all the money you didn't spend on a posh bed in the first place). The 'down topper' is possibly the most scrumptious (and relatively new) bed accessory on the market. It is a great fat ploofy layer of fluff that you fold over the mattress before putting the sheets on. All very dreamy and comfy and bouncy. So much so that you may decide to stay in bed all day, and who could blame you?

(v: Insomnia)

Being boring
We're against it.
(v: Bores)

Benders
Sometimes in life you just have to let go. Going on a bender is traditionally seen as a male preserve but increasingly women are doing it too. Sometimes benders creep up on one. You know, the promise of a quick drink with a friend at the end of work turns into a big night out, or a Friday night out with mates turns into a very long, alcohol-fuelled weekend (occasionally culminating in eating tripe, shoeless, in a workman's café at 5 a.m. on a Monday morning).

A great bender is a holiday from real life: a spontaneous way of marking the end of a relationship, a divorce or to celebrate a landmark birthday. It's often a rite of passage for friends, male and female, confidences are exchanged, relationships consolidated and the unspoken rule is, as a mark of your deepening respect and love for one another, that whatever your various states of disrepair nobody's going to remind you of your extravagant pole-dancing in Tranny-shack in Soho. Or maybe just a little bit . . .

In fact, a key feature of a bender is that you probably

won't remember anything when you wake up, you may well have lost a number of your belongings and you may end up in a hotel room, though not necessarily the one that you had booked for yourself the previous evening. However, fragments of memory WILL begin to return during the course of the morning and you will probably find yourself looking into the mouth of hell. You may discover that drunk-dialling and a toxic bachelor or two have entered the mix, which is the point where regret, self-doubt and paranoia begin to creep in. The two solutions are either to butch it out at work or go to bed. Relief will finally come at about 7 p.m. when the miasma begins to lift. You can, of course, attempt to guard against all these things – eat carbohydrates before you go out; drink a glass of water after every glass of champagne; appoint a drinks monitor; only take one credit card with you, and so on and so forth – but look into your heart and ask yourself truthfully and honestly whether such an evening really counts as a bender?

(v: Alcohol, Booty-calls, Booze, Breaking the rules, Cocktails, Dipsomania, Drunk-dialling, It seemed like a good idea at the time, Make the most of it, Regrets)

Bereavement

'He was not in charge of grief. Grief was in charge of him.'
– *Pulse*, JULIAN BARNES

'This is not the time to repress your feelings. Allow yourself to go mad as you like.'
– NICHOLAS ARDIZZONE

(v: Age of grief, Counselling, Grief, Loss, Therapy)

Be warm

Happy people aren't especially lucky or beautiful but they connect well to others and as a result they tend to have rich personal relationships. In adolescence we assume nihilism is cool. But as you get older, warmth becomes a seriously hot property. Stop worrying whether people will find you weird and intense. Other people are generally nicer than you think. And if they're not? Your goodwill combined with good behaviour is the best form of body armour.

If you insist on maintaining your ice-cold *froideur* you will eventually become an empty fridge. If you reach an understanding that it doesn't matter what people think about you then you have become entirely free.
(v: Secret confidence)

Be well informed

There is no excuse not to be. The radio, newspapers, websites or well-chosen periodicals, such as *Week*, will keep you up to date. It's important to take a view on politics but remember to change the subject if it looks as though your radical views on Sarah Palin, global warming and the royal family look set to ruin somebody else's beautifully organised dinner party.
(v: Good stuff that's free, Libraries, the Queen)

(The) BF

'A friend is, as it were, a second self.'
– CICERO

Your BF, usually but not always, is the closest thing you have to family without being family: she is the person you can be most honest to; she is utterly trustworthy; never judgemental, she is the keeper of your innermost dreams and desires. Although she may from time to time point you in the right direction and administer a necessary pep talk, she is also the best of fun and you can literally spend days at a time talking on the phone or chatting on the beach. If you don't spend enough time with your BF, because of the demands of family and work, you will miss her enormously but once you are together again it's as though she has never been away. It is also the mark of a BF that she never really makes demands. If this sounds too idyllic prepare for the occasional twinge of irritation, that's a reality, but also recognise that you quite simply can't imagine life without her and celebrate that fact.

(v: Catching the bouquet, Pep talk from a fiery redhead)

Bien dans ta peau

This charming French expression is true, elegant and simply means 'to feel happy in one's skin'. If you are *bien dans ta peau*, you are not self-conscious, or mirror grabbing or in need of constant flattery.

(v: Flow)

Big babies

'Oh give me a break' is the battle cry of those who have the onerous task of having to deal with a 'big baby' on a regular basis. This could be your lover, your darling child, your BF or a colleague at work. Big baby-ism has no regard for age or gender. Warning signs are that they moan constantly. The big baby (and this is the really irritating bit) makes an absolute meal of helping anybody else out, to the point where they become no help at all and quite simply you wish you hadn't asked them in the first place. A big baby is also perennially moody and basically just way too delicate for modern life. Have we striven so hard to free ourselves from the shackles of a patriarchal society to have to put up with such nonsense? The answer is NO. The solution is DON'T DO IT. So to all you BBs out there, 'Spare us the labour pains and, quite frankly, grow up!'

Birthdays
They come, and they go, and they come again. Taking a fluid attitude to your own is probably the best idea, as life changes, and with it your ideals.
(v: (A) little bit of what you fancy does you good)

Bitches and hos
For heaven's sake! Where has this ridiculous kind of chat come from? The pointy finger turns towards America and, in particular, to rap music, but loads of men and, sad to say, a few women – whatever their economic circumstances or the colour of their skin – have jumped on this pernicious bandwagon. Stop it now!
(v: Caveman moment, Rap)

Blaize, Immodesty
(v: Confidence, Role models)

Blame
Blame becomes increasingly ugly as one gets older, and there is something rather forlorn about a grown woman still blaming her parents. Either park it in the long-term car park and throw away the keys or, if you still feel weighed down by burning resentments stemming from childhood experiences, the time has to come to take responsibility for them

yourself and go to see a therapist. Long-term grievances should not be allowed to fester. Also, it is surely, unless grotesque abuse has taken place, the place of the grown-up child to smooth the path for ageing parents. Olive branches can grow anywhere, especially with global warming. Start cultivating your olive grove now. The ability to forgive is one of the greatest of all human qualities.

(v: Big babies)

Blogging

Gives you a voice and a presence in a very noisy world. From Julie Powell who cooked all of Julia Child's recipes (immortalised by the film, *Julie & Julia*) to sexpert Belle de Jour, a micro-blog can become a global hit. You may even get paid-for advertising. But remember the male blogosphere can be bruising. Ignore the trolls!

Bloodsports

'Sex is a bloodsport. Making love to real people is dangerous. It comes with the risk of rejection, humiliation, jealousy and abject failure. And the possibility of bliss.'
— GERMAINE GREER
(v: Camiknickers, Contraception, Creative corsetry, Mercy fuck)

Bloom

'The day came when the wish to remain tight in a bud was more painful than the risk it took to blossom.'
— ANAÏS NIN
(v: Rain)

Blow-dries

A blow-dry is not a replacement for a good haircut but it can lift morale faster than a large glass of wine. It's a good idea to have several salons on speed-dial for a last-minute appointment. And shop around. A blow-dry can cost anything from £15–£65 but think ahead, it may not be worth paying a small fortune for a senior stylist if you're going to go wild swimming tomorrow.

(v: Necessary vanity, Secret confidence, Wild swimming)

Blow-jobs

'Do as you would be done by' is our motto here. It's also terribly good for the cheek muscles, ladies, and some people claim that it can trigger the start of labour. Do keep it up!

(v: Childbirth)

Blueberries

1. Possibly the ultimate super-food. Many nutritionists believe that if you make only one change to your diet, add blueberries. Bake them in muffins, snack on them at your desk to beat sugar cravings ... Keep a bag in the freezer, so you always have some to hand.

2. Just 100g (4oz) of blueberries contains the same amount of age-defying antioxidants as five servings of most other fruit and vegetables. To remind you: antioxidants help guard against a range of cancers, heart disease, asthma and age-related neurological diseases. They do this by preventing infectious bacteria from clinging to the wall of the gut, bladder and urethra. Blueberries also offer protection against cystitis.

3. High in vitamin C and a good source of fibre, blueberries

contain a compound, pterostilbene, which acts to protect the heart in the same way as cholesterol-lowering drugs. They also contain anthocyanins, which give blueberries their blue colour.

4. Blueberries contain polyphenols, which combat the effects of free radicals, a key cause of wrinkles, so they keep skin looking younger for longer. They also help the body to make collagen, which keeps skin supple.

    a. It's good to eat lots of red or blue plants (watermelon, cranberries, bilberries, grapes, prunes) that contain anthocyanins – many new cutting-edge beauty products contain them because of their cell-protective powers.

5. While we are on the subject, look out for make-up containing an ingredient called Purpulyn, which has anti-ageing benefits. It is found in blueberries and also in plants such as dark tulips and black orchids.

(v: Banana, Detox, Eat your greens, Super-foods)

Blues

The blues have a special quality that is different from depression, grief or all round low spirits. They are characterised by weepiness, flashes of intense sadness and the feeling that one is secretly unable to cope. They can be triggered by a variety of things, both small and big: remembrance of things past; the passing of the seasons; a dear friend moving to live abroad; sheer tiredness; the intense hormonal changes that can come with the birth of a baby; the prospect of a family event, but whatever the trigger it is worth taking them a little bit seriously. Vitamins, exercise, a good night's sleep, cutting out alcohol for a bit, a brilliant and engrossing book, the companionship of old friends can all help to combat the blues. From a creative point of view, happiness writes white, while some of the best poems and songs in history have been inspired by a good dose of the blues.

(v: Babies, Christmas, Depression, Winter)

Body management

'Many young girls are constantly consumed by controlling and managing their body image to the extent that they are much more involved in the production of the self than in living.'

– SUSIE ORBACH

Bohemians

Many people are afraid of bohemians because they think they are like hippies and are smelly and don't wash their hair. Most bohemians are incredibly sophisticated, fabulously inspiring people who have an unconventional approach to life, be it in appearance and/or behaviour. They tend to be free spirits who rarely moan, cf. the journalist Jeffrey Bernard as they chopped more and more bits off him, and don't give a fig what other people think of them. They do have a tendency to get a little bit repetitive when they have drunk too much, but who are we to cast the first stone? Gather as many around you as you can.

(v: English eccentrics)

Bolt-hole

This might be a palace, a wattle-daubed cottage, a teeny beach hut on a windswept shore, a spare bedroom or even a garden shed, but it's your kingdom and yours alone where you can grab a bit of 'p and q' and gather your thoughts.

Or not. Sometimes just a little light gazing out of the window does the trick. Women, in between work and home, are not granted much personal space, so your only option may be to grant it to yourself. If you are of an Arts and Crafts bent, have fun doing up your bolt-hole and making it your own. It's somewhere where you can finish that book, write poetry, do some embroidery, or simply read the newspaper. Somewhere where you can just 'take five'.

(v: Beach huts, Embroidery, Infinite vistas, Poetry, Separate spaces, Studio)

Bombshells

Pulled up, pushed in, and generally shaken all about, the Bombshell is a name given to a drop-dead gorgeous siren. It is also the name for the ubiquitous cocktail dress, which can cover an absolute multitude of sins and dress you up like a knickerbocker glory. You need nothing more than a cardie and a pair of slingbacks to go with it and you're away. With ruched panelling and a sort of superstructure that would have made newspaper magnate Howard Hughes, who among other things designed the ultimate bra for Jane Russell, green with envy, every Dangerous Woman about town needs at least one or even two of these babies in her wardrobe.

(v: Body management, Frocks, Marilyn Monroe)

Bones

Plenty of sunshine, lots of exercise, as well as calcium in the form of milk, eggs, cheese, yogurt, oily fish, sardines, salmon, tuna, spinach.

(v: Exercise, Knees)

Boobs

Voluptuous curves are back. And people really do love a proper bosom. It's one of life's pleasures. Women probably spend even more time admiring them than men. 'Breasts really are the new guns', a triumphant girlfriend said recently, and in the twenty-first-century there is nothing more fascinating than a woman who owns her sex appeal.

Of course, it helps that the current rise of tailored shifts, corsets and stockings are so flattering to curvy birds, and it's wonderful that the days of *La Dolce Vita*, when women were supposed to have milky white globes spilling over their dresses are, gloriously, back. The French have a lovely phrase for it too: '*Elle a tout le monde dans le balcon*' (she has everyone in the balcony). But how does one dress the breasts? Or rather, how low should you go?

It's so easy to make a sartorial faux pas with cleavage. Party frocks with a daring neckline can look very good on the hanger, but get it wrong and everything goes into free-fall. You need to understand structure. The perfect breasts are pert not pendulous. So think in 3D, and sort out the bras, and/or the corsets to go with each frock. Too much cleavage can make the difference between being perceived as a gorgeously sexual human being and a cartoon slapper. For those of us over the age of 35 there are clear rules for exposing skin. Make sure you're well supported, avoid slashed to the waist affairs (tit tape doesn't work), never wear a crossover neckline (you get that awful crêpey crease), and don't expose too much leg if breasts are on show.

But not everyone has to do boobs. If you are a flat chester, enjoy revealing toned shoulders – the new erogenous zone, cf. the Duchess of Cambridge and Michelle Obama.
(v: Bras, Creative corsetry, Curves)

Booty-calls

You may or may not have been on the receiving end of a booty-call but it works like this. It's about 10 p.m. You are planning to have an early night when your phone goes. It's a bloke who you have met once or twice, you may even have slept with him. He is sitting in the pub with some friends and he is a little bit drunk. The conversation is genial but the meaning is clear, he wants to have sex. So far so good but the tricky part of all of this is, do you? If you are confident and ready to throw caution to the wind, put on a pair of clean knickers, jump into a cab and make the connection, or is it going to be a firm 'no' and a cup of hot milk and early bed? It's a difficult one and much depends on how you are feeling about yourself. If the answer is confident and sexy and up for anything, then go for it while taking the necessary precautions. However, if you are feeling in any way miserable, vulnerable or lonely, turn your phone off, put on your fluffy slippers and reach for your battered copy of *Gone with the Wind*.

The good news is that our survey shows that if you want to make a booty-call yourself you will have a 99.9% success rate. It's great to know that in the battle of the sexes women sometimes have the upper hand.

(v: Alcohol, Drunk-dialling, It seemed like a good idea at the time, Mercy fuck, Regrets)

Booze

(v: Alcohol, Ballooning weight, Booty-calls, Champagne, Cocktails, Diets, Dipsomania, Drunk-dialling, Grappa, Martini, Quests)

Boredom

'. . . that state of suspended animation in which things are
started and nothing begins, the mood of diffuse
restlessness which contains that most absurd and
paradoxical wish, the wish for a desire.'
– ADAM PHILLIPS

Bores

'Blessed is the man who, having nothing to say, abstains
from giving us wordy evidence of the fact.'
– GEORGE ELIOT

'Only dull people are brilliant at breakfast.'
– OSCAR WILDE

We all know one or two bores and if you are becoming one
yourself we suggest you snap out of it sharpish, although,
of course, a key characteristic of being a bore is that you
don't know you are one.

An atypical bore is somebody who collars you at a
jam, and then does something unutterably rude, such as
grill you about what A levels you took when you are
trying to laugh and drink a Martini. A bore is somebody
who doesn't realise that a party is for amusing chitchat,
and that it is everybody's duty to be a little bit up and
light and amusing. If in trouble with a bore, courtesy
dictates that you talk to them for a long five minutes but
then you can make your excuses pronto and dart off to
the loo, or pretend that you have to go outside and make
a call. Chances are there will be smokers out there and
they are usually much more fun.
(v: Guests, Walking away)

Botox

To Botox or not to Botox, that is the question. Most women spend 90% of the time saying they wouldn't have Botox and then when they meet somebody who has had it done they have a panicky ten minutes wondering whether they should go ahead themselves.

An alternative is facial acupuncture, which was used as a beauty tool for hundreds, if not thousands, of years by the empresses of China. Practitioners claim that facial acupuncture stimulates collagen production, helps minimise the appearance of fine lines, reduces the depth of deeper lines and improves skin tone, but whereas Botox freezes muscles this form of treatment can stimulate and revitalise them.

Facial acupuncture also reviews and addresses the internal reasons for poor skin or premature ageing by stimulating the function of organs such as the heart and the liver and helping to improve digestion. Patients report additional medical benefits, including a resurgence of energy and improvements in circulation. It's well worth investigating as an alternative to the dreaded cosmetic surgery.

(v: Necessary vanity)

Bouncing back

The ability to draw a line underneath an unhappy event and move on is the thing to aim for.

(v: Bereavement, Depression, Despair, Grief, I don't)

Boundaries

Boundaries can encompass personal space, emotional vulnerability, legal rights, or simply the right not to let anybody else use your toothpaste. Strong boundary setting is seen as a cornerstone of a healthy relationship. People who are very good at setting boundaries are often confused with people who are just very good at getting their own way by those who are not very good at setting boundaries. But if in doubt make a list of the behaviours of those around you that are repetitive, intrusive and get you down, e.g. interrupting while you are the phone, leaving dirty washing on the floor, smoking skunk in the living room or not taking it in turns to put out the rubbish, and decide to do something about it. People don't like changing so be prepared to face criticism, anger and possibly even derision – but don't be derailed. Keeping calm while remaining assertive and polite, but at the same time sticking to your guns, is what boundary setting is all about.

(v: Anger, Co-dependency, Taboos)

Boyfriends

It's nice having a boyfriend but it's not essential to your happiness.

Boxing

Traditionally associated with the male of the species, after *Million Dollar Baby* came along it became commonplace to see women boxing at the gym. It may not suit all of us, but it turns out that boxing can be fun. It's a focused way of releasing aggression (or, in turn, discovering it) in a safe environment. It is also particularly good for core strength, upper arms, busts and, very importantly, waists. Check out what your local gym has to offer boxing-wise: either one-to-one or a boxing class. If you discover that you enjoy it, invest in a good pair of boxing gloves. You don't have to 'enter the ring' to reap the benefits, but it's pleasing to know that, if necessary, your right hook is up to scratch.

(*v: Ballooning weight, Helen Mirren, The Third Sex, Waist*)

Bras

According to the experts, we've nearly all got it wrong in the brassiere department. Apparently 76% of the female population wear ill-fitting bras every day and probably have drawers full of wrong 'uns. The most common mistake is to buy a bra with too big a back and too small cuppage. This can be dire as it pushes the bosom outwards as opposed to inwards.

Sadly, we have also discovered that even weight changes will not help you remould the bosom. So it's simple. Get a fitting! Most good department stores offer this service. If you are over 35 invest proper money in two good bras. We promise you won't regret it.

(*v: Boobs, Creative corsetry, I can't afford to buy cheap*)

Brazilian

'It's the leaf around the flower, the lawn around the house. You have to love hair in order to love the vagina.'
– *The Vagina Monologues*, EVE ENSLER

(*v: Hairiness, Pornification*)

Breastfeeding

We are not going to go into the practicalities but it's clearly important and fulfilling to breastfeed if you can – sixteen weeks is a good target. However if you can't, and there are myriad reasons why it may not be possible, don't beat yourself up about it. What a baby needs most is a calm mother

who is getting enough sleep, not an exhausted and strung-out harpy angsting about whether her baby is getting enough milk or when the World Health Organization says it's the right time to start weaning. There are plenty of well-balanced strapping young men (and women) brought up on formula milk and tinned chocolate pudding to prove the point.
(v: Allergies, Babies, Boobs, Implants)

Bridesmaids
The film that changed the female landscape.

'If we had a message, it was that we didn't want people to think you have to be married, because you don't.'
– KRISTEN WIIG

(v: Hen nights, Female comedians)

Brothers
You can feel incredibly close and familial with your brothers when you see them but at the same time also very far away. They are, after all, blokes and as soon as childhood is left behind their daily concerns and interests may be very different from yours. Once they have steady girlfriends or settle down with a partner or wife you will have to make every effort to include this partner as that may be a vital route through which to remain connected to your brother.

However, although you may not talk to your brothers every day they can play a very important role in your life and you in theirs. They can help you think like a man, particularly in matters of the heart. They can tell it to you straight when others cannot (after all they know you very well indeed). They can offer measured advice in a way that an over-controlling over-anxious father may not be able to do and they can offer insight and support if you find yourself alone bringing up teenage boys. In the long term, a good relationship with brothers, indeed with all your siblings, is vital if you find that you have to make difficult decisions about the care of elderly parents. Much depends on whether you actually like each other beyond loving each other and to a certain extent that is in the lap of the gods.

(v: Family therapy, Teenagers, Think like a man)

Bullying

Bullying is generally associated with childhood and adolescence but adults can bully people too. Bullies are generally people who at some level feel insecure, over-competitive, inadequate, intensely jealous of others and unloved, however successful they may or may not be. Bullies can just be copying others because they are too immature or too stupid to take an independent view themselves. However, if you are a victim of bullying all you can see in your oppressor is the tyrannical, manipulative, unpleasant aspects of his or her nature. It's deeply unpleasant and often very frightening. Sadly, bullying at work and at home is common, and mothers take note, if you face, and put up with, a barrage of criticism every day from your children you may well be being bullied. The first step is to confront the bully and set some boundaries about the future, but to do this you may need professional support.

(v: Boundaries, Co-dependency, Domestic violence, Sexual harassment)

Bundling

This is a term to describe going to bed with somebody who you probably quite fancy but in the event decided by mutual

agreement not to have sex. You may cuddle and kiss and chat for a bit but then you bundle up together and go to sleep. But be warned, you may end up off piste after all.
(v: Bachelors)

Bury the hatchet

Walk on the wild side. It's a hard thing to do. But if you can overcome the visceral sense of rage, you will find yourself floating ethereally above the physical world; you just have to manage it without choking. Constantly weighing up behaviour on the great scales of injustice just means that you will become bitter and twisted. Concentrate instead on your blemish-free soul. In the worst-case scenario, if someone dies on that rift without reconciliation, there is no going back. Ever.
(v: Killing with kindness)

Burkinis

Nigella's Lawson's decision to wear a burkini on the beach revealed our national media obsession with women's bodies and how they should or shouldn't be displayed.

On a beach, a woman is expected to expose her body, so when Lawson chose to defy our social conventions to protect herself – both her privacy and her skin – the newspapers declared war. Given that famous women's bodies are endlessly scrutinised for extra bulges, cellulite and tell-tale signs of ageing few women can fail to understand Lawson's urge to wrap up. Women live daily with their imperfections (too fat, too thin, too womanly), while the male body is venerated and protected. Women endure the indignity of mixed changing rooms in many high-street stores; men have separate cubicles to protect their modesty.

Surely the whole point of fashion is that it's about expressing our identity – our tribal allegiances and our rebellion.
Many items of modest dress have already been adopted by
the high street as fun, guerrilla fashion – turbans and
scarves; wigs and hairpieces; hoods, high collars and
snoods. We have even seen harem pants becoming a popular
teenage street fashion trend.

What is heartening is the way that both feminism and the
pro-modesty movement can share common goals – among
them, the insistence that women should be free from sexual
objectification, viz the SlutWalk protests. Whether you are
considered overdressed or underdressed, discreet or brazen,
depends entirely on who is actually making the rules, so in
this life why not make your own.

(v: Armoury, Pornification)

Bye-bye baby

Yes. This is tough. Yes it hurts but you have to be brave.
When your children leave home of course you will feel the
loss of the baby you fed on the hour, every hour and loved
and hugged so much. You will probably spend several days,
if not weeks, wandering round the house feeling like a giant
electric socket without a plug and wondering, 'Where did
the time go and what is left to me?'. You never stop being a
parent. At the same time, mists clear, horizons beckon and
you will discover a new independence.

(v: Adventure, Babies, Infinite vistas)

❧

Camiknickers

Our grandmothers knew what they were up to. Classic but sexy, comfortable, practical and flattering, camiknickers are a wardrobe essential. Buy them in light colours: cream, pale pink, violet blue and silver-grey ... darker colours can be ageing, with the exception of red. Red camiknickers are particularly cheering in winter. If this sounds extravagant, see the glossary for e-shops that do an excellent and reasonably priced range. Camiknickers will cover lumpy bottoms, make thighs look trim and, most importantly, wearing them will give you secret confidence.

(v: Affairs, Cinq à sept, Creative corsetry, Secret confidence)

Cancelling Christmas

'Have a great Christmas, but only if you want to.'
— ROB RAYNER

It is okay to do this unless you have very young children. This time of year can be a very difficult and stressful and lonely time for many people. One way of getting round it is to volunteer to do charitable work and encourage your lazy parents to join in, i.e. helping the homeless, or deprived or traumatised children, or housebound old folk have some kind of Christmas. This means that you are doing something worthwhile, you will actually enjoy yourself and you are avoiding the hideous materialism that epitomises the Christmas season. However, it has become increasingly fashionable to volunteer and so you may find your offer of help is turned down. Don't be down-hearted as you are now entirely within your rights to fly to the nearest non-Christian country and stay there for some time, but do think about offering your services to a local charity in a more sustainable way in the New Year.

(v: Christmas, Going to prison, Hell, Volunteering)

Cancer buddy

Cancer is virtually a pandemic in the western world. The likelihood is that one in three of us will get some form of cancer during their lifetime and may even die of it. Breast cancer is the commonest form of cancer in women so you will probably know somebody who has it, has had it, or you may even be a sufferer yourself. The good news is that the treatment of breast cancer has been so broadly successful that the disease has been re-classified as a chronic illness rather than a life-threatening disease, but whichever way you look at it cancer is not fun and chemotherapy and radiotherapy can leave patients feeling more ill, more exhausted and more demoralised than when they were first given their diagnosis. Whether you are becoming a cancer buddy, or are looking for one, the job description is as follows:

1. This is not about you. However upset you are that your friend is ill you must put those feelings to one side and concentrate on your friend and her family.

2. A regular commitment to spending time looking after your friend is a nice offer. Don't just say I'll do anything to help, plan ahead and come up with a variety of suggestions – whether it's accompanying her to hospital while she undergoes chemotherapy, taking her to see a movie or simply suggesting a walk in the park on a sunny day. Let your friend choose.

3. Lovely surprise gifts such as flowers, scented candles or cosy bedsocks will be greatly appreciated but don't forget practical tasks too. Offering to make a meal, clean the house (chemotherapy patients are very susceptible to infections), walk the dog, drive the car, or pick up the kids can be as blessed as a bottle of delicious scent.

4. Having cancer is boring. If your friend wants to talk about it ad infinitum it's fine but your job is to be cheerful, life-enhancing and up and as far as possible to normalise what can be a grave situation. It's important to inject some fun into the proceedings and if your friend is bedridden some good gossip can be very diverting indeed.

5. Be sensitive to the needs of her family and other friends. Don't monopolise your friend or take control of her life, requests or requirements, or worst of all become competitive with your friend's other cancer buddies. Sometimes the best thing you can do is just to leave a flask of soup by the door.

6. Remember to celebrate any good news your friend may receive, and there will be some in the course of treatment, even if the long-term prognosis isn't great.

7. You are allowed to feel sadness too but you need to take responsibility for this and process it at home.

(v: Hair loss, Hospital etiquette, Leaving the party, Making a will, Memory boxes, Ward wear)

Candles

In almost all faiths, votive candles are part of ritual observances. In modern times there is something incredibly cheering and festive, particularly in the depths of winter, about taking the time to light strategically placed candles around the house. The clutter disappears, ditto the cat hair, the peeling paintwork. You don't even have to wait until twilight falls, in Scandinavia candles are lit any time of the day or night.

However, a word of warning. Candles – like cushions – are a girl thing. Men are baffled by them. And yes, you can have too many in a household. As columnist Julie Burchill hilariously observed, 'I bet you could prove with pie charts that the more scented candles a woman buys, the less orgasms/job security she has.' Ouch.

(v: Magic spells)

Can't

Or won't? 'There is no such word as can't.' If you ever find yourself saying, 'but I can't . . . ', simply replace the phrase with 'I'll try', unless your personal safety is at risk or your actions will deeply hurt somebody you love. The results can be extraordinary.

(v: I don't)

Carbohydrates

Nowadays it's almost socially acceptable to have a glass of wine or a line of coke but should one piece of bread pass your lips you know that you will be damned for all eternity.

Boring though it is to have to admit it, and although in theory we don't believe in dieting, ditching the carbs does help knock off the pounds. This basically means doing the Atkins, without doing the Atkins. Or doing a sort of Atkins, but with a tiny bit of carbs on the side. It still works.

Carbs are also addictive, so the less you eat them, the less you want them. This will help you keep the weight off once you have lost it. So let's re-frame the idea of 'dieting' as 'slightly changing the way you eat' and we'll throw in some super-foods too for good measure. Why the hell not? *(v: Ballooning weight, Blueberries, Diets, Eat your greens, Going to prison, Waist)*

Cars

'A car, a car, my kingdom for a car.'
– 'My Kingdom for a Car', PHIL OCHS

It's less important if you live in a city but if you are single and want a car, you need to have a man who knows his carburetor and his big end and who you can go to and wring your hands and say, 'Can you sort this out please, as I have to go away, ooh, and by the way I don't have much money.' It's counter-intuitive feminism. The 'damsel in distress' is usually a very good turn where a jalopy is concerned, simply because men love to be macho and practical, and they also love to help out. This is the perfect conduit for their frustrations. Having said that, please don't forget to sign up with the Automobile Association or equivalent. If you discover that the aforementioned male doesn't know his carburetor from his callipers then the AA will prove invaluable.

Many women bang on about cars being unnecessary,

but they are vital if you want to visit friends in the country and/or have kids and generally buzz about the place not carrying a coat.

(v: Counter-intuitive feminism, Taxis)

Cashmere

Handwash in 'volumising' shampoo. It will make your Cashmere even softer and very, very fluffy.

(v: I can't afford to buy cheap)

Casual sex

An awful lot of moralistic drivel is written about casual sex. Ultimately it's your choice.

(v: Bachelors, Contraception, It's a gift, No sex before marriage, Twice is polite)

Catching the bouquet

If '27' is the new '18' then the age limit for bridesmaids has risen exponentially. What was the preserve of tiny tots, your best friend from school, your sisters and virgins or at least the unmarried is now open to pretty much anyone of any age – not least your newly divorced godmother. So let's not be ageist about brides-maiding. Choose the women, whatever their age, you love best to accompany you through the preparation for the profound ceremony of marriage and don't forget that nowadays no single woman is too old to catch the bouquet. However, if you feel you are really too elderly to totter down the aisle in peach chiffon behind your three times already married best friend you are allowed to say so.

(v: BF, Wearing white dresses, Wedding cake)

Cats
Forget clichés about elderly spinsters in shapeless house-coats with cat hair in the butter, cat owners are true sensualists. You get a graceful, tactile, independent admirer in four-legged form. Cats are pretty low maintenance: they don't mind you going out to work – and they do wonders for your physical and mental well-being. Relationships with cats are (largely) free of the psychological games inherent in human relationships. Pets don't have mood swings or meltdowns and they never talk back. They are great levellers. Plus, they're elegant. Cats are super-groomers – and never have a bad-hair day.

It's often better to get two kittens. They are company for each other and not much more expensive. Or, if you don't have time for rearing young cats, choosing an older, house-trained moggie from a pet rescue centre is a great solution. Never give them embarrassing names (cats have their pride). And do invest in pet insurance from day one. Just make sure their dental bills aren't higher than yours!
(v: Blow-dries, Hope)

Catnapping
Whether you are a cat, a master of the universe, a cockney sparrow or Spanish having a siesta, having a power snooze, having a little lie-down, taking a nap, taking forty winks, sleeping in the afternoon is one of the joys of life. It is restorative in every sense. An hour in the afternoon is worth about three hours sleep at night, and can take the edge off exhaustion, lift your spirits and prepare you for a long night out.
(v: Bolt-hole)

Caveman moment

Fiery feminists or not, we all have to admit to having a caveman moment from time to time. That swoony guy who could surely sling you over his shoulder, gather wood, make a fire and then go and kill something for dinner with no mucking about reading poetry to you either. Grr. The thing is, he is often quite cavemanish in other respects too. So after the initial swooning and OMG moments, you are left with, er, a caveman. We all love a hunk who can chop down a trunk but in the cold light of a twenty-first century dawn we may decide we need other qualities in a man for a longer-lasting relationship.
(v: Bitches and hos, Fur, Rap)

Champagne

'I drink it when I'm happy
And when I'm sad.
Sometimes I drink it when I'm alone.
When I have company I consider it obligatory.
I trifle with it if I'm not hungry
And I drink it when I am.
Otherwise I never touch it, unless I'm thirsty.'
– MADAME LILY BOLLINGER

Let's also raise a glass to the heroic Madame Clicquot Ponsardin who in 1805, aged 27, took over the company on her husband's death and developed the now ubiquitous Veuve Clicquot. How extremely clever and very progressive of her to use her widowhood to name and brand her champagne, restore her family fortunes and give so many people so much pleasure down the ages.
(v: Artisan mustard, Booze, Cocktails, Dipsomania, Drunk-dialling)

Charm

Is a double-edged sword.

(v: Bachelors)

Chastity

It has become fashionable to opt for chastity as a way of protecting oneself from potential abuse and subsequent heartbreak at the hands of the hordes of emotionally inadequate men who roam our streets and frequent our parties. But you do have a choice, so exercise it.

Don't go to bed with a man who you know isn't going to be nice to you in the morning.

(v: Entering a convent, No sex before marriage)

Cheating

In card-games or life cheating has an underhand quality that is deeply unattractive. It suggests a desire to win whatever the cost and an inability to respect fine qualities and genuine abilities in others. Cheats tend to be found out, cf. Lord Archer, Lord Black, Bernie Madoff, and are universally despised except by other cheats. Women tend to cheat with a little more style and a great deal more sex appeal, cf. M'Lady in *The Three Musketeers* and Mata Hari, and so we can forgive them almost anything.

(v: Poker)

Chess

Alongside crossword puzzles, sudoku and pub quizzes, chess exercises the functions of the junctions and stimulates the neural paths in one's brain. Allegedly this prevents Alzheimer's. It's probably worth a try.

Chia seeds

One of nature's highest plant-based sources of complete protein. Just 100g contain as much calcium as two cups of milk. Eaten whole or crushed they can also be used in baking or as a thickening agent. The best way to add chia to your diet is to sprinkle a teaspoon over muesli or porridge. You can also add them to smoothies, salads and stir-fries, or use the milled flour in muffins and cakes.

In the States you'll see the grain on menus, in health-food stores and at juice bars as the growing wave of 'chia evangelists' are working the superfood into dishes at celeb-studded vegan hot spots. But, in fact, chia, a member of the mint family, has always been a superfood – the third-most important crop for the Aztec empire, after corn and beans.

Chia seeds are packed with omega-3s (the essential fatty acids linked to lean muscle mass, clear skin and heart health). They are also fibre-rich, with more cancer-fighting antioxidants than blueberries. Simply add them to the food you love – and they fill you up. Best of all they have very few calories and are gluten-free.

(v: Ballooning weight, Cooking: eat your greens, Meditation)

Childbirth

Quite a lot of fuss is made about childbirth.

(v: Fertility, Five Element acupuncture, Pregnancy, Ward wear)

Childfree

One in five women aged 45 is now childfree. Analysts suggest both men and women want to work and play harder for longer before settling down. For some, it's enough of a challenge to meet a significant other for cocktails and mini-breaks, let alone think about rearing a child together, but the good news is that being childfree – a far more positive phrase than childless – is now quite socially acceptable.

There are a number of women who actively choose not to have children. They prefer to put their lover, their job and their freedom first and not everyone craves the traditional nuclear family or is automatically maternal.

If you don't have children, there is more time for holidays, parties, time-consuming hobbies and enduring friendships and the right to have fun – and yes to be selfish – without apology. It's also increasingly seen as a green choice.

But it is still an issue of pain for many. Fertility is never a given, so smug parents please go gently, plus becoming childfree can creep up on you while you are busy doing other things. It isn't necessarily a conscious decision. It's hard to know exactly when you're grown-up enough to be a parent – or even to be in a committed relationship. Men, bless them, will always have a get-out clause but the risk for women of starting (or ending) relationships later in life is that you may find it's too late to sprog.

(v: Aunts, Babies, Quests, Termination)

Chocolate

Handmade artisan chocolate is the new Châteauneuf-du-Pape. New waves of chocolatiers are cooking up extraordinary flavours – everything from chocolate with chilli to pineapple confit with ylang-ylang – in their laboratories. It has become the grown-up dinner party gift of choice.

All of us deserve decent chocolate, but for those of you worrying about ballooning weight the mantra is eat less but eat better. A single, exquisite, jasmine-tea truffle is better value than a box of brand-name chocolates. The higher the cocoa content (70% plus is good), the less sugar and saturated fat it contains.

Chocolate gets a bad press (mostly from men), but chocolate is also the reward you give yourself when life is going badly. It's the perfect way to cancel out a bad date, to calm a hangover or simply to grab supper on the run. Chocolate has amazing flavour and complexity, and it's the only form of nourishment that melts at body temperature. More emotion is invested in chocolate than any other foodstuff: it has a Proustian interplay with memory, perception and fantasy. It makes you friends and takes you out of yourself.

Chocolate can be deeply sexy too.

(v: Ballooning weight, Diet)

Choirs

Forget cabaret or stand-up, choirs are one of the best ways to meet new people. At the end of the evening you can all pile into the café or pub, you get to travel to performances and competitions, and you will learn to love being part of an ensemble, something bigger than yourself. And there is the sheer physical joy of singing.

Choirs are democratic. Every person brings a different dynamic to the group and the interaction between you – on a personal and social level – sets you apart from any other kind of band. It's the exact opposite of an *X Factor* audition. Memories of school choir practice might put you off, especially if you couldn't read sheet music and were asked to mime, but with the new 'indie' or 'scratch' choirs, it doesn't matter if you're not formally trained.

Communal singing is a powerful way to bond. With indie choirs, you don't have to turn up to millions of rehearsals. Often the call goes out via Facebook and what could be

more human and more fun than a bunch of people shedding
their ordinary lives to meet once a week to make music?
(v: Churches, Flow, Get out of a rut and get involved)

Christmas

'One Christmas was so much like another, in those years
around the sea-town corner now and out of all sound
except the distant speaking of the voices I sometimes hear
a moment before sleep, that I can never remember whether
it snowed for six days and six nights when I was twelve or
whether it snowed for twelve days and twelve nights when
I was six.'
– *A Child's Christmas in Wales*, DYLAN THOMAS

Christmas can be a testing time if you are prepared, as some
are, according to Martha Stewart's 'Christmas Count Down
to the 25th Holiday Calendar' to repaint the Sistine Chapel,
install plumbing and electric lights in the gingerbread house,
and bear a son, swaddle, and lay him in a manger. It's up
to you, of course, but it's also okay not to overdo it.
(v: Blues, Hell)

Churches

Churches are everywhere, like the corner shop or the pub,
but all the more splendid because they are there to escape
to and to take solace from, whomever your God. Sit and
soak up the divine and offer up prayers if you so wish. If
not in a particularly spiritual frame of mind, open your eyes
to the architecture and marvel at the stained-glass windows.
There is no judgement in the house of God.
(v: Day-tripping)

Cider vinegar
A teaspoon in a cup of hot water is regarded by many as the absolute dream ticket to re-boot your drowsy metabolism and making you bright eyed and perky. Quaff on a twice-daily basis and true believers swear you will shrink and glow with good health.
(v: Climacteric, Diets, Skin)

Cinq à sept
The magic time between five and seven p.m. (as the phrase denotes) when lovers meet, and the phrase was invented by Parisians. Moral concerns aside, by leaving work a little early you will still have enough time to make your assignation and then get home in order to shower, change and sit down to supper with your respective partners. You will discover too that afternoon sex has its own particular pleasures and rewards.
(v: Affairs, Arrangement, Creative corsetry, Twice is polite)

Cleaning
'Behind every immaculate house is a very dull person.'
– ANONYMOUS

Cleaning is both overrated and underrated. A little mess here and there, plus a couple of cobwebs, never did anybody any harm. However, if you want to create a bit of mental space there is nothing quite like a calm well-ordered home.
(v: Allergies, Flow, Housework, Infinite vistas)

(To) Cleanse or not to cleanse
Choose a product gentle enough for your skin. You are trying to remove oil and retain water (moisture) – something

too strong will dry your skin out and stimulate oil glands to produce more. The trick is to apply heat (a warm cloth) to your pores so oil can be melted otherwise it will stay under the first layer of skin – and you'll get spots.

Morning or night, a good dollop of cleanser massaged into your skin, in upward and outward circular movements, and removed with a warm muslin cloth leaves it clean and revived. The cloth helps gently exfoliate your skin's surface.
(v: Beauty industry)

(The) Climacteric (menopause)

Oceans has been written about this period of transformation in a woman's life and we provide some reading suggestions in the bibliography. Some people hardly notice 'the Change', for others it's a gruelling and miserable experience that can come with huge physical discomfort and emotional upset. However, the key thing is to understand that it is not an illness and that an awful lot can be done to help if symptoms are acute. Diet and exercise can play their part and if you are contemplating HRT, we urge you to research bio-identical hormone replacement therapy instead.
(v: Contraception, Eat your greens, Fertility, Flaming)

Cocktails

Cocktails are girl heaven, an escape from what Kingsley Amis once described as the three most depressing words in the English language, 'red or white'. Cocktails give confidence and class – and take the edge off a dull day or a difficult everything. There's always an excuse to sink a strawberry daiquiri with a girlfriend. It can be like starring in your own private film and there's a whiff of danger too. Cocktails were invented during Prohibition in the United States in the 1920s and drunk secretly in 'dives'.

Even today, the best bars remain discreet and the American TV series *Mad Men* has made cocktail drinking cool again. Back in fashion are strong-tasting spirits – bourbon, rye whiskey and gin – made using classic recipes with a modern twist. But don't be apologetic if you yearn for creamy concoctions with paper umbrellas and Carmen Miranda-style fruit garnishes. Long drinks can be better for the wallet – and the head.

Decor is crucial. Old-school sophistication is what you are looking for. Champagne bars at railway stations inspire childlike enthusiasm: but don't meet up on the day you're supposed to actually catch a train.

There are a few ground rules for the great last-minute cocktail fling. Dress up. Remember to eat or the waiters will regret letting you through the velvet rope. And do watch those rounds. Beauty comes at a price. You may be sitting in art deco heaven, but then most cocktails will start at a minimum of £10 each. And however much you are tempted, we really don't recommend drinking more than two or, at a stretch three, in one sitting – unless of course you are on a bender.

(v: Alcohol, Bad habits, Benders, Bombshells, Booze, Champagne, Dipsomania, Drunk-dialling)

Co-dependency

A term that is bandied about a great deal, sometimes jokingly. However, it is worth understanding what it means and how it might be affecting you. Addiction is a family disease and co-dependents are people who find themselves in relationships with people who are alcoholic or drug dependent. There are over 50 varieties of addiction and

while co-dependents may not be addicts themselves, there may be a family history of addiction. Co-dependents sometimes, though not always, have also suffered from some form of abuse or grievous loss at an early age that enable them to develop highly sophisticated coping mechanisms to face the world, but which overlay great suffering and vulnerability. To the outside world, co-dependents may appear to be highly functioning, successful and extremely charming, but secretly they can suffer from a crippling lack of self-worth and be super critical of themselves and others. In their efforts to keep control of the deteriorating family situation they find themselves in they may actually enable the addict in his or her addiction.
(v: Dipsomania)

Cognitive behavioural therapy (CBT)
Is very à la mode in therapeutic circles and is a useful tool if you want to change repetitive and depressive thinking and destructive patterns of behaviour. It's essentially about pressing the re-set button.
(v: Depression, Visualisation)

Cold showers
The infamous Scandinavian secret is the power shower, which jumpstarts the system and makes you run like a Duracell bunny. Can and should become a serious habit.
(v: Skin)

Colour
We rather took the mickey out of Colour Me Beautiful image consultants at the time when it was launched but in retrospect it's an extremely useful tool. The sight of armies

of students, office workers and shoppers clad in unrelenting funereal black is drab, drab, drab. So bring back the Sixties and rock on flower power.

Popping colours can give you zing and totally alter your mood, as well other people's. Prints and tangerines are prettier to look at, full stop. Everybody has certain colours that really work with their shade of hair and skin tone, so it is worth finding out if it is turquoise, scarlet, violet, canary yellow or lime green that works for you. Colour is a tonic all round. Not for nothing is shocking pink called the navy blue of India. If you can't say goodbye to darker tones, lighten up a charcoal grey cardigan with a dazzling scarf or a pair of red tights. We dare you.

(v: Bombshell, Twee)

Comfort zone

'Life begins at the end of your comfort zone.'
– NEALE DONALD WALSCH [author]

We all need to get out of our comfort zone and out there. Getting damp and chilly is one of the best ways of making you feel alive. We spend far too much time grumbling about the weather while lurking in our cosy, heated office or home 'pods', where the worst thing that can happen is a heel snaps. Getting on a horse, jumping in a river, rowing a boat, sleeping outdoors in a tent, these are all ways of getting back to basics and out of your comfort zone. Reaching a destination, cold and wet, after a hard and taxing journey, is lovely and will make you feel both challenged and proud. Even walking up the stairs to the office is, for many, a goal achieved. If you live in the country there is no excuse. If you are a city dweller, you still have access to parks, heath

and rivers where all sorts of organised activities can be found, whether hiking, riding, rowing or bicycling. But whatever your plan, ensure there is a hot shower and a decent supper at the end of it.
(v: Adventure, Flow, Wild swimming)

Commitment phobia
(v: Emotional availability)

Companionship
'It is the friends you can call up at 4 a.m. that matter.'
– MARLENE DIETRICH

Companions are part of the joyous sense of our lives. They know what makes us tick and what makes us laugh and they travel alongside us.

Romantic love can be selfish – 'I want you alone' – while companionship means making the most of the time two people have, not just for being together, but togetherness.

The truth is companionship is just as important as sex. Ask most couples why they chose their life partner, and they'll most likely answer, 'We enjoy each other's company'. It is impossible to foresee what our interests and likes and dislikes will be 20 years down the road – people mature differently – but the true measure of companionship is one's ability to accept development and change in a friend or partner without feeling it threatens us in any way.

There is nothing worse than feeling 'uncompanionable'. It is arguably more upsetting than a lover's tiff. We take pride in our friends, pleased that they have chosen us and that we have chosen them. They 'get' us and reinforce our sense of self.
(v: BF, Good husband material)

Complain

The service is bad. The food is revolting. The shop assistant is rude. Your face is puce, your heart is pounding, you feel resentful and you want to throw something through the window. Don't! Transfer the guilt back to the shop/service/ annoying thing in hand, and merely ask, 'How can they make this up to me?' Embellish naturally (a woman's prerogative), 'I bought this for my mother/It's my birthday/ I'm going away tomorrow' . . . that sort of thing. One of the few upsides of the Big Brother age is that all companies are now hidebound by recorded conversations and fear bad press from even the most lowly of customers. So stay calm. Take control. Insist on speaking to a manager! Don't take it out on the ill-paid, powerless employee who has the awful task of trying to fob you off over the phone. Remember courtesy and good behaviour at all times, but you do deserve that upgrade. Ask!

(v: Counter-intuitive feminism, Good behaviour, How to get an upgrade)

Complete wankers

Quite a rare beast but if you come across one of these men you will know instantly that you have. Their defining characteristic is that they have no redeeming qualities whatsoever. Don't bother to argue with them, it's a waste of your extremely valuable time, make your excuses and leave at the earliest available opportunity.

(v: Committed bachelors, Emergency exit, Narcissus)

Condoms

You know your options. In these days of snazzy new contraceptive devices (implants under the skin of your arm, indeed!), it's easy to overlook the simple, practical, chic of the condom. Safe to use, they are cheap and easy to obtain.

Being prepared doesn't make you a slut. Carrying condoms shows a willingness to practise safe sex and shows respect for a partner's and your own sexual health. Stash a pack in your handbag and simply forget about them until needed. Do occasionally check that they are in date.

Barrier contraception is key at any age because it not only protects you from unwanted pregnancies, but also from a number of very much unwanted STDs. It's important that you protect and survive especially if you are dating casually. Be assertive: you know what's best for your body so say exactly how you feel.

Don't let anyone sweet-talk you into having sex without a condom because 'it feels better'. Put bluntly: if it's not on – it's not in, and wave goodbye to that man if he tries to make life difficult.

(v: Contraception, It's a gift, STDs)

Confidence

'There's no mystery to confidence, it's just about self knowledge. It's the savvy to know which of our flaws can be changed, and which ones to accept and let go. Then, making the best of the good points.'

– IMMODESTY BLAIZE [Icon]

It is the heart of the matter. If you are genuinely confident you remain unflustered about what other people think of you, are interested in the outside world, can be open about your feelings, but are not seeking approval from others.

(v: Bien dans ta peau, Necessary vanity, Secret confidence)

Container gardens

All you need is outside space – anything from a window box to a balcony or a yard, where you can have planters and troughs. The more low maintenance the better.

There's no point in having anything that you will under- or overwater or will be kicked up by boys, dogs or footballs. No fragile blooms. No succulents. Stick to drought-resistant plants.

The joy of a container garden is that if there's room it's like having an extra room in the house, which you can decorate with chairs, a table or chaise longue. Plants can be grown in virtually anything provided you add some drainage holes. We've seen herbs growing in shoes and rows of beans sprouting from upturned hats. Recycle old suitcases, sinks and trunks too.

Plus there is the sheer joy of walking around a garden centre. Forget the plants, it's the people. There's something rather wonderful about watching folk from opposite sides of the class divide bonding over cottage garden flowers.

But just don't expect all your green-fingered friends to approve of your new container 'scheme'. They'll remark that the *Fatsia* is unhappy or insist that New Zealand grasses might have been a better choice. Don't forget that gardening can be the sport of the Borgias.

(v: Day-tripping)

Contraception

(v: Condoms, It's a gift, STDs)

Control freaks

They love to impose their beliefs and foibles on others and therefore are often draining company. The 'live and let live' ethos passes them by as they go about their business, bossily policing people's lives, going through their bins, metaphorical or otherwise, and giving a great deal of unsought advice. But beware. There's a little bit of a control freak waiting to ignite in all of us and once it takes hold it's a very hard habit to break. Step back while you can and begin to listen more instead.

(v: Advice, Bullying, Co-dependency, Dangers of overplanning, Exquisite listening)

Conversation (art of)

Agh. The art of small talk. The *je ne sais quoi*. Sadly, unlike politicians and state leaders, we don't all get furtively briefed with a finely honed precis, such as, 'This is Matthew. He's a spy and likes jumping on and off trains and making quick exits from hotels', which is, of course, potentially riveting. No. Mere mortals such as ourselves have to take our courage in both hands and pretend that we are wholly comfortable with the social scenario we find ourselves inhabiting, however unconfident we may feel. If one is feeling very shy, a good way of protecting one's inner core is to be extremely charming and ask questions of and be totally interested in other people. It turns out that everybody secretly loves talking about themselves and they will be very flattered by your interest in them. Let them. Inquire, make jokes, be self-deprecating. You will seem gracious and relaxed and if there is a dread pause in the conversation, 'Can I get you another drink?' always works very well too.

(v: Be well informed, Bores, Self-confidence, Small talk)

Cooking
Ready, steady, yes. This is what women the world over do several times a day.
(v: Anna Del Conte)

Cosmetic surgery
(v: Climacteric, Diets, Facial acupuncture, Tummy tuck)

Counter-culture/Occupy movement
After the great decades of political protest (Greenham Common, Rock against Racism, the Miners' Strike), came the era of rampant materialism. It seemed young people, brought up on Nintendo Game Boys and designer labels, were politically indifferent.

But now we're seeing a whole new generation dis-illusioned by global capitalism. The Occupy movement takes on the greed and indifference of the City ('Occupy Wall Street. Bring tent'); students mount colourful protests against fees and cuts; while young feminists (Shoreditch Sisters, Daughters of Eve) campaign against sex trafficking, female genital mutilation and sexual violence (SlutWalk). Most recently, Pussy Riot dominated the world's headlines and went to prison for scrutinising Putin's 'brave new Russia'. It's just like the 1970s again – we say nostalgically. Been there, got the poster.

But actually it's rather different. No longer broadly right- or left-wing, the new activists tackle single issues with wit, panache and bravery. The absence of elected leaders in the traditional sense may confuse us – but it's what keeps the movement fresh. Stanford MBAs Ori Brafman and Rod Beckstrom have called it 'starfish power' –

cut a leg off the starfish and it automatically regenerates ...
(v: Fairness, Demonstrations, Be well informed)

Counter-intuitive feminism
Essentially female behaviour that may look atavistic but
which masks an iron will to ensure that you get your own
way in the end.
(v: Cars, Mrs Thatcher)

Country weekends (weekend retreats)
Even if you weren't born with a peerage and a family motto,
you can always jump the class barrier and stage your very
own *Gosford Park* house party – as long as your chosen
destination has a long drawing room for pre-dinner drinks,
four-poster beds and a croquet lawn. (Organisations such
as the National Trust or The Landmark Trust rent out very
charming stately piles for just this kind of purpose.) City-
dwellers often underestimate the rejuvenating power of a
weekend away. The minute you hit the motorway, your
spirits will lift at the prospect of rolling countryside, long
walks and roaring fires. A word of warning about the
country, however, it's very green. There are no shops and
to get mobile phone reception you probably have to climb
on top of a barn. Plus, if you're staying in someone else's
country house, there's a bewildering etiquette to learn.
Should you help yourself to breakfast in the morning? How
does the bloody Aga work? How do you address the house-
keeper? Key to getting it right with your hosts is to bring at
least a couple of bottles of decent wine, an additional present
such as some lovely soap or a slim volume of verse and
always, always, always write a proper thank-you letter.
Arguably the more 'natural' and at ease with yourself you

are, the more rewarding the country experience will be. Even uptight townies unwind in the end. Climb a stile, get muddy, swim in a river: you'll come back glowing with health, having spent a weekend in an elegant bubble, only smelling slightly of wet dog.

(v: Bolt-hole, Comfort zone, Courtesy, Guests, Seaside, Wild swimming)

Courtesy

A little of this can go a very long way; and there are certain key attitudes that even a post-feminist man should adhere to. If common courtesy could be rolled out around the world, what a sweeter place it would be.

To have the door opened with the words 'No, after you', is a delight. An instant 'Let me take that for you', at the sight of a woman struggling with bags of shopping and staggering to the bus or car is music to our ears. Asking 'How are you getting home?', 'Shall I call you a cab?' and then walking you to the aforementioned cab (and opening the door) earns a man five gold stars.

This may sound like charm-school stuff, but it used to be a blueprint for male behaviour across society. In particular, we despair that men no longer get up for pregnant women on busy Tubes and trains. So how do we bring common courtesy back? Answers on a postcard please.

(v: Manners, Twice is polite)

Crash pads

You're on to date number five. After a movie, supper and flirting, you suggest going back to their place.

Never mind that it's Zone 3 with a £50 taxi fare. The

Date looks into your eyes and says coolly, 'Damn it, let's get a hotel!'

Crash-pad hotels are the latest trend. Instead of trekking home on public transport, you can check into a chic boutique hotel without breaking the bank. If all is going well you won't have had a decent night's sleep and you'll arrive unfashionably late at the office, but if the reverse you can at least console yourself that you've gone to work early looking revived and refreshed and will impress your boss.

The crash-pad model is based on no-frills timeshare-style hotels – the sort you get at airports or train stations. But it has none of the seedy associations of the 1970s shag pad. You'll get a state-of-the-art entertainment system, mini bar and even a New York-style wet room.

Instead of worrying about how tidy your bedroom is, or whether you've got anything to drink at home, you can focus on pure pleasure. Frazzled couples who have managed to get a babysitter for the night might even want to book in for the whole evening.

The unspoken message of the crash pad is clear: you are here, only briefly, to rest and recharge. Everyone deserves to feel like a rock star for a night.

(v: Creative corsetry)

Cream

The word. The texture. The colour. The sound. The 'everything' about cream is sexy. Whipped, poured, Chantilly: it's a luxury that feels automatically orgasmic. Even the sound of the word makes for a better day. You are the cream in my coffee or even the Alexander in my brandy cocktail. Treat yourself.

Creativity

Is not linked to IQ. You may not be able to split the atom, but boy, can you pack a punch as a dancer, artist, poet, writer, craftswoman, actor … the list is endless. The latest brain research shows that just changing small, regular, hidebound habit boosts your creativity, as can being creative.
(v: comfort zone, Live as well as you dare)

Creative corsetry

Every over-40-something Oscar-winning actress and mother of three is bending over backwards (literally) to be on the cover of *Vanity Fair* wearing a corset and suspenders and not much else, claiming that she's beginning to explore the dark side of her sexuality. We blame Madonna. So to remind you of the rules, this kind of kit is only to be worn on stage at the Folies Bergère in Paris or Caesar's Palace in Las Vegas or in the privacy of your own bedroom or hotel room.
(v: Affairs, Crash pads, Have you got the kit?, Pornography)

Credit cards

We all have a love/hate relationship with credit cards. On the one hand they enable us to buy beautiful and expensive shoes, on the other they highlight the poisonous relationship between 'consumers' (by the way, when did we stop being people?) and banks. If you find yourself in trouble with a credit card, and many of us do, there isn't an excuse. You need to face the problem, respond quickly, work out a payment plan, set up a standing order and stick to your budget. And don't forget to cut the card up.
(v: Angry birds, Grasping the nettle, Money matters, New financial intimacy, Opening brown envelopes)

Crisis

When you are having a meltdown it's annoying to be told by the office know-it-all that in Chinese the word crisis also means opportunity. However, there is a grain of truth in this old adage so instead of kicking the door in or sitting down to write a suicide note, think about the dramatic and sometimes positive alternatives that a crisis might be offering you. Whether it's the abrupt end of an increasingly unsatisfactory relationship, losing a job that ultimately you don't like very much or facing bankruptcy, you are finally being forced to confront problems that have probably been simmering away for quite some time. This could be liberation.

(v: Opportunity, Suicide)

Cross-generational friendship

These days it's not unusual to see a 38-year-old and a 70-year-old having dinner together. We are all beginning to understand it is unhealthy to hang out exclusively with your own age group. A true friend is someone who makes you think differently, who is willing to share the risks that any increase in complexity brings – that's why cross-generational friendships are so rewarding. It's important to look beyond your obvious social group.

Older friends bring wisdom and perspective and teach you not to waste time on regrets. They tend to be less judgemental and less competitive. There's very little they haven't lived through, and they enjoy your strengths. Plus, they can be a humbling reminder to us that we ain't seen nothing yet when it comes to hedonistic rule breaking.

Younger friends keep us on our toes – whether it's recommending new shops and bars, tweaking our wardrobe, ('yes' to the leather jacket, 'no' to the kitten heels) or teaching us to download the latest apps. As a more assertive generation with liberal parents, they have a refreshing – and surprisingly good – take on sex and love. They are less likely to obsess about work and they understand pleasure. And they take us out of our comfort zone. They do need a bit of guidance and support too, but it's rewarding for us to feel we can reciprocate.

It's a huge compliment to be adopted as a friend by somebody who is 20 years younger or older than you. But no one is asking you to be a neo-parent or an old-age pensioner's carer. True cross-generational friendships are fun, not worthy.

(v: BFs)

Crosswords

(v: Chess, Mental exercise)

Crushes

Crushes make the world go round. Anything that puts a sparkle in your eye, makes you brush your hair in the morning and get to work on time, has to be a good thing. Having a crush is like having a pulse – it makes you feel alive.

However, you can't always choose your crushes. Sometimes they just sneak up on you and before you know it – ooh, heavens – who was that?

Adolescent crushes are a trial run for real emotion and a real relationship. They help us understand which qualities we notice and like in another person, and maybe a few that we don't like. If we're older, particularly if we are rendered shy or giddy or tongue-tied by the experience, it can be a nostalgic reminder of teenage rites of passage.

Our crush may never guess the extent of our feelings. Or it might be a mutual crush, where there's a shared but silent acknowledgement that in another life you could have been far more to each other than you are in this one, and there is a pleasurable sadness in acknowledging that. Crushes should be, by definition, a fun flirty pleasure, an escape from real life, or even a tricky patch in a long-term relationship.

But be wary if you find a crush tipping into a full-blown adult obsession. We've probably all been tempted to do a little bit of phone and cyber stalking, cf. Princess Diana, but it rarely ends well. Remember the rules of good behaviour still apply.

Likewise, if you're on the receiving end of unrequited attention try to be kind: it's a compliment, but never let anyone behave in a way that makes you feel funny or uncomfortable. That's not a good crush. That's harassment.

Let's not be hypocritical either. Part of the test of crushes for people in long-term relationships is accepting your partner will have them too.

Often we're mortified if the other person realises we're smitten. But the greater truth is that after the age of 35 everyone loves having admirers. You can never have too much positive attention.

(v: Quests)

Cunt

According to Wikipedia, etymologists cannot completely agree about the origins of the word cunt though it is thought that it is of Norse/German origin and must also bear some relation to the Latin word *cunnus*. It was in common usage during the twelfth century but by the sixteenth century had become a term of abuse. The reasons for this remain unclear but are (presumably) misogynistic in origin. The word appears several times in *The Canterbury Tales*, within a bawdy context, but at this point in its etymological career the word is not considered to be obscene. The main character of *The Wife of Bath's Tale*, who in her own way epitomises the idea of a Dangerous Woman in the Middle Ages, has this to say on the subject:

'You would have my quente alone?/Wy, taak it al! Lo, have it every deel!/Peter! I shrewe yow, but you love it weel;/For I wold sell my bele chose,/I kould walke as fresshe as is a rose;/But I wool kepe it for yor owene tooth.' which translates as:

'Is it because you'd have my cunt alone?/Why take it all, have every bit of it;/Peter! Beshrew you but you're fond of it!/For if I would go sell my belle chose,/ I could walk out as fresh as is a rose;/But I will keep it for your own sweet tooth.'

Interestingly, after close textual analysis, what looks like a slightly risqué chat reveals a much subtler exploration of the loaded relationship between sex and love, money and power.

Three hundred years later John Donne's sly but loving tribute to the cunt – 'sucked on country pleasures, child-ishly' – in the sexy and magnificent sonnet 'The Good Morrow' marks the time when a shadow was beginning to fall on the open use of this word, but whatever it's genus, as Germaine Greer remarks, 'it is one of the few remaining words in the English language that has a genuine power to shock'.

(The) Curse

'I was ten. I had noticed something was weird earlier in the day, but I knew from commercials that one's menstrual period was a blue liquid that you poured like laundry detergent onto maxi pads to test their absorbency. This wasn't blue, so ... I ignored it for a few hours.'
— *Bossypants*, TINA FEY

Old-fashioned slang for menstruation that reflects the loaded associations that come with being a daughter of Eve. Luckily advances in science, combined with good vitamin advice and specialist medication make having your period a less onerous task and something that can be talked about in public, though not necessarily at supper.
(v: Menstruation)

Curves

(v: Ballooning weight, Bombshell, Boobs, Creative corsetry, Petticoats)

Cutting ties

'The truth will set you free. But first, it will piss you off.'
— GLORIA STEINEM [feminist and journalist]

Your time is too precious to spend on people who let you down, jobs that crush your potential or hobbies that you have outgrown. By all means research the situation carefully first. It would be awful not to give a friend or lover the chance to change. Maybe you can meet halfway so whatever happens you don't burn your bridges. But if when you've thought it through properly you still want to cut ties, do it quickly and cleanly. The more quickly you begin the process, the faster it's over. There's no need for bitchiness. You can thank the person for their friendship and say goodbye. But don't look back. It's kinder for everyone – especially you.

(v: Emergency exit)

Cycling

Is a fab and practical thing to do, though a challenge if you are whizzing round in a major city surrounded by mad men in haulage trucks. Have clip-on lights and, even though it's not terribly fetching, wear a high-visibility jacket, which you can roll up to nothing and slip into your bicycle pannier, and a helmet. It's vital you practise your hand signals.

In contrast, cycling in the countryside is a truly blissful way of travelling about, especially in the summertime.

(v: Adventure, Ballooning weight, Flow, Sideburns)

Daddy damage

'Every woman adores a Fascist,
The boot in the face, the brute
Brute heart of a brute like you.'
– 'Daddy', SYLVIA PLATH

If only we had world enough and time to do due justice
to the complex relationship between fathers and daughters.
At best it can be an incredibly important paradigm for
your future healthy relationships with men. At worst, and
it can get very bad indeed as the mountains of misery
memoirs testify, it can almost destroy your life. If you
feel your present is over-shadowed by an unhappy past,
or you find yourself in repetitive patterns when it comes
to relationships with men, it may be that revisiting past
events, in the context of your relationship with your
father, within a therapeutic setting – understanding what
happened, reliving the pain and then moving on – is what
will set you free.
(v: Daughters, Family therapy)

Dancing

'I did everything he did but backwards and in high-heels.'

– GINGER ROGERS on Fred Astaire

(v: Ballroom dancing, Dancing with the devil, Flow, Raves, Tango, Tap-dancing)

Dancing with the devil

Go on, take to the floor! You'll need something to talk about in the old people's home.

(v: Co-dependency, Control freaks)

Dangers of over-planning

'We must be willing to get rid of the life we've planned, so as to have the life that is waiting for us.'

– JOSEPH CAMPBELL

Very few people say they enjoy that runaway feeling when there's so little time and so much to organise, e.g. Christmas, but are we, in the Western world, in danger of over-planning our lives away? Is that dreaded but meaningless contemporary word, 'stress', a modern-day response to atavistic fears that the world is a frightening and dangerous place, i.e. if you are worrying in the middle of the night that the colour of the table napkins is wrong for tomorrow's party, is it just your brain going into overdrive because you need approval from your social group because otherwise you will be left to die in the forest?

(v: Christmas, Co-dependency, Control freaks, Safety)

Dating

Always keep the door open. Love stories start every minute of the day: you never know what is round the corner. Keep shaking things up, breaking the rules and changing your habits. A recent scientific report suggests that by changing our routines we change our luck.

(v: Comfort zone, Complete wankers, Safety)

Dating sites

Ten years ago, people would rather have hung naked over a crocodile pit than admit they met through a lonely hearts ad. The very name screamed 'loser'. But now, thanks to cool online sites and classified ads, everyone has dabbled. Of course, it's lovely to meet in 'real life', where you can judge chemistry instantly. The fact that someone has walked across the room and chosen you is a great help. But over a certain age that room begins to get smaller. Sign up to a dating website and immediately you have more than 1,000 matches. You won't always fancy each other. But choice is everything. Don't spend too long e-flirting (it can be disappointing if you invest too much in the correspondence). After a couple of phone calls, arrange to meet. To be honest, the first time isn't a date. We can all be kind and convivial for an hour. Don't agree to a second date out of guilt, but be generous in your dismissal.

(v: Almost date, Dating, Good husband material)

Daughters

Daughters are one of life's great delights. It's lovely to have a Bonsai you. However, your daughter will need to separate from you at some point during adolescence and this can be a very painful process, not least because the warfare can be cruelly verbal as opposed to physical. Accept that this disconnection has to happen: pass the baton on, offer support and empathy but don't get in the way of your daughter's emerging independence.

(v: It's a girl, Mothers, Raising Girls, Sisters, Sons)

David Attenborough

Is David the sexiest man in Britain? Well, yes, probably. He is certainly the world's most powerful and influential naturalist. He has changed the way we understand ourselves and the species we share the planet with. He appeals to every age group. Evidently totally intellectually brilliant, he remains modest, warm, humane, funny and empathetic. He is the guest of honour at our top table.

(v: Good husband material, Top table, Will you marry me?, Zoology)

Day-tripping

If you are too stressed to holiday abroad, there's real joy in planning road trips with female friends. Pack up the car, print off maps and keep a copy of Pevsner in the boot. Build the day around a 'place of special interest' (castle, stately home, sculpture park, novelist's house), but make sure it's a day of total pleasure. Who cares about being single and not-exactly thin when you are whizzing down a country lane with your friends? You can keep an eye out for single arty men, but let's be frank, straight men rarely call their friends and say, 'Hey mate, I'm feeling a bit down. Fancy a trip to a National Trust property?' This is a day for female bonding. Make sure you have a lovely lunch: a glass of rosé with fish and chips. And then, of course, on the way home there's always a garden centre. It's not a proper day-trip

unless you return home with a car full of pots of herbs and perhaps the odd small tree.
(v: Container gardens)

Dealing not coping

Women are very good at coping but sometimes the coping overwhelms the dealing. Problems become repetitive and, paradoxically, developing successful coping strategies can mean that you begin to take a much bigger share of responsibility while never resolving the underlying problems. The result is that you become exhausted, snappish, irritable and controlling. You feel exploited but can't quite explain why. So a home truth: many women complain endlessly about how much they have got to do and how little time they have to do it, but won't let anybody else help. So don't be a martyr. Delegate what you can. Grasp the nettle and write down a list of the things that are bothering you and take action.
(v: Big babies, Boundaries, Bullying, Co-dependency, Grasping the nettle)

Debt

'Annual income twenty pounds, annual expenditure nineteen nineteen six, result happiness. Annual income twenty pounds, annual expenditure twenty pounds ought and six, result misery.'
– Mr Micawber, *David Copperfield*, CHARLES DICKENS

'All I ask is the chance to prove that money can't make me happy.'
– SPIKE MILLIGAN

There is no excuse to be in debt, although probably most of us are in one way, shape or form. Take control. Buy an accounts book and work out your income and your outgoings. Then make the necessary cuts coalition style. It hurts, of course it does. But you'll get immense satisfaction from managing your money more effectively and once you cut unnecessary spending habits you'll begin to value the things you do spend money on, and enjoy planning for your future.
(v: Credit cards, Grasping the nettle, I can't afford to buy cheap, Money matters, New financial intimacy, Opening brown envelopes, Pensions)

Décolletage

Ooh la la. Ding dong. This is the coyest, sexiest part of your body and one you should know how to work and exploit, should you wish to do so. French women are all very good at protecting and projecting this area, but it needs daily attention. A combination of creams, massage and exercise will work well together but don't forget the vital element – the importance of posture. The overall aim is to have a dainty show of crêpe-free bosom, which you can expose with a certain amount of flirtation. If the male gaze is important to you, neglect your décolletage at your peril.
(v: Boobs)

Deferment of pleasure

It is a truth universally acknowledged that the survival of the human race has depended on the fact that women will defer their own pleasure for the sake of the greater good. In modern times we remain experts in this particular field and it's incredibly useful for all those not quite grown-up men around us that we do. Even the media, supposedly

dominated by liberal types, absolutely consolidates this view. However, is there a slight whiff of martyrdom in all of this? Of course, it is good to meet your responsibilities: some would say that it is only by meeting them that we set ourselves free, but nowadays we seem to want to add even more great expectations to the mix. Can we only really let ourselves have a good time when we've stacked the dishwasher, lost ten pounds and recovered the lost ark of the Covenant? Ten years later we might look back at a photograph and say: 'Heavens, I did have rather nice arms after all. I could have gone dancing and had fun and maybe got home a bit late and neither I nor the people I love would have been any the worse for it.'
(v: Orgasms)

Del Conte, Anna [icon]

'There is nothing which bonds a family together more than a delicious meal enjoyed around a table. While you eat it conversations blossom, laughter explodes, discussions and arguments arise. In three short words: life becomes alive. There is nothing which expresses love more than good food, carefully and properly prepared, or at least that is what I hope since I have spent the best part of my adult life cooking and I have enjoyed every minute of it.'
(v: Cooking)

Delusional behaviour

It's delicious being irrational for a day or so. As hard-working grown-ups we all need time out from being sensible. Maybe we can still be a diva at 50. It is, of course, possible the boss is secretly in love with you ... But when friends and family start to look at you with sympathetic faces, it's time to rein in, before you tip over into full-scale lunacy.

(v: Benders, Crushes, Female logic, Mad women, Magical thinking, It's not all about you, Ranting, Benders)

Demonstrations

'I think you should take your job seriously, but not yourself.'
– JUDI DENCH

Please do go on these. You should not be deterred by scaremongering newspapers. Terrible things are done in our name by politicians who we have voted into power. You have the right to protest about them. Just don't go round carrying a rock in your hand, or torturing policemen with poetry.

(v: Angry birds, Lipstick, Poetry)

Department stores

For everything but the kitchen sink, but they do sell kitchen sinks too! A department store is NOT a large shop with lots of concessionary shops within it. A department store is where you can go and buy a pair of camiknickers, a dishwasher or just a needle and some thread and know with certainty that you will be treated with absolute courtesy whatever your age, weight or spending power. If you take time to look, you will also uncover all sorts of useful treasures, such as candle-snuffers, L-shaped pillows, egg coddlers, strapless bras and beautifully made, black suede evening gloves. We cannot recommend department stores highly enough.

(v: Lipstick, Very public inconvenience)

Depression

'If you want the rainbow you gotta put up with the rain.'
– DOLLY PARTON

'In the midst of winter I found within myself an invincible summer . . .'
– ALBERT CAMUS

'Noble deeds and hot baths are the best cures for depression.'
– *I Capture the Castle*, DODIE SMITH

Depression is a generic term that covers a multitude of sins. For some people it's a phase, for others a spiritual event, or for the most unlucky it's a life-long illness that has to be managed like any other chronic disease. Psychotherapists and psychiatrists are often at war when it comes to the treatment of depression, but don't be afraid to take medication despite the scaremongers. It can help enormously, if only to give you a break.
(v: Blues, Freud, Jung, Self-pity)

Detaching with love

A phrase that has eased itself into common parlance alongside the proliferation of Alcoholics Anonymous and other related self-help groups. In essence, it means that we can allow ourselves 'to love the person but not the disease', but that we do not have to, nor should we try to, engage with the emotional or practical carnage that often surrounds the addict. It is also a useful behavioural tool for daily life, actually you can detach with love from just about anybody who you feel is giving you a hard time. If this all sounds far too po-faced for its own good, be reassured, the phrase 'I'm

detaching with love' can also be used to comic effect in a range of social situations, e.g. if you need to leave a party pronto, disengage from a bender or decide not to go to bed with a man you've recently snogged.
(v: Bad boys, Benders, Co-dependency, Dipsomania, Emergency exit)

Diamonds (are a girl's best friend)
Tradition suggests that a man should spend three months' salary on the engagement ring for his intended, and that nothing less than half a carat* will do. If there is a lovely man in the wings, this is the moment to fulfill your heart's desire. However, we all know that the path of true love doesn't always run smooth. Nowadays many a single gal buys her own ring, and all power to her elbow.

Make sure you buy the best diamonds you can afford. They come in all cuts and colours and are as hardy as hell, so don't just keep them for special occasions. Pink, to make the boys wink, is especially pretty. These sparklers will go with everything in your wardrobe and are a great investment, so bear that in mind too. Last but not least you can choose your stone then ask an à la carte jeweller to create something for you to your own design. How classy.
(v: Engagement)

Diets
'Never eat more than you can lift.'
– MISS PIGGY

---

* A carat is 0.20 grams.

Yo-yo dieting is a feature of many women's lives but it can be bad for your health, and can ironically alter your natural metabolism, which makes it extremely hard to lose weight. What's important to understand and accept is your natural body shape, but what nobody wants to do is put on too much weight. Jill Shaw Ruddock rightly claims that we must concentrate on the noun rather than the verb.
(v: Ballooning weight, Carbohydrates, Cider vinegar, Eat your greens, Trampolining)

Dignity
This may sound like a preposterous, perhaps old-fashioned, characteristic but it's rather like necessary vanity or secret confidence. It's a character-defining quality that can shape your life for the better. If you can manage not to lose your temper, whatever the slings and arrows of outrageous fortune, people will respect you for it. However, if you are holding your head up high while all around are losing theirs don't take the moral high ground. That just makes you a prig.
(v: Good behaviour, Grace)

Dilation
Cervical
When you are having a baby your cervix needs to dilate to ten centimetres. It's one of the rules. If it doesn't you will probably have to have a Caesarian. This will necessitate an epidural, which in the circumstances can be quite a relief.
Pupils
If your pupils are dilating it may be to do with shock or pain or fabulous sex or it may be that you have taken too many recreational drugs. If the latter, it's a telltale sign easily

spotted by canny teenagers and inquisitive bosses. Expensive sunglasses are helpful in these circumstances or you could just ease up on the hallucinogenics.
(v: Babies, Childbirth, Drugs, Sunglasses)

Dipsomania

An old-fashioned word for alcoholism. There are very broad definitions of what makes an alcoholic and also very narrow ones, but the governmental diktat to restrict yourself to a certain number of units a week is rather a blunt tool, which it seems the majority of regular drinkers find risible and routinely ignore. We are not natural killjoys but women are drinking more and more and for a variety of reasons it is no doubt injurious to our well-being. If you are worried about how much you are drinking, take a break. A little self-restraint from time to time is a good habit to acquire and one way forward is to abstain one day a week, one week a month and one month a year. Your health will benefit in all sorts of ways.
(v: Alcohol, Benders, Booty-calls, Booze, Champagne, Cocktails, Drunk-dialling, Emotional overdrinking)

Dishwashers

Many people spend more time loading and unloading the dishwasher than having sex.

This is unwise.

Divorce parties

It may be that once the financial settlement has been agreed it's appropriate to crack open a bottle of champagne, but this may not be a triumphant gesture, rather a recognition that a long and usually agonising process is now thankfully

over. As for divorce parties, isn't that the equivalent of dressing head to toe in black crêpe for a wedding?
(v: I don't, Lawyers)

DIY

Girls have solo sex too. *Sex and the City* blew the doors off with the episode that featured the Rampant Rabbit. No one needs to put up with bad behaviour in a lover when you have all the resources you need for self-satisfaction. Plus there's some rather promising kit out there. Don't ever let anyone make you feel lonely or inadequate about having solo sex. Men have been feeling great about it for centuries.
(v: Le gadget)

Dogs

'Dogs are owned by men and men are bludgeoned by fate.'
– *Lassie Come Home*, ERIC KNIGHT

If you are newly single, or your children have just left home, or both, then maybe the time has come to think about getting a dog. It's a commitment. Like small children, they need a routine you can stick to, but in return they offer devoted companionship. They will also force you to exercise, a minimum of half an hour a day, and wherever you go you will make new friends. It's wise to get a '57 Varieties' mutt/mongrel (they won't suffer from congenital health problems in the way that some purebred dogs do). Do your research into the dog's provenance and its parents' sociability before going ahead, but look forward to a long friendship.
(v: Ballooning weight, Cats, Diets, Exercise, Waist)

Do tell!

Well, sometimes it is appropriate and sometimes it isn't. Generally information needs to be passed around, that is one of the functions and rewards of being part of a bigger society. However, if somebody asks you to keep their secret then you must do so and if somebody asks you to reveal somebody else's secret then you must resist. But we are all vulnerable to siren songs so don't beat your BF up if she lets slip.

(v: BF, Gossip, Secrets)

Don't!

'To tell a woman everything she may not do is to tell her the most she can do.'

– SPANISH PROVERB

Down the rabbit hole

Sometimes in our over-controlled and over-planned lives we need to just let things happen to us and the more chaotic, abstract and hallucinatory the better. If, like Alice, you find yourself falling down a rabbit hole, i.e. every intention and expectation you had about your life is being tested and everything you face is about to be transformed, succumb – in retrospect, the experience will be life-changing.

(v: Adventure)

Drawing a veil

Unless life and limb are under threat, or human rights are being compromised, let it go. The Yankee Doodles say 'Don't sweat the small stuff', and we second that. Life's far too short.

(v: It seemed like a good idea at the time, Regrets)

Dreams

'Be not afeard. The isle is full of noises,
Sounds and sweet airs that give delight and hurt not.
Sometimes a thousand twangling instruments
Will hum about mine ears, and sometimes voices
That, if I then had waked after a long sleep,
Will make me sleep again; and then, in dreaming,
The clouds methought would open, and show riches
Ready to drop upon me, that when I waked,
I cried to dream again.'
– Caliban in *The Tempest*, III. ii., WILLIAM SHAKESPEARE

'We are such stuff
As dreams are made on; and our little life
Is rounded with a sleep.'
– Prospero in *The Tempest*, IV. i., WILLIAM SHAKESPEARE

'Dreams . . . they've gone through and through me, like
wine through water, and altered the colour of my mind.'
– *Wuthering Heights*, EMILY BRONTË

'Dreaming is free.'
– '*Dreaming*', DEBBIE HARRY
(v: Freud, Jung)

Drugs

Are as old as the hills. Folk the world over have been sniffing
convivially and smoking and imbibing companionably since
the golden age, obviously because by and large they are
extremely enjoyable pursuits. Artists have always been
attracted to substances that heighten feeling and produce
altered states, as have shamans and religious visionaries. In
the twenty-first century a gin and tonic and the occasional

jazz cigarette or the like is not anyone else's business but yours and can be a good way of unwinding after a hard taxing day. Your body may well be a temple, or a Bedouin tent for all we know, but you are grown-up enough to make an informed decision. But all kinds of drugs including pharmaceuticals, and yes, boring old aspirin, tend to be addictive and their use needs monitoring so you do not get hooked.

If you have got teenagers and you come across any 'substances', you need to discuss them calmly and as soon as possible. The alternative is where addictions lie. Threatening hell and damnation will only make the kids go underground. You need to keep the debate ongoing and in the open. The bigger picture is that the illegal drugs industry is now worth trillions of dollars and brings criminality, destruction and death in its wake. But the genie is well and truly out of the bottle whichever way you look at it. The case for proper education about, taxation of and decriminalisation of drugs has never looked stronger.
(v: Dilation, Drunk-dialling, Insomnia, Meds)

Drunk-dialling

You are, of course, over the affair. You are out with friends, it's a Friday, and you are boldly looking forward to the future but after that third drink the small voice of doubt creeps in. Maybe it was my fault? Maybe I need to tell him how much I do love/hate him? Is he with somebody else? Is he missing me? It wouldn't do any harm to make the call. And so on and so forth . . . by closing time doubting Thomas has turned into a huge green glittering snake exhorting you to eat the apple. Before you know it, you are hitting speed-dial. At this point your BF will attempt to ascertain what is going on and then try to wrestle you to the floor, grab your phone and throw it in the nearest river – and not without reason, because she has spent every spare waking moment of the last three months listening sympathetically to your outpourings of rage and grief and the promise that you will never, ever speak to him again. But it's too late, the die is cast, you make the call. Even as you are doing it, you already know somewhere in your heart that when you wake up in the morning, whatever the outcome, you are going to absolutely hate yourself. There is only one solution: it's tough but mercifully simple. When an affair is over delete all phone and email addresses from all relevant technology and keep it that way. He can always find you again if he wants to.

(v: Bad habits, Booty-calls, Booze, Cocktails, Dipsomania)

Dullness

Is there any real excuse for dullness? There is surely little or no reason why people can't put effort into being amusing and entertaining company. A few anecdotes up your sleeve, some good jokes and a dash of piquant gossip are recommended. Be ready to be 'on'.

(v: Bores, Conversation [art of])

❧

Ease

'What if we just acted like everything was easy?'
— MARY ANNE RADMACHER

Eat your greens

Mother was right: you should eat your greens. The importance of dark green vegetables in our diet is, quite simply, not to be trifled with. From decades of exhaustive research, by the men and women in white coats, we have the indisputable facts: foliate and antioxidant-rich leafy vegetables can provide everything from a boost in your skin's radiance to a significant reduction in the risk of cancers and birth defects. We know that just three cups of fresh leaves a week can be invaluable to your health. If you find it all a bit goody two-shoes, the next time you are tucking into a bowl of salad greens consider the suggestion that you are eating sunshine. Sounds ridiculous but as any seven-year-old schoolkid will tell you, plants get their emerald hue from chlorophyll – a unique molecular structure, which allows them to capture and store the energy of sunlight.

But whatever you wish to ponder as you chew, the main reason to eat green leaves is, of course, how they taste –

elegant, complex and sophisticated. They look beautiful too. So toss them jauntily in a large bowl with a drizzling of balsamic, fresh lemon juice and extra-virgin olive oil and top them with all kinds of seeds and nuts, if you are so inclined. Divine.

(v: Ballooning weight, Climacteric, Diet)

Elderly primagravida

The average age for a woman to have her first baby in the UK has risen from 26 to 29.4 in the last ten years. The term elderly primagravida is the term used to describe a woman of 35 years or older who is expecting her first baby. Given that we are starting to have babies later and later, expect to hear this term more and more frequently – you may even be one yourself.

The pros of having a baby later are that you are far more likely to be calm and patient, and you won't worry about not going out to parties. However, it can be physically challenging and extremely exhausting.

(v: Babies, Childbirth, Fertility, Pregnancy)

Elegance

'The only real elegance is in the mind; if you've got that, the rest really comes from it.'

– DIANA VREELAND

(v: Beauty treatments, Camiknickers, Creative corsetry, Exercise, Petticoats, Necessary vanity, Secret confidence)

Email XXing

Of course we don't really LOVE them. But the screen 'X' is women's secret weapon: a way to lighten up a bossy email to a co-worker, or shorthand for 'we're still cool' after a slightly tricky missive. A couple of hundred years ago, it might have been an open sexual invitation. Now it's just a nice, platonic way of saying, 'Thanks for fixing the photo-copier'.

(v: Technology, XXXs)

Embroidery

Most of us claim that we are far too busy, our lives are too stressful, our time too limited to engage in a hobby. Blah, blah, blah. We've heard it all before. It's important that we have something to focus on apart from work. The truth is that it is truly life-enhancing and rewarding to take up a new interest. It can be anything from bee-keeping or collecting vintage cars to growing old roses, but if you want something that you can simply pick up or put down at a moment's notice at home then knitting, petit point, quilting or embroi-dery could be for you and you might even create a family heirloom in the process. If, as most of us are, you are over-exposed to modern technology there is something enor-mously soothing about shutting off the over-active brain and concentrating on making something beautiful with your hands. And, rather like a handwritten letter, there is nothing quite as nice as receiving a handmade present.

(v: Flow)

Emergency exit

Whether you are simply at a ghastly party, at the back of a disorderly queue or floundering in a relationship that is making you extremely unhappy, don't be afraid to use the emergency exit. That's what it's there for.

(v: Crisis, Leaving the party)

Emotional overdrinking

Yes, alcohol is the symptom but it's the self-hatred the next day that is ruining our lives. We wake up hungover, our body flooded with stress chemicals, which, apart from anything else, affect our metabolism.

Try to have at least one alcohol-free day a week. Avoid friends who are simply looking for a drinking partner. There are ways of resisting peer pressure with little white lies, such as 'I'm on antibiotics' or 'I've got a hangover from last night'.

Instead of pouring that glass, pamper yourself in different ways, e.g. a long aromatherapy bath, a massage or that DVD you've been meaning to watch.

(v: Alcohol, Booty-calls, Cocktails, Dipsomania, Drunk-dialling, Wine)

Empty Nest

You went away that
Summer's day
And I understood then
For all mothers
The strongest band in the universe
And I stand proud to be a member
I did not pop tears at the farewell
I had watched you with your grin
And charm
With your green eyes
More familiar to me
Than my own hands
As you told me of plans
You had made
For my quiet stoicism is nothing compared to

Mothers of soldiers
Mothers of prisoners
Mothers of the quiet starving.
I took those mother paces backwards
And like a twitching bird
Gathered myself
To walk away.
– 'July', SARAH-JANE LOVETT

Engagement

People make a fuss of you when you get engaged and so they should. Enjoy every last minute.
(v: Catching the bouquet, Hen nights, Wearing white dresses)

English eccentrics

Fascinate and amuse with their slightly daffy differences and the way they stick out like a sore thumb in today's homogenised society. Bring them on, we say. Often geniuses or aristo-bohemians, they are usually preoccupied or obsessed with an idiosyncratic way of living, and have a tendency to strange garb and unusual habits. However, they often achieve wonders and are to be treasured accordingly. They make life much more funky.

Enigma

It's hard to remain an enigma when we live in a world where everybody is intent on revealing every little thing about themselves at parties and then revealing it again on the interweb. But do try it. If in doubt, cast your mind back to *Brief Encounter* and imagine how the whole caboodle would have been blown out of the water if Celia Johnson had received a text at the wrong minute. Being enigmatic is a very sexy quality indeed.

(v: Instinct, Power, Sense of self)

Entering a convent

Who hasn't had that fleeting moment while watching Julie Andrews in *The Sound of Music* when you think, 'Surely I'd look great in a wimple?'

Before the emancipation of women 'becoming a bride of Christ' was a career opportunity. It meant that one could escape an arranged marriage and the attendant risks of childbirth and have some hope of a rudimentary education. Historically, women of a certain class could seek refuge in a convent, sometimes because of political necessity, cf. Eleanor of Aquitaine, or simply because they wanted to withdraw from a secular life.

Nowadays to become a nun, one must be Catholic, female, unmarried and sane. Women who are not virgins can become a nun (this is a big breakthrough) but Roman Catholic women who are divorced may not generally become a nun unless they have received an annulment from the Catholic Church. They must prove that the marriage was somehow invalid or contracted under false pretenses in order for an annulment to be granted.

A widowed woman may become a nun, but generally she must have raised any children to the age of 18 prior to taking vows, since these vows would supersede the care of her own children.

Some nuns are religious scholars, and sometimes it may be necessary to have a college education prior to joining an order. Twenty-first century nuns can work as nurses, teachers, doctors or psychologists and often play an active

role in the service of their local communities. So, if you're a dab hand at running up dirndl skirts made out of damask curtains this may be the job for you.
(*v: Chastity*)

Equality

'We are all equal wearing a swimming cap.'
– ANONYMOUS

Erotica

'Pornography is about dominance and often pain. Erotica is about mutuality and always pleasure.'
– GLORIA STEINEM

Desire begins in the head for many of us and women are just as entitled to visual stimuli as men. It may be looking at sensual photographs, buying rock star underwear or a visit to a burlesque club, but erotica is about falling in love with yourself a little: giving yourself permission to act out private fantasies – alone, or with a Significant Other. The erotic shapes our life in a very important way. It adds texture and spice to life. Don't let go of that just because you hate porn.
(*v: Creative corsetry, Pornification*)

Ethical banking

'There is a better way for banking – but it relies on us voting with our financial feet.'
– DEBORAH ORR, *The Guardian*, 13 July 2012

In an age where we can't trust the banks to have our best interest at heart (NB, several have also been charged with money laundering in third-world countries), we need to do our research.

The bank manager of 20 years is not our father! We can switch our account from the big banks to ethical, local or mutual alternatives (www.moveyourmoney.org.uk). Thanks to electronic banking, it's never been easier to shift your financial dealings. It's fine to open a new account alongside the old one and move things over gradually.

Even self-confessed lazy maths girls (!) can make an effort to use local companies that will reinvest in your community, rather than multinationals that will suck it away. For example, does your bank or building society employ British call-centre workers rather than cheaply outsourcing to poorer nations?

As feminist columnist Janice Turner observes: these days we should be judged not by what we do in the bedroom, but what we do with our bank accounts . . .
(v: Lazy maths girl, Opening brown envelopes)

Eve

'He would declare and could himself believe
That the birds there in all the garden round
From having heard the daylong voice of Eve
Had added to their own and oversound,
Her tone of meaning but without the words.
Admittedly an eloquence so soft
Could only have had an influence on birds
When call or laughter carried it aloft.
Be that as may be, she was in their song.
Moreover her voice upon their voices crossed
Had now persisted in the woods so long
That probably it never would be lost.

Never again would birds' song be the same.
And to do that to birds was why she came.'
– 'Never Again Would Birds' Song Be the Same', ROBERT
FROST

Everyday sexism
After a decade of indifference, feminism is properly back
on the agenda. And there are some powerful political movements afoot – from the Campaign to ban page 3 in the *Sun*
to raising awareness about the horror of FGM (female
circumcision). Look out for the Everyday Sexism Project
(www.everydaysexism.com) where women can catalogue
instances of sexism experienced on a day-to-day basis. It's
hardly surprising after the Jimmy Saville scandal and the
culture of sexual harassment revealed at the BBC that
young women are protesting. The wider context is that
women's groups are forming all over the world (cf. *The
Pink Sari Revolution* by Amana Fontanella-Khan), but this
doesn't mean the fight-back has to be humourless – see the
publication of new book of essays *50 Shades of Feminism*.

(The) Ex (plural)
Oh the ex. The ex is only really the ex when you simply
don't fancy him anymore. Of course, he probably won't
ever believe that to be the case and he will fondly (or
otherwise) imagine that you will carry a torch for him until
your dying day. But now he has run off with the au pair,
someone else can do your dirty work, and gradually the
love and agony you feel will turn to anger and hatred and
probably end up as ambivalence. If, however, the very
sound of his dulcet tones has you running for the vodka
bottle, just steady yourself, make a written note of the things

you wish to relay to him pertaining to the children in words of no more than two syllables and sentences of no more than ten words. Then have a stiff one.
(v: Agony, Divorce)

Exercise
(v: Arms, Boxing, Comfort zone, Cycling, Pilates, Tap-dancing, The Third Sex, Trampolining, Wild swimming, Yoga)

Expanding universe
Try different music you haven't heard before. Tune into a different radio station. Learn another language. Try new foods. Mix things up sometimes just to get a fresh perspective. It could be as simple as moving the furniture, or sleeping on the other side of the bed.

Push the limits of your body by taking up martial arts. Learn to do a handstand. Try meditation or open your mind to other political or religious points of view. Even if you don't agree, you'll be able to argue much more intelligently.

People report that learning a new thing every day makes them happier than sex. Whatever you learn encourages new neural pathways in the brain and, over time, with repetition, you gradually become better at something. The human brain is infinite, we use about an eighth of it. You can keep learning until the day you die. Queen Elizabeth II has made it a lifelong habit to learn a new fact every day.
(v: Comfort zone, Handstand revolution)

Expensive
You will always treasure something lovely and probably

ridiculously expensive, whether it's a diving watch, a loud-print Italian dress or a delicious and fragrant face cream, and make really good use of it because you have invested in it and for very good reasons. It is probably beautiful, well made and of exceptional quality. Wearing or using it can often make you feel like a million dollars, which is just as well.

(v: I can't afford to buy cheap)

Exquisite listening

'If we develop a more listening mind, we can become more centred, more focused, and in that way we can deepen our powers to heal and to help.'
– SISTER STANISLAUS KENNEDY

As we struggle to be heard in the cacophony of noise around us it is worth remembering that the ability to listen well is becoming something of an art form.

Whether it is listening to an elderly parent reminiscing about squandering the time carelessly as they did in the golden age, a child who is formulating his or her first long sentence or a friend who is having a bad time, listen carefully. We may long to get our own point across but resist the impulse.

Stay silent, suspend judgement, experience the world from another's perspective.

Extended families

In fluid and/or 'blended' families, the general feeling is, the more the merrier. So park any annoying, grinding irritations that you have with your in-laws and your daughter's puerile boyfriend or ex-husband's trophy wife, and swiftly opt for the 'killing with kindness' policy. Where children and elderly parents are concerned, put aside your differences, there is no point in making other people's lives miserable because you can't sort out your own. Life, as they say, is far too short and you will feel quite angelic to boot. The children will love to see everyone getting on and, as a proper grown-up, you owe it to them to make that happen.

(v: The Ex, I don't, In-laws, Teenagers, Stepchildren)

Eyes

The windows to the soul and our greatest natural asset. Eyes matter: for communicating, bartering, flirting. They speak even when you are silent. In the twenty-first century, well-shaped eyebrows can open up the face and take ten years off us and false eyelashes are no longer the preserve of drag queens.

(v: Dilation)

Facial exercises

Eva Fraser, glorious facial fitness diva of a jaw-dropping 84 years, explains that muscles sag in the face unless you work them out and stretch them. Creams, however good they are, cannot lift the facial muscles. You really do 'have to take your face to the gym'. Whilst Botox can be seen as the quick fix, it makes the other muscles weak in the meantime and you have to keep it up. Facial Exercises offer a facelift by natural means which doesn't cost a penny. The only way you can start looking young is by actively moving the muscles in your face and neck. Try and use them all.
(v: Blow-jobs)

Fairness

The demand for social justice has never looked so lively. And the new buzzwords are 'equity' and 'fairness'. The nation is both united and appalled by a world where the rich, both individuals and large corporations such as Amazon and Starbucks, don't pay their taxes while ordinary working people are struggling to make ends meet, and where social mobility has effectively ground to a halt. We demand a redistribution of resources and we need a level playing field.

Fairness is the sign of an open society: it helps us aim high; fosters loyalty and ambition; and protects those more vulnerable. It's a keystone of one of the oldest democracies in the world (i.e. ours) and it's one of the loveliest words in the English language.

(v: Be Well-informed, Counter-culture/Occupy movement, Demonstrations, It's not all about you)

False eyelashes

Invented by DW Griffiths in 1916 for the heroine of his epic movie *Intolerance*. Stars such as Dietrich, Hayworth and Lamarr understood that a languorous close-up could be stronger than a thousand pictures. Post the sixties, false eyelashes went into decline and became largely the province of transvestites, but in the last couple of years there has been a 'falsie' revival. Now everyone is experimenting with extensions, lash-regenerating mascara and magic re-growth formulas that are applied nightly.

Michelle Obama wears false lashes. Lady Gaga sports feathered lash sets. Shu Uemura has made custom-designed mink lashes with diamonds for Madonna. Long eyelashes are associated with youthfulness, lashes get shorter as you grow older and hormone levels change, and glossy eyelashes are signs of health and fertility and raw sex appeal.

Falsies are a great way to change your look without having to do something invasive. You can choose from one or two spider's legs added to the edge of the eye to enhance a sexy flutter, or go for the full caterpillar effect.

Lash extensions (£85–£140) are more costly but last up

to three months if you have top-ups. All you need to do is comb them in the mornings.
(v: Necessary vanity)

Family

'Happy families are all alike; every unhappy family is unhappy in its own way.'
– *Anna Karenina*, LEO TOLSTOY

They drive you mad, push your buttons and no one knows better how to get under your skin than a member of your family. But it's the only one you get. We all have a vision of how we'd like family life to be, but we may have to let go of those fantasies. While a shared past can be a bond, we also know rather too much about each other.

Birth order, age difference and gender may also give us different perceptions of the same childhood experiences – differences that can be hard to reconcile.

No family is the same. For some raised voices could be traumatic; for others this could be the usual form of communication. If all parties are willing to hang in there and change direction when they make mistakes, the relationship can be rescued.

If you're dealing with a silly spat that can be resolved informally, take the plunge and phone. Better to sort out a problem before it becomes a major haemorrhage.

Treat each other with the courtesy and respect that you would extend to friends and colleagues. If necessary lie politely. Then go home and have a very large gin.
(v: Brothers, Daddy damage, Daughters, Family therapy, Mothers, Sisters, Sons, Teenagers)

Family therapy
Can be agonising, but also surprisingly helpful.
(v: Brothers, Daddy damage, Daughters, Mothers, Sisters, Sons, Teenagers)

Fasting
Biblical in many senses, fasting is worth doing to blast your system. Most people eat way too much so, once in a while, warm water and lemon for a day or two is to be embraced. You feel very worthy afterwards, which is why so many religions encourage it: it helps cleanse the system, re-boots your metabolism and can give you a slightly heady weight-less feeling, which may make you susceptible to heavenly visions. However, don't try and fast if you are pregnant, have a chronic or life-threatening illness, have a busy working day or you are breastfeeding. It's not fair on anybody, least of all yourself.
(v: Cider vinegar, Diets)

Fear
'All that ever holds somebody back, I think, is fear. For a minute I had fear. [Then] I went into the [dressing] room and shot my fear in the face . . .'
– LADY GAGA

Feet
Never begrudge spending money on your feet. It's not just girlish vanity. Feet are the foundation of the body. Feet keep you standing upright. A foot can sustain enormous pressure, several tons over the course of a one-mile run, and provide flexibility and resiliency. There are 26 bones (one-quarter of the bones in the human body are in the

feet), 33 joints and over 100 muscles, tendons and ligaments in each foot.

And there's no need to be ashamed of your feet. A good chiropodist or podiatrist can rescue the worst corns and calluses – and often give you back the feet of a child! We're not just talking a colourful toe varnish, a medi-pedicure is as important as visiting the dentist. Bad foot care is akin to poor oral hygiene.

First your therapist will uses a scalpel, lancet or drill to eliminate corns, calluses or thickening layers of skin (you will feel nothing, it's all dead). Next they will file and reshape the nail – straight, not too short to avoid ingrown nails. Then during a lower leg and foot massage, each muscle, tendon and joint is manipulated to liberate the bones. Women who wear high shoes need to keep their feet mobile. Podiatrists see women of 35 and over who can no longer put their back heel on the floor. Invest in regular massage to prevent you having the joints of an 85-year-old.

Please, please, please look after your feet. They deserve to be treated with respect.

(v: Flats, Orthopaedic footwear)

Female bankruptcy

For the first time ever, the number of women plunged into bankruptcy is equal to the number of men. Debt experts say it is not driven by women buying Ferraris or luxury holidays, but a sign of how they are struggling to survive this double-dip recession, possibly past a divorce. The long-term impact is massive, because a black mark on our credit history lasts for six years. This means we are unlikely to be able to take out a mortgage, a credit card or a loan.

It's an important feminist issue to understand more about how money works. It doesn't all have to be scary, alienating facts about spreadsheets – money is also about life goals, friendships and our relationship with ourselves.

(v: Lazy maths girls, The new financial intimacy, Opening brown envelopes)

Female breadwinner

These days women are just as likely to hold the family purse strings as men – supporting partners who have taken a career break, gone back to college or are working in a low-earning, creative profession (playwright, artist, carpenter, etc.). The upside of this new breed of alpha wives is women feel like equals in the relationship, but yes there is the stress of supporting the mortgage and all the living expenses. Resentment can creep in – especially when you're rushing out of the door for a morning meeting at 8 a.m., and he's in pyjamas clearing up porridge.

It's a delicate balancing act keeping everyone's ego happy. It turns out being a househusband is very much like being a housewife – what gender you are makes very little difference. There are huge rewards to being the major caregiver of children but little time to yourself – no mulling over emails, surfing the web or Friday nights in the pub with the sense of another week complete.

To make sure we don't disparage – or stop fancying – men who stay at home, just chuck them a pink ticket and let them run away for a bit. Off for a jog, to the pub, to see some mates. Do not lose respect. Just because someone is the househusband doesn't mean you are their keeper.

(v: Alpha females, Ambition, House-husbands, Mating in captivity, Think like a man, Top table)

Female comedians

A great female comedian is like an unexploded bomb in a handbag. She might go off at any minute – voicing extreme rage – or she might apply her lipstick and play nice. From Tina Fey to French & Saunders and Miranda Hart, the best writer-performers find a way to say the unsayable. From cancer to suicide and disability, no subject is too sacred. Women and gay men – who routinely see themselves caricatured on TV – respond to the raw power, the amorality of the great female comedy performer. They make us howl, they make us blush ('I can't possibly admit that I do that'), they make us rightly furious. But dear God they make us feel better about ourselves.

Female foe

There is a particular type of Single White Female who, while pretending to want to be your best friend, actually wants to take on your life. She may start by copying your clothes, then the way you laugh, she may adopt your friends and/or your parents and turn up for Christmas and expect a stocking. She will probably end up by stealing your man. It can seem quite flattering to begin with but behind the scenes she is already reading your diary in secret and thieving small possessions, such as lipsticks and silk stockings. This can become a form of psychological torment. So beware of the signs, confront her immediately and send her on her way.

(v: Frenemies, Mistress, Well put together)

Female lechery

Is it OK to ogle a hunk in trunks (cf. the parade of beautiful bodies at the Olympics)? Or is it an act of blatant object-

ification? Only you can decide, but if you have been subject to blatant objectification yourself that may give you a clue.
(v: Caveman moment)

Female logic
A term primarily used by men to describe a range of behaviours and thought processes that would be seen as inherently feminine. For example, when a woman changes the subject or angle of a discussion, hesitates over the bill or (rather adorably) puts her handbag in the fridge. One of our fathers refers to this as 'grasshopper mind'.

Amusing as it may be, too often it's an excuse for misogynistic humour, such as: 'How many women does it take to change a lightbulb?' 'Just one. She holds it still and waits for the world to revolve around her.' Yawn.

But you know we may well have the last laugh. Men may acquire information better and orient themselves more accurately. But they also focus exclusively on one task and become irritated when asked to settle another problem at the same time.

In women both cerebellar hemispheres function at the same time, which is why we can watch TV, talk to a friend and cook dinner at the same time. We may simply take the A roads as opposed to the motorway, but, as any fool knows, off piste is generally more interesting and lots more fun.
(v: Counter-intuitive feminism, Gossip, It's a girl, Lazy maths girls, Satnav)

Female sports presenters
Irritatingly men tend to like female sports presenters, especially if they are cute. However, they are not really necessary.

There are plenty of men who can talk about rugby extremely well. One of our number takes serious umbrage at the sight and sound of a female sports presenter giving commentary and doing interviews after a full-on rugby or Test match. As Al Murray, the Pub Landlord would say, 'No. A pint of beer for the gentleman and a glass of white wine for the lady'. It really is off-putting to see these women involved with these blokey sports. Fair enough if it's tennis, netball, badminton or swimming. But come on here. There is no place for women in rugby, football or cricket. Just leave the men to it. Life will go on. Is it half-time yet?
(v: Annoying women who like football)

Fertility
The received wisdom is that in one's teens and twenties one is ridiculously fertile, but this lessens once we hit our mid-thirties and if you haven't had a baby by the time you are forty you may face some challenges if you want to get pregnant. However, everybody has a story to prove the opposite and it is also clear that some couples can get pregnant more easily than others. Sadly infertility, despite all the advances in health and well-being, has become some-thing of an epidemic in the western world and hand in hand with that epidemic a major medical industry has evolved. Older male gynecologists tell us that we are just leaving it too late and that by selfishly pursuing a career we only have ourselves to blame if we can't get pregnant. The more enlightened baby-makers will recommend some form of medical intervention if we don't get pregnant within a certain time frame. Poor diet, stress, lack of exercise and PVC packaging are all cited as additional reasons for infer-tility and so people trying to get pregnant can find them-

selves in a very stressful cycle of self-improvement, often driven by very conflicting advice, as they try to create the perfect body environment for conception. Our suggestion is Five Element acupuncture, but if the clock is ticking seek medical advice.

(v: Contraception, Elderly primagravida, Five Element acupuncture, Magic spells, Pregnancy)

Festivals (etiquette at)
All sorts, musical, literary or otherwise, have mushroomed all over Britain in the last ten years. Alongside Ascot, Henley, Wimbledon and Lords and the Queen's garden parties you haven't really done the season now unless you have been spotted hanging at at least one of the following events: Bestival, the Great Dorset Steam Fair, Hay, Glastonbury, Latitude, Port Eliot, Hard Rock Calling or The Curious Arts. However, it doesn't matter whether you have got a VIP pass (and it's access all areas) or you are camping in your grandfather's old Army tent. Good behaviour and courtesy to others is absolutely the order of the day. As we all know, vast quantities of alcohol are consumed and a variety of drugs ingested at these kinds of festivals and if you are going with your kids, or meeting your kids while you are there, you may have to agree that what goes on tour stays on tour.

Festival must-haves include wet-wipes, perfume, moisturiser, sun block, a hip flask of brandy, a hat, deodorant, dry shampoo, cigarettes or tobacco and papers (for those among us who smoke) and energy bars. If you are camping but lucky enough to be travelling in a car, take a proper mattress and pillows plus clean linen.

(v: Wet-wipes)

Film club (start a)

Finding it difficult to drag someone along to see the latest Almodovar? Prefer documentaries to blockbusters? Then start a film club. *Ciné-clubs* were originally set up in Paris in the 1920s to bring film lovers together in an informal situation to watch screenings that were hard to see in mainstream cinemas. There was usually delicious food and drink on hand too.

You can take it in turns to hold a film club. All you need is a decent DVD player, or a projector and a white wall. Alternatively, look out for hotels and independent cinemas with their own cine clubs: they will often include lunch or supper as part of the event. It doesn't have to be a room full of earnest film-makers in black polo necks. There are sci-fi film clubs, mini foreign film festivals, screwball comedy and Eighties nostalgia nights.

Film is a brilliant way to connect with new people. In contrast to stilted conversation at parties or private views, there's a brief initial chat over a glass of wine and then you get to sit in the dark for two long hours – and wallow. After the screening everyone is so fired up that the evening flows freely. You are bound to meet like-minded people sooner rather than later, and whether you find a lover or discover your new best friend, you know that you share a mutual passion.

Finances
(v: Frightening bank managers, Money matters, Pensions, Something for a rainy day)

Fires
If you are lucky enough to have a fireplace, lighting a fire in the family hearth is one of life's great pleasures and is one

of the few upsides of the arrival of November and the start of a long winter. A fire brings warmth and the natural element of wood into the home. And in the depths of a bleak mid-winter it can bring soul, cosiness and good cheer. Summer fires, lit late at night with the windows open against the backdrop of a velvety blue sky, have their own strange beauty and outside fires or fire-pits can bring a pagan grandeur to any occasion. If you live near the sea and can collect driftwood it will add the sulphurous colours of blue and green to the flames.

Some people are instinctive fire-makers – although there is no rhyme or reason to this – but, if in doubt, do keep a stash of firelighters handy (they are not expensive) and use them liberally.

(v: Candles, Magic spells)

F is for funny

'You can't really be strong until you can see a funny side to things.'
– *One Flew Over The Cuckoo's Nest*, KEN KESEY

And 'funny' puts the wind in your sail, the cream in your coffee and the screw in your screwball. If you can be around funny people and folk with fizz, your life will be impeccably leavened forever. The chintz may be sagging, a higgledy-piggledy state may reign slightly more than it ought to on the domestic front, but hey, if someone or something can stick a smile on your face then everyone is singing for their supper.

Fishing for compliments

We prefer deep-sea diving.

Fitting in

Nobody loves pedantic, fussy, demanding women and there is nothing more ageing. Go with the flow. It's what makes the world go round.

(v: Flow, Old ladyish behaviour, Satisficers)

Five Element acupuncture

Originally based on the Tao, Five Element acupuncture was a preventative system of medicine favoured by the 'princes' of Ancient China. By balancing the body's Five Elements, boosting the immune system and ensuring the free flow of 'chi' or life-energy, the healer would also treat each individual in relation to his or her community. In the twenty-first century medical experts have found little proof through scientific study of its efficaciousness and remain sceptical of its healing powers, even though hundreds and thousands of westerners, who visit acupuncturists on a regular basis, swear by it. So how do we bridge this contradiction? It seems unlikely that acupuncture is the cure for chronic illness but it is also possible that the very physical connection between acupuncturist and patient and the time that the practitioner spends with a patient has a life-enhancing effect. If you feel well, you are well. If you are finding that more conventional forms of medicine and therapy are not doing the trick it may well be worth giving it a go – particularly for depression, fertility problems, insomnia and low libido.

(v: Botox, Facial acupuncture, Fertility)

Flaming

Posting angry messages online about another person's behaviour can be tempting. But do be careful. Sometimes a mere spat escalates into an all-out 'flame war', where users

bombard an individual with offensive messages. Tone is notoriously hard to judge online. Unlike a row over email or the phone or even in public, a Twitter spat plays out in real time in front of everyone who cares to follow you, anywhere in the world. Engaging in angry words with an ex is rarely helpful (the acrimonious Goldsmith and Rothschild). Best to err on the side of humility and be courteous when posting or sending messages. You can always throw darts at their photo on the fridge.
(v: Anger, Angry Birds, Ignore the Trolls)

Flats

Oh the deep, deep peace of flat shoes after the true agony of bone-bending stilettos, cf. *The Little Mermaid*. Occasionally it really is worth giving up on 'girl' shoes. You'll save a small fortune on plasters and blister dressings. Men will respect your speed and dexterity (if, indeed, you care about their good opinion of you) and you'll lose weight (because you can walk further). Plus flats don't have to be dull – think handmade brogues, ballet pumps, roll-up real cotton ballet shoes in your handbag just in case, delicate flip-flops, silver sneakers or kick-ass biker boots.
(v: Feet, High heels)

Flirtation

It's all in the eyes, so take off your sunglasses. Be very interested, even if you are not.
(v: Sunglasses, Trysts)

Flow

All of us know that wonderful feeling of being so caught up in something that we stop watching the clock. It's particularly important to experience this in the busy lives that we lead. Positive psychologists call it 'flow'. Virtually anything can be a flow activity – reading, telling a story, ice skating, painting, singing in a choir and even socialising.

You will know if you have had a 'flow experience' because you will become immersed in whatever you are doing and remember it afterwards as highly gratifying and fulfilling. Scientists say it raises our level of happiness because we are most 'ourselves' when we are caught up in the moment and when we are able to forget temporarily the daily grind: bad hair days, irritating in-laws, tax bills.

The trick is to identify our key flow activity – the thing that gives us most pleasure – and factor more of it into our lives. *(v: Choirs, Reading groups, Yoga)*

Flowers

A woman carrying flowers always looks gorgeous – it implies an admirer has just sent you a bouquet, or that you are taking them to a friend, which means that you are a wonderful and generous human being. But whatever and whoever they are for, they will make you happy. Buy yourself a bunch of flowers, however small, once a week and put them by your bed. If your budget is tight, and the onset of autumn is making you feel gloomy, invest in some basic terracotta pots and bulbs: plant crocuses, hyacinths and daffs in October in pots and keep in a dark cool place. They will flower about Christmas time and will keep you going through winter and into spring. A vase of dead flowers can also look rather spectacular in its own kind of way, but don't go too Miss Havisham.

(v: Catching the bouquet, Container gardens)

Food
(v: Anna Del Conte, Carbohydrates, Cooking, Gelati, Old-fashioned Italian restaurants)

FOMO (Fear of missing out)
Coined by the young and refreshingly honest, you've sort of either got it or you haven't. Some souls plough their furrow and are happy to really not give a damn what others think of them or what they are doing. Others, however, are constantly pinging on the fruit machine of life to wonder whether, where or when and what should I wear to the next party? To be twitching at the light on the blackberry and checking for when to scoot off is not a good look. FOMO is essentially also a massive insecurity that others could be having a damn good time without you. And how could they ever dare to do that?

Frankness
Political correctness has somewhat muddied the waters around lasses simply being able to speak their mind, which is something of a shame as treading on eggshells is so dull. As long as you are not planning to scare the horses, being clear about your feelings and saying what you think is a way of being true to yourself, although it may be best to hold back where the boss or mother-in-law is concerned.
(v: Anger)

Freelance
(v: Portfolio careers)

Frenemies

'Always forgive your enemies; nothing annoys them so much.'
– OSCAR WILDE

'Keep your friends close and your enemies closer.'
– Michael Corleone in *The Godfather Part II*

Occasionally there are people in your life who you liked once but for some reason, often lost in the mists of time, you like no longer. You still see them about, you are still reasonably friendly towards them when face to face, but secretly your inner dog doesn't like their inner dog very much. However, at some unconscious level you are unable to detach from them completely. Our view, which may feel initially unpopular, is stay with your frenemies. There is probably an undiscovered reason why you still feel connected to them at some level, and while you work out what that is it's probably better having them inside the tent than not.
(v: Female foe, Persephone, Schadenfreude)

Freud

When in doubt, read Freud. From dreams and errors to jokes and symptoms, the father of psychoanalysis is never dull, although in many areas discredited. Like the Victorian gentleman he was, he believed women should be sweet domestic creatures, but he was one of the first to acknowledge women had sexual desire, and that repression of that sexual desire could make us supremely lonely or hysterical (just like men). He also made us sound bloody interesting, declaring, 'The great question that has never been

answered, and which I have not yet been able to answer, despite my thirty years of research into the feminine soul, is "What does a woman want?"' To be honest we're still puzzling that one out ourselves. But it's nice when someone asks. For that alone we can forgive him penis envy.
(v: Depression, Dreams, Jung)

Friends
(v: Aloneness, BF, Frenemies, Schadenfreude)

Frightening bank managers
They don't really exist nowadays because so much banking is done on the Internet. If you need a loan, an emergency overdraft, a mortgage, a pension or advice with what to do with a small nest egg, you will be put through to the relevant department and advised accordingly. However, if you are summoned to the bank to be grilled by the powers that be, always wear a suit and carry a broadsheet newspaper or a copy of *Whoops!* by John Lanchester (a riveting and terrifying account of what banks do with your money, even if you haven't got any). You will be taken much more seriously.
(v: Debt, Money matters, Pensions, Something for a rainy day)

Frocks
From little black dresses and shirtwaisters to Diane von Furstenberg's forgiving wrap dresses, it's all about the frock. One-piece dressing is practical – you don't have to co-ordinate a frock with anything else, saving time in the morning. A dress will take you from day to evening (for posh, simply add a necklace and heels). Coat dresses are

even better if you are forgetful, or just can't bear carrying stuff to parties or the theatre.

But it's the 'frockness' of the frock that needs celebrating. Nothing skims curves more kindly than a dress: it can give you a nipped-in waist and a hint of cleavage and exudes grown-up femininity. If you tend to be a jeans girl or are simply addicted to casual dressing, the power of putting on a frock once in a while cannot be overstated. People melt.

The trick is to find your best shape. The silhouette matters. Apples suit tailored shifts; those with a *Mad Men* va-va-voom figure are best with 1950s styles; long lean types can go shorter than they think, especially with opaque tights, God's own gift to women.

Make sure you go for a lined frock (no wrinkles) that allows you to bend, reach, etc. without embarrassment or the loud splitting of seams. The rule of thumb is low neckline OR lots of leg, but not both: no one wants to be mutton dressed as vamp. Remember, sleeves can cover a multitude of sins, so add a lace cardigan or shrug to a sleeveless shift. Pockets tend to divide the fashionistas: yes, they slightly spoil the line, but heavens, women need secret spaces for lipstick, credit cards, etc. A great fabric is like a walking painting. Don't underestimate the power of colour – it can be too easy to stay in black. A low-cut back or asymmetric sleeve adds amusement. You don't have to be traditionally girlie: Coco Chanel's exquisite navy and white shift dresses took their inspiration from nuns' habits and military uniforms.

Hemlines are a barometer of social and economic change. Dior brought in the New Look after the Second World War. The return of luxurious fabrics after rationing revolutionised the figure. Conversely, Mary Quant's Sixties mini tunics were designed to allow women (normally trussed up in suits and pearls) to be able to run and skip, just like small children.

Dresses allow you to play out discreet fantasies – who am I today? Businesswoman or femme fatale? Sometimes it's fun to be restrained and ladylike. At other times you want a great no-fuss summer dress that reminds you of your teenage self. There's one for every mood and for every social encounter. Also, frocks are very helpful for dates with carnal conclusions (easy to take off without fumbling). And remember, men love buttons (don't even question it). But actually, frocks are for women. Frock envy is what makes the world go round. So please don't wait until you lose three stone. Every girl deserves a great dress.
(v: Bombshell, Colour, Pears, Shapes, Waist)

Fruit

Many of us struggle to make our five a day but snacking on fruit can give you a fantastic boost. Berries are best and accompanied by cream make the most delicious and easy puddings ever invented.
(v: Blueberries, Cooking, Diets, Eat your greens, Hospitality)

Funerals

Always write a letter of condolence first. Try not to cry so much that you draw attention to yourself, which can be very embarrassing unless, of course, you are a professional mourner and get paid to do so. And, if you feel it's all going to be too much, there is nothing to stop you having a brandy with a friend before the event. Make sure you have a good hanky or two, your outfit is smart, leave plenty of time to get to your destination and make sure you know exactly where it is. Be very sensitive with the immediate family, and follow the general flow with the seating in church, i.e. do not squish yourself into the front row. Think it through. Remembering something funny, loving or meaningful about the deceased to tell their family and friends at the wake can be helpful and cheering. Take some flats in case it turns into a party.

(v: Grief, Leaving the party)

Fur

'All fur coat and no knickers' is a slight aimed at a so-called 'common' gal. It implies louche morals and general all-round bawdiness. But who can deny the touch of glamour derived by a hint of mink or a wrap of raccoon? Of course, you need to bear in mind that these beautiful and fetching items have been borderline non-PC for several decades, but as long as the pieces you are wearing are vintage and have been dead as a doornail for quite some time it is silly not to do them the honour of wearing them. Toasty warm, heart-stoppingly sexy, throwing on a fur is a quick way to add some old school pizzazz to your outfit. And, for what it's worth, the heart of a caveman beats in most blokes, they are suckers for a fox in a fur.

(v: Animal prints, Caveman moment)

❧

Galleries

Keep your visual stimuli high. You don't always have to do a three-hour blockbuster exhibition. Get into the habit of dropping into smaller galleries or museums. Revisit a favourite painting in your lunch hour, go round with an audio-guide or ask the gallery attendant at least one question that will shed new light on your favourite artist. Alternatively, take a day off and embark on a galleryathon. Reading artists' biographies can give you a richer understanding of their goals and, yes, love lives. Don't worry that you have to understand art intellectually before you can appreciate it. Your immediate response and own interpretation is the cornerstone to developing a critical sensibility. Maybe the piece will awaken a long-forgotten memory or a strong emotional feeling will wash over you. Whatever happens, it's all good. You might even become inspired to try something new when you leave, cf. Tracey Emin's bed, and don't feel guilty just dropping in to use the café or shop. Anything that inspires the gallery habit is legitimate!

(v: Day-tripping)

Gap year

Everyone is doing it and it's not necessarily poverty theme park tourism. Why not rent out your home for a few months and pad off with a partner or friend to one or two places where you have always wanted to go? You don't have to be in search of anything except the spirit of adventure, the chance to learn new skills and maybe the opportunity to share yours around. Those with teaching degrees can go forth and earn a living almost anywhere, the possibilities are endless. However, resist the temptation to sell property to fund a year out. It's a dangerous move. After all, you need to be able to come home in due course.

(v: Adventure)

Gardens

(v: Container gardens, Day-tripping)

Gay best friends

Gay friends are a joy. But they are your friends first and foremost – and gay second. No one goes out hiring based on sexuality. These days it's all about blended friendships. The term 'fag hag' is an affront. And – let's get this straight – gay and lesbian friends are not automatically any better at interior design, shopping or cushion plumping than anyone else. They're just as likely to be mad about football or *Top Gear* and they may also be married with children.

What GBFs are good at is pleasure. Our younger trailblazing GBFs get there first on every trend – from nightclubs and lectures to great venues for birthday parties. Just check out their Facebook sites for their latest downloads.

Their judgement is impeccable – and they have the best address books. They don't blanche about going to expensive restaurants or paying for taxis.

If you're not part of the 1.8 nuclear family, GBFs can prove to be a gift from God over Christmas. They will offer open house with a five-course lunch, champagne and karaoke. You can bring a mother or two (if she behaves), but it's quite clear who's in charge.

Lesbian and gay friends tend to be sexually liberal and politically informed and they certainly won't let you become complacently liberal. Homophobic bullying remains a hot issue for gay men and women. They'll sharpen up your wardrobe and give great relationship advice. But you have to earn their friendship. GBFs can see through the smug marrieds who just want a godparent for their offspring.

If a gay power couple splits, your loyalties can truly be torn. Unlike many straight couples, you tend to like them both equally. But after the initial grief of parting, ex-gay partners often end up friends, they may even go on holiday together with their new lovers. It's all so bloody civilised. Clearly we heterosexuals have a lot to learn.

(v: Cocktails, Cross-generational friendship, Escaping your comfort zone, Imaginary love affairs with gay best friends)

Gelati

The ultimate girl food. *Gelato* – Italian ice cream – has a smooth texture with a burst of intense flavour and is amazingly low in fat (less than half the fat of traditional British ice cream). Forget boring old vanilla or raspberry ripple, these days flavours include pine nut and fennel seed, hazelnut meringue, pumpkin, mascarpone or apple and cinnamon, alongside versions of Italian classics such as pistachio, *stracciatella* and dark chocolate. Sometimes it's a relief to skip the main course and head straight for the dessert bar. And you can always top up with a little brandy. It goes down a treat.

(v: A little bit of what you fancy does you good)

Get out of a rut and get involved

The two go hand in hand. There's no better way to blow off the cobwebs, to recover from the end of a relationship or seize the moment than by getting involved with other people.

(v: Bouncing back, Cancelling Christmas, Choirs, Churches, Film club, Gap year)

Getting it right

Formal dress, what to wear to not get it wrong. Ascot decrees that there should be no skirts above the knee and no hats with a smaller base than 4cm. This rule, designed to eliminate miniskirts and fascinators, is probably a good benchmark for formal occasions at which you need a good heel, a good back, a hint of fur maybe, and a beautiful drape and tailoring. Stockings, chiffon, a shirt with a satin ruffle, dressy wide slacks and a whoosh of Pucciesque print work like a dream.

Tea dresses which come below the knees are perfect for summer parties and smart events. Equally smart with a sling back or cowboy boot.

Opera is long frocks and full evening glam. Arm candy in black tie is the final touch.

(The) Giddy limit

A Cockney expression that equates with the phrase 'the last straw.' Essentially, it is an old-fashioned way of saying 'enough is enough'. Said in exasperation rather than anger, it is a very useful tool when faced with other people's bad behaviour because it doesn't invite anger in return.

Gigolo

The true gigolo isn't out to humiliate women. He's only passing through. No doubt he'll end up with someone younger or older than you but for a summer, he's yours. And that might be worth picking up the tab for. For women there is more equality in this relationship than you might think, and a healthy dose of realism. Seasoned women get company, emotional support and – sometimes – sex. And there's a lot that a gigolo can learn from their Mrs Robinson.

Girls

Lena Dunham has changed the TV landscape with her glorious TV series, *Girls*. If *Sex and the City* was about empowerment through credit cards, *Girls* takes a much more complex view of life as a twenty-something female New Yorker. Funny, dark, sad, lost? All those things and much more.

(v: Bridesmaids)

Girl crush

It could be your boss, or Alison Goldfrapp, or that fascinating woman at the library. It's like a mini love affair. You quote her all the time, start watching the DVDs she recommends, and wonder out loud if it's 'too soon' to ring her. You want both to be her, and be her best friend. Usually

non-sexual in nature – sorry boys – but no less thrilling.
(v: Baby dykes)

Gloves

'A lady is known by her shoes and her gloves.'
– *Mrs Dalloway*, VIRGINIA WOOLF

The opening chapter of Mrs Dalloway – as Clarissa searches for the perfect white gloves, 'above the elbow', with pearl buttons – packs the punch of an emotional thriller.

But then gloves, from bejewelled lace to buttoned kid, have always been about seduction. Gloves embody practical elegance. And to be damn practical about it, they keep you warm and stop the spread of germs. They are also a brilliant punctuation point: if you need a moment to impress, or slow conversation down, there's something rather thrilling about watching a woman take off her gloves, finger by seductive finger, cf. *The Age of Innocence*.
(v: Department stores)

Gluten-free

Life's too short.
(v: Carbohydrates)

Godmothers

Let's be frank about this. Godparents have little to do with God, or in fact parents. Godchildren are essentially the love child of a friendship born in your twenties or thirties (sometimes even further back) and it can be a relationship that struggles to survive the trials and tribulations of their divorce, or yours. If you ask a cross section of disgruntled teens 'What have your godparents done for you lately?' the answer is probably, 'Not enough'.

That is not to say that there aren't masses of kids with cases of port maturing slowly in order to be cracked open on an eighteenth birthday and guzzled by a group of motley Facebook friends, but on the whole, godparents are a slack lot, often very self-absorbed and once they have their own kids even less interested in their godparenting duties.

So if you are a godmother, focus on your inner 'fairy'. If you are not good at remembering birthdays, stow away the odd bit of cash in a post office account. (Godparents are duty-bound to give small but meaningful amounts of money to godchildren at odd times.) However, the occasional lovely lunch or a trip to the theatre can be a real treat for your godchildren too. A letter at important moments in their lives, a phone call, a postcard from abroad, all show you've thought of them. And the thought really does count.

(v: BF, Technology, Teenagers)

Going to prison
Probably the best lie-down you can have on the cheap. A chance to catch up on your reading, learn to garden, keep down your phone bills, and somebody else cooks Christmas dinner. You can look forward to your freedom party too.

(v: Bolt-hole, Infinite vistas)

Good behaviour
One of life's great protective mechanisms.

(v: Courtesy, Dignity, Grace, Punctuality)

Good husband material

'Chains do not hold a marriage together. It is thread, hundreds of tiny threads which sew people together.'
– SIMONE SIGNORET

'Only choose in marriage a man whom you would choose as a friend if he were a woman.'
– JOSEPH JOUBERT

As Gloria Steinem wryly notes, we are becoming the men we wanted to marry. Assured, self-reliant, economically independent, sexually liberal, with a credit card and (hopefully) a rather nice apartment.

This fact is often used as a stick to beat single gals – cue the hilarious joke: 'Single women over the age of 35 are more likely to be killed by a terrorist than get married.' But, you know, it's a good thing. We don't need a husband to do the DIY/fix the car/deal with the bank. We can either do those things ourselves or pay someone else to do it. Just as men don't need a little woman to cook, clean and home-make. It's all up for grabs.

What does make good husband material is kindness, respect, adventurousness, curiosity – and a dynamo in the bedroom. A keeper, basically.
(v: *A good man is hard to find, Dating, David Attenborough, I don't, Top table*)

Good stuff that's free
(v: *Churches, Galleries, Libraries, Parks, Seaside*)

Good turn for the day
Cheesy. No. More old-school Scouts or Brownie operandi. Without being Holier than Thou, doing one good deed a

day, even if it's providing company, coffee, carrying a bag
or pushing a job over to a mate, is the best way forwards.
Particularly for the strugglers with huge bags of groceries
and babies in tow who are all too often left floundering at
the bottom of an escalator or staircase.
(v: karma)

Googling yourself
This has a peculiar and vaguely masturbatory quality about
it. Try it once, but from then on it should be avoided at all
costs unless you wish to go truly barmy.

Gossip
(v: *Small talk*)

Grace
'Happy is your Grace,
That can translate the stubbornness of fortune
Into so quiet and so sweet a style.'
– *As You Like It*, II. I., WILLIAM SHAKESPEARE

We all have a higher self somewhere inside us. This is where
your capacity for kindness, wisdom and courtesy meets
your love of family and your generosity towards your friends
and workmates transcends any negative or bad feelings you
have had. Graciousness reigns in this realm and if you can
access your higher self in times of strife it may well get you
out of all kinds of trouble and bring with it a feeling of great
calm and serenity.
*(v: Dignity, Good behaviour, Old-fashioned Italian
restaurants)*

Grappa

The grown-up *digestif* of choice. You only need a slug to experience the heat, kick and the high alcohol content (between 40% and 60% by volume). Made from the leavings of the grapes after winemaking, grappa is primarily served as an after-dinner drink to aid the digestion of heavy meals. The fine versions come in beautiful hand-blown bottles, but in Italy they also use grappa as a medicine or as disinfectant to clean down the bar.

(v: Alcohol, Benders, Booty-calls, Dipsomania)

Grandparents

Be extremely nice to your children's grandparents, give them the keys to your house, and ask them to help with your babies. Their goodwill must never be abused.

(v: Babies, Divorce, Family therapy, Extended family, In-laws)

Grasping the nettle

The truth is it hurts – most people would prefer to stay in bed for three days to watch the entire box set of *The Sopranos*, or stage the Trivial Pursuit Olympics to avoid doing it – but the anticipation is worse than the pain itself. The sting only lasts for a little while. So whether it's phoning your frenemy to apologise for last night's behaviour or facing up to a bullying colleague at work – do it! It is difficult, but the more you are prepared to grasp the nettle, the easier it becomes.

(v: Money matters, Frenemies, Opening brown envelopes, Pensions)

Green exercise

Just five minutes of exercise in a 'green space' can boost mental health. It could be walking, gardening, cycling, boating or horse-riding in locations such as a park, garden or nature trail. There is growing evidence that combining activities, such as roller skating or cycling, with nature boosts well-being. An even greater effect comes from exercising in a green and blue space – an area that also contains water, such as a lake or river. Our lives get out of balance living in an urban environment. As human animals we need to be in nature: feeling the ground beneath our feet, touching the grass. You need to see a horizon in a city of tall buildings. And we all need more vitamin D. Green exercise breaks the tyranny of the gym. Best of all, it's environmentally sound and it's free. Beautifully, the Japanese call it 'green-bathing'.

(v: Ballooning weight, Comfort zone, Flow, Good stuff that's free)

Green living
This is very popular. However, recyling your batteries may not be enough to save the planet. We need big sweeping international change, radical policies and unswerving politicians, who are prepared to make difficult and unpopular decisions now, in order that our grandchildren can live in a viable world. Time to demonstrate.

(v: Demonstrations, Eat your greens, Get involved, Green exercise)

Greer, Germaine [icon]
'You're only young once, but you can be immature forever.'

Grief
'Don't grieve. Anything you lose comes round in another form.'
– RUMI

'Grief is different. Grief has no distance. Grief comes in waves, paroxysms, sudden apprehensions that weaken the knees and blind the eyes and obliterate the dailiness of life.'
– *The Year of Magical Thinking*, JOAN DIDION

(v: Age of grief, Bereavement)

Guests (how to be a good one)

The Chinese say that, rather like fish, guests go off after three days. There is definitely something in this. A good guest cannot be dreary and spoil the fun. Good guests bring a bottle of wine/flowers/chocolate/something homemade if invited over for dinner. You will have already been keeping a keen ear out for tips, so you know what your host or hostess will really like. Good guests offer to walk the dog, load the dishwasher, and go on any trip proposed, even if they don't want to. They do not discuss their personal health, or anyone who is dying. If people go pink when you share your views on the Taliban, drop it, and go back to talking about some foodie phenomenon, or the latest wind turbine.

Clean the bathroom after use and air your room. Fling compliments around about the house, including 'God how do you manage to do all this?' Leave by 4.30 p.m. on a Sunday and always send a thank-you letter and all should be fine.

One 'killer-guest-stroke' was witnessed at an impromptu picnic in Devon. It involved a cool box, containing vodka, tomato juice, sherry, horseradish, Lea & Perrins, Tabasco and celery salt, being unexpectedly produced from the boot of the car. Complete with two bags of ice. The devil, as they say, is in the detail.

Guillem, Sylvie [icon]
'Having limits to push against is how you find out what you can do.'

Guilt
Guilt is a woman-shaped word and can have the same poisonous, intense quality as envy or shame. We can feel guilty about almost anything – for being ambitious, for neglecting our family, skipping the gym, for lying about buying that new dress. But as many psychotherapists will tell you, guilt is not a real emotion. It's the default position we occupy when we won't accept the truth about our real feelings. Obviously we do things that upset people, such as breaking your sister's vase. You know you didn't do it on purpose, so logically you should have no reason to feel guilty about it. Yet you can't stop beating yourself up about your clumsiness, and how you could have avoided it. Now the question becomes: what does feeling guilty do for you? Is it secretly oddly comforting?
(v: Truth)

Gynocrats
These are men who dig strong women and would rather hang out in all-female company. They have no problem with women taking the lead or having the best lines. These are the men you want at your top table.

Gynocrat comes from the noun gynocracy or gynae-cocracy: a government or society ruled by women. Though more often found in myth and science fiction, matriarchal societies have existed in many civilisations, including the all-female Amazon culture reported by Herodotus (484–425 BC). For many years 'gynocracy' was a pejorative word used by anti-feminist men to describe 'angry wimmin' who wanted to take over the world, after doing the washing and ironing, presumably.

But all that changed in 2009 when novelist, author of *The Rachel Papers*, and father of three daughters, Martin Amis, outed himself as a gynocrat. In fact, Martin added helpfully: 'I was quoted by, I'm pleased to say, Germaine Greer, as saying that all men should be locked up until they're 28. Boot camp. That would knock some sense into them. We're terrible. We can't help it!'

It's a heartening re-appraisal by a former *enfant terrible*. *(v: Middle-aged novelists, Top table)*

Hadid, Zaha [icon]

'You really have to have a goal. The goal posts might shift, but you should have a goal. Know what it is you want to find out.'

Hair

'Sometimes I think not worrying about your hair anymore is the secret upside of death.'
– NORAH EPHRON
(v: Blow-dries, Necessary vanity)

Hair dye

Has sort of changed everything. Before the Fifties very few women dyed their hair and even in the Seventies the artist Francis Bacon famously chose to touch up his roots with boot polish, but dye has been a massively liberating product for women, who almost as a matter of course all dye their hair at a certain age. Don't ever underestimate its restorative powers.
(v: You're only young twice)

Hairiness

Wouldn't it be nice if we could all be a bit more grown-up about being hairy? Body hair is there for a reason. It protects the skin from chafing, transfers heat into and out of the body and absorbs drips and fluids. Plus denser areas of hair are sites of scent-releasing glands that trigger sexual attraction in others.

(v: Bikini wax, Brazilian, Necessary vanity)

Hair loss

Whether it's the result of stress, the menopause or chemo-therapy, hair loss can feel depressing and undermining. Hair loss doesn't just affect the scalp, it can affect eyebrows, eyelashes, nasal hair and pubic hair. The lack of eyelashes and nasal hair are particularly irritating as it can mean you catch eye infections more easily and have a permanently runny nose.

The truth of the matter is it ain't fun and it's vital that you try and keep your spirits up, so perhaps now is the time to invest in that Hermès scarf you have always wanted (or a good fake). Or dig out your mum's retro-Seventies Elizabeth Taylor-style turban and add a sparkling paste brooch for extra panache. However, if you are not in the mood to make your hair loss a fashion feature, you can simply buy yourself a very good wig. Bravest of all is to shave your own head. Surely it's time for the return of the Rude Girl . . .

(v: Cancer buddy, Climacteric, Ward wear)

Halos and how to wear them

Homer described Minerva crowning Achilles with a 'halo of golden-cloud from which she kindled a glow of gleaming fire' and the simple aura of light has crowned the heads of many of history's most famous figures, from the Virgin Mary to Napoleon.

Although not gracing the canvases of our modern world, the halo still encapsulates the notion of a pure, divine grace that suffuses the soul. While the selfless care of others may not be the most fashionable of contemporary qualities, every so often a person or occasion calls for you to wear a halo, so why not bask in the golden glow of humility and goodness, just as virgins, saints and martyrs have always done.

(v: How to be good, Bury the hatchet)

Handbags

'I have this Ferragamo hot-pink bag that I adore ... I mean, how can you be unhappy if you pick up a big pink bag?'
– HILARY CLINTON

'Clinton is absolutely right. A woman's handbag is an extension of her self, the only place where all the different parts of her life converge – which is why looking inside other people's bags is so interesting ... On the outside, you see a woman in a suit, "done" hair, discreet make-up. On the inside of her handbag, you see her real self: an iPhone, a BlackBerry, a lipstick in a colour she'd never wear to work, sachets of Calpol, a pack of wet wipes, the cigarettes she doesn't admit to smoking, the pills for stress headaches you'd never dream she had because she seems so able, an old love letter, a child's teddy ... Someone I know who was eternally single used to carry her passport around in her bag, in case she met a wonderful man who

whisked her away to Paris on the spot. I can't think of a sweeter manifestation of hope springing eternal.'
– *The Sunday Times*, 20 February 2011, INDIA KNIGHT

God. Don't we love handbags? They are like sweeties for big girls or penises for women. All you need for a tip-top handbag collection is a good eye and a slightly impulsive nature. We have bought bags from all around the world: the best of the swag is a rather brilliant Louis Vuitton one for ten dollars from a yard sale in Florida. Of course, you need all sorts of different handbags for different occasions. They don't all have to be super luxury items. All they need to do is catch your eye, cheer you up and be capable of carrying at least keys, cigs and a lipstick. Have a checklist when you move the contents of one to another.
(v: Elegance)

Handstand revolution
Doing a handstand against a wall can help you reset and recharge your metabolism for the day. It reverses gravity allowing much-needed rest for your legs and feet, it improves upper body and core strength and the rush of blood to the head is great for your face and skin. Forget dreary old weights and rowing machines, handstands remind us of when we were very young and filled with dreams.
(v: You're only young twice)

Handwritten letters
Letters were once the only way to conduct long-distance relationships. We waited weeks for them to arrive from pen

pals or boyfriends who had gone to India in their gap year, kept them scented and be-ribboned in our knicker drawers (surely what they were invented for) and in return poured our hearts out onto paper-thin airmail letters or Basildon Bond writing paper – and practised our best italic hand-writing with beautiful fountain pens.

Sadly, in this new age of mass communication letters have lost some of their importance but, much as we all adore instant messaging, is anyone seriously backing up emails and tweets for posterity, apart from those rather frightening corporations in Silicon Valley? Are we convinced that the expression of our hearts and souls will not all be reduced to memory sticks? We still fantasise about long discursive letters. They're part of our emotional history. So go and find that dusty bottle of ink and get weaving.

Letters excel in conveying a true message. Whether it's a thank you, a love note, or for saying you are sorry in a way that is hard to ignore: for putting across the tricky, difficult, private or loving. Still feeling cynical? Go to the penultimate scene in *Persuasion* and you will change your mind.

(v: Affairs, Accepting invitations)

Handyman

You need a handyman in your little black book because, try as you might, the battle with the drill and the spirit level may be *un peu de trop*. Give him a list and start with the most important task, especially if it involves the roof, then work your way down to the more cosmetic adjustments. Don't let him spend days doing paint effects when he can be putting shelves up. Because he can handle a hammer,

you will naturally think he walks on water, so beware of having a 'cavewoman' moment. Make sure he clears up the debris before he moves on and, whatever you do, don't sleep with him or he will, ultimately, cease to be useful.
(v: Caveman moment)

Have you got the kit?
Although donning a pair of stockings and suspenders in a dusty tent in Glastonbury may not be your idea of fun it's not un-sensible to be a little bit prepared for the booty-call, the wild weekend away or just simply the romantic advances of the man you love. A lovely bit of kit or even just a beautiful bra, tucked away in the back of a chest of drawers quietly awaiting the right moment, can instill secret confidence.
(v: Affairs, Booty-calls, Cinq à sept, Creative corsetry, Twice is polite)

He reads she
After school and university – where we inhabit the same library – it's very easy to read completely different books from men. Difference is healthy, but we all yearn for shared references. A friend of ours recently compiled a 'Feminist Reading List' on the Kindle for her husband, downloading all the books (*Jane Eyre*, *The Second Sex*, *The Beauty Myth*, et al.) that had been important in her life. When he goes out walking he's also got a pile of 'Talking Books' on the go. He may not agree with all her choices, but it's been an invaluable insight into the key feminist debates – and the mercurial female psyche. Now all she needs is HIS list.
(v: Be well informed, Middle-aged male novelists)

(The) Heart

'It is only with the heart that one can see rightly. What is essential is invisible to the eye.'
– ANTOINE DE SAINT-EXUPÉRY

Heckling

Has its place. Make your target lazy politicians, they are three a penny.
(v: Demonstrations)

Hell

'If you are going through hell, keep going.'
– WINSTON CHURCHILL
(v: Christmas)

Hemlines

Supposedly the great economic indicator. When stocks are soaring, skirts rise to mini length. When markets head down, hemlines drop. But every woman is the arbiter of her own hemlines. Don't be bullied into wearing anything that makes you uncomfortable. Many of us prefer above-the-knee in winter and longer in summer when everyone starts baring flesh. As a rule of thumb you can probably go shorter than you think or chance a flirty dress, worn with a long jacket. But before interviews and dates, check out that optimum length by sitting in front of the mirror. There's nothing worse than the wrong sort of 'skirt drift'.
(v: Elegance, Frocks)

Hen nights

Time to make a stand against bunny ears and penis-shaped lollipops. Do you really want to spend a small fortune in a nightclub with people with whom you have nothing in common, bar the fact that you share a friend who happens to be about to get married? Ask any woman and she will have at least one story of hen-night-related humiliation. However, it is important to mark a rite of passage. There are far more grown-up ways to celebrate – especially if it's a case of late love. One friend organised a screening of her favourite film at the British Film Institute, followed by cocktails and supper at Claridges. Another designed a brooch, worn by all the hens on their weekend away, to keep as a memento. Part of the pleasure of the modern hen night is making an age-old tradition fun, personal and a bit grown-up.

(v: Catching the bouquet)

High heels

If you're normally a Converse All-Stars kind of girl, don't just roam off in a virgin pair of high heels and hope for the best. Hobbling is not the look you are aiming for. A little baby lotion around the edges of the shoes and a practice trot around the house are vital. You are aiming for an upright posture and a gracious gait. Jerry Hall suggests 'Think book on the head, and a light bounce in the walk'. Practise standing on tippy-toes to strengthen tootsies and this may be the moment to think expensive. A well-made pair of high heels will allow your body to rest slightly back on your heels, realign itself and balance accordingly, as opposed to a shoddily made pair of stilettos which will throw your hips and body weight forward. This will make you look like Jack Lemmon in drag in *Some Like It Hot*.

(v: Feet, Flats)

Hoarding vs mess

Hoarding can be quite a pejorative word, and if you are a hoarder you will find that you are often accused of being sentimental and untidy. Ignore men-folk at this point. They love to throw things away because it's easier than tidying up. However, the total horror-show of out and out clutter can be tackled with the aid of a steely eyed sibling or friend who will galvanise the clear-up, and help sort out the piles for 'clean', 'keep', 'store', 'charity shop' and 'chuck it out'.

Huge clear bags from places like IKEA cost a couple of pounds and mean you can stash away in the attic (or other grottos) clothes and shoes and other prized possessions that a darling daughter will adore to inherit when she comes of age. They ensure that all is clean and dry and will also be readily identifiable.

Buy plastic folders with about 40 pages, and file your newspapers cuttings, old photographs, tickets stubbs and pressed flowers here. There is nothing nicer than keeping old diaries, love letters, writing poems, school reports and 'stuff'. So long as everything is clean and organised and parked in a suitable place, your children, grandchildren and/or godchildren will be the beneficiaries in due course.

(v: Good stuff that's free, Green living, Memory boxes, Passing stuff on)

Holidaying with girlfriends (pleasures and pitfalls)

What could be nicer than a holiday with your best girl pal? No irritating relatives. No moody men. Just cocktails and fun. However, the bad news is, relations with friends can sometimes be strained to near breaking point by character traits you only begin to notice once you're on the road.

Do you have the same attitude to money? Do you both drink? What if one of you likes to be in bed by 9 p.m.? Will there be a clash between the beach and the art gallery? Will it be a disappointment if you don't meet charismatic men? Does she actually eat food at all? Even the best of friends can hide these sort of details from each other.

It's often better to do a mini-break or weekend away first, as a trial run. Many singletons are simply not used to spending 24 hours a day with another person, so tolerance can be sorely stretched. Your lovable taxi habit may be the very thing that brings her out in a cold sweat. Ditto her snobbery about contemporary art. Even the nicest people can end up arguing about table manners or when to open the car window.

Do discuss the following:

1. How much time will you spend together each day?
2. How far are you prepared to travel to your destination?
3. Do you want to share a room (factor in heat, snoring, possibility of seduction)?
4. Do you want an all-inclusive holiday offering hassle-free relaxation, or a self-catering apartment or villa?
5. Is sunshine important?
6. Do you want to drive while away?
7. Would you prefer to visit many places during the trip or stay in a single destination? Some of us get palpitations about packing up every two days!

(v: Anger, Day-tripping)

Honorary girls

Contrary to the film *When Harry Met Sally*, it is possible for men and women to be friends without erotic tension. There's a huge relief in hanging out with a male pal who understands your jokes, reads the same books, can give you impeccable advice on a shopping trip and can understand the dark arts though not practise them. As it happens, you wouldn't necessarily want him to. He's not competing with your girlfriends, rather he's part of the pack. Alpha males can stop sniggering at the back right now: being an honorary girl says nothing significant about sexuality but it does mean a man who gets you. Truly great and lasting platonic friendships are worth fighting for. And the more exposure you have to the way the opposite gender thinks, the better, but do watch out for his slightly green-eyed new wife. She may find your mutual, easy intimacy a threat and if she does, be merciful.

(v: Good husband material, Gynocrats, Top table)

Honey

'If you want to gather honey, don't kick over the beehive.'
– DALE CARNEGIE

The ancient Egyptians considered bees the symbol of sacred femininity. Honey was also used for healing wounds and as a preservative (due to its antibacterial properties). Raw, unprocessed honey is a super-food that provides anti-oxidants, minerals, vitamins, amino acids ... you name it. Stick to darker honey. The pollen from flowers that produce dark honey contains the most micronutrients. It's never been more fashionable to be an urban beekeeper: sign up for an apiarist course in your area. Those without gardens are using rooftops or balconies for their hives; or you can buy a fabulous plastic bee house structure. We particularly like those sexy hats with veils.

(v: Container gardens, Skin, Super-foods)

Hope

'Hope begins in the dark.'
— ANNE LAMOTT

Hope is possibly the most beautiful word in the English language. Hope is what keeps us going. Hope is the future and increasingly we are told to visualise our hopes so that they become a reality. In our darkest hours, hope gives us the possibility of a way forward. You need hope as much as you need the air that you breathe.

(v: Cancer buddy, Quests, Visualisation)

Hormones

Who hasn't gone to bed a perfectly sane woman and woken up as a wailing banshee? A hormone imbalance can have a drastic effect – causing everything from teenage acne to PMS, endometriosis, infertility, thyroid malfunction and depression. You are not being neurotic, this is a real thing. Don't let the doctor belittle you or treat you like a naughty schoolgirl.

From our teens to our late thirties, the battle is to keep our hormones on an even keel. According to women's doctor Marion Gluck: 'They work like a symphony together. When they are out of whack, we are out of whack.' An imbalance can cause bloating, irritability, low moods. By our late forties/early fifties, it's all in freefall. As women approach menopause, oestrogen levels decline. We may opt for HRT or tailor-made bio-identical hormone replacement therapy, or simply sail through. But we need to be well informed about the options out there.

Hormones get an unfair press – they really are a girl's best friend. They regulate every function in our bodies: from intellect to metabolism, from building bone strength to helping us cope with stress. They make us tick. They are the chemical messengers that continuously circulate in our bloodstream. They rule – and sometimes ruin – our lives. Rather thrillingly, no two women have the same endocrine system – like our fingerprint, it's totally unique.
(v: Eat your greens, Climacteric, Exercise, Vitamins)

Hospital etiquette

Observe visiting times unless otherwise advised. Bring magazines, fresh fruit and sparkling water. Flowers are not allowed. Be up and light and tune in. Stay for as long as the patient requests and no longer. If close family arrive, say a cheerful farewell and leave without a fuss. It's not about you.
(v: Chemotherapy, Childbirth, Ward wear)

Hospitality

'A house may draw visitors, but it is the possessor alone that can detain them.'
– CHARLES CALEB COLTON

Generally, hospitality has nothing to do with money. It can be a fresh pot of coffee after a long journey. It can be a muffin and buttered toast with tea. It is the warm arm around your shoulder and a warm feeling in your tummy. It could be an offering of a bowl of soup, a spaghetti dish made from what's in the fridge, washed down with a bottle of rough red. Or, to warm the cockles of the heart, a slinky sloe gin with a dash of fizz. Whatever your notion of hospitality, provide food when there is hunger, drink when there is thirst and a metaphorical stable for the night. Hospitality is biblical in its resonance and one of the loveliest of human instincts.

(v: Cocktails, Cooking)

Househusbands

It sounds brilliant doesn't it? And some very high-powered women can run their lives because their husbands stay at home (sometimes in conjunction with a nanny) and look after the household. However, it takes a very particular kind of man who is able to subdue his ego in this manner without suffering side effects, often the most immediate being the loss of libido. In this scenario, Jung would argue that the animus/anima that are present in every archetypical partner relationship have fallen out of balance. If you and your partner are thinking about organising life in this way, look long and hard into your hearts and minds and work through a shipwreck scenario before making a final decision.

(v: Jung, Shipwreck scenario)

Housework

'I think housework is far more tiring and frightening than hunting is, no comparison, and yet after hunting we had eggs for tea and were made to rest for hours, but after housework people expect one to go on just as if nothing special had happened.'

– NANCY MITFORD

(v: Cleaning, Flow)

How to be good

When it comes to the survival of the species one might argue that 'how to be good' is the million-dollar question.

Existentialists might contend that the universe and everything in it is the outcome of brutal, random acts of violence over which we have no control. We remain detached, anonymous beings, free to roam the world without any connection to the other-worldly, the spiritual or the sublime. Romantics, on the other hand, lovingly suggest that love and spirituality lie at the heart of humanity, forming the core of our existence.

Yet the idea of being good surely acts as a bridge between these two world views. The world has become a difficult place, so whether you have faith or spirituality, or just keep your feet firmly on the ground, the notion of being good might be just the key to making it a better place.

Indeed, geneticists have long argued that the animal kingdom's ability to come together and work collectively is the key to survival. Yet the idea of being good – a notion that has for so long been entangled in faith and religion – in what is now a largely secular, objective age, proves difficult. It might involve a good deal of self-denial which will never gain the popular vote. But as ecological Armageddon draws ever closer, this may be our last chance to discover being good again.

(v: Bury the hatchet, Halos and how to wear them)

Hysteria

Can it have been so long ago the ancient Greeks imagined our wombs were rampaging all around our bodies. Possibly not if the current hash of politicians are to be canvassed. But lo, it was so deemed that this strange imbalance meant that women could not hold any high office or serve in any position of consequence in ancient times. Cause and effect springs to mind.

I can't afford to buy cheap

This is extremely sound advice. Essentially, if your monthly budget is tight and you have little money to spare for non-essentials, it is better to save it and then spend it on a truly beautiful jewel-coloured cashmere cardigan, an elegant pair of well-made boots, a gorgeous frock that can be dressed up or down, or a string of pearls, rather than blow it at Primark on a load of stuff you will only wear once or twice. Similarly, an extra hundred pounds spent on a washing machine may give it an extra five years of life, ditto on a proper mattress or a well-sprung sofa. You will discover that even when something begins to fray at the edges, it remains beautiful and stylish and you will go to heaven for being so 'green'.

(v: Elegance)

I don't

Divorce is very high on the list of top traumas, but those who bounce back quickest are the people who are able to manage their expectations. There is enormous fear of change and the unknown. It is scary to have to reassess who we are and who we might become. However, one of the most exciting and liberating things that can happen to a woman is to find herself on the road to post-divorce recovery. A lot of women over 40, having got through a divorce, are having the time of their lives.

As divorce lawyer Vanessa Lloyd Platt says, 'In my mind the way forward is "Marriage Lite". It involves respect and companionship, but absolutely without taking one another for granted. It's not about picking up socks and sharing money and paying dreary bills. It's the enlightened choice for the emancipated woman and may even become "marriage à la mode".'

(v: Affairs, Companionship, Depression, Family therapy, Grief, Lawyers, Money matters, Teenagers)

Imaginary love affairs with gay best friends

It's incredibly easy to fall for your GBF without knowing it's happening (because he is so perfect), and fantasising that it might just be reciprocated. Often it comes from a good place – as a way to avoid bruising masculinity or get over daddy damage. There's a reason we're all a bit in love with Tom Ford. We dream of someone who gets our taste in films/books/clothes. Who smells fabulous. And understands our strengths and weaknesses. But actually there's something self-destructive about desiring a man who doesn't want/need to sleep with women. And, of course, it's fatal if you're single. Poor, flawed straight men can never compete with GBFs for kindness and solicitude and treats and compliments. They set the bar way too high for heterosexuality. It's a lovely fantasy. But gay friends are just that. Friends.

(v: Gay best friends, Top table)

Implants

'For this kind of money, they'd better be looking at them.'
– DOLLY PARTON on people who stare at her surgically
enhanced breasts

Love them or hate them they remain an option. At some
point you may need implants. A little bit of padding can
help repair the wear and tear of the slightly beleaguered
upholstery, which may have fed several babes and now
could do with some perking up. With the best will in the
world, once you've expanded from a 34C to a 40D and
back again, even the most hopeful exercise regime
won't get you pinging back. If you want to have implants
and have the means to do so and you think it will make you
feel tip-top, then frankly you owe it to yourself. Do your
research, go and see the best consultant available and see if
you can talk to somebody who has experienced the same
procedure.

But beware, implants are not a teeny undertaking but,
for many, a couple weeks of severe discomfort may be worth
it if you finally have the chest you are happy with. After all,
it's got to last you a lifetime.
(v: Boobs, Bras, Cosmetic surgery, Creative corsetry)

In Bluebeard's castle

One of the most devastating leitmotifs in Bartók's opera
Duke Bluebeard's Castle is the sound of the sighing of the
dead wives who have been incarcerated within the castle
walls. Widowers can be a very attractive proposition to
Dangerous Women: they are vulnerable, often deeply traumatised and desperate to love again as quickly as possible
and they often come with ready-made families and nice

houses. But beware, dead wives, however imperfect, can cast a long shadow. There will be enormous expectations all round which are hard to meet and the man who will eventually emerge from behind the widower you fell in love with may be a very different and much more difficult proposition.

(v: Good husband material, Stepchildren)

Incest and folk-dancing

'Try anything once apart from incest and folk-dancing.'
– SIR THOMAS BEECHAM

Independent bookshops

In a world of three-for-two, it's extremely tempting just to shop at the retail blockbusters. But indie booksellers have a breadth of knowledge that's hard to match. They'll recommend new authors, order a long-forgotten title, even give you a mini-bibliotherapy session if you're bored by your bookshelf.

If you value authors – and the small independent presses who discover them – it's a nice gesture to pay full price. Independent book and record shops matter.

They offer expertise and choice. So shut down the laptop and walk across the road to a proper shop.

(v: Be well informed)

Infinite variety

'Variety's the very spice of life,
That gives it all its flavor.'
– 'The Task', WILLIAM COWPER

'Age cannot with her, nor custom stale
Her infinite variety.'
– Antony and Cleopatra, II. i., WILLIAM SHAKESPEARE

(v: Adventure, Comfort zone, Get out of a rut and get involved)

In-laws

Can drive you insane or save your life. Sometimes it's a mixture of both.
(v: Divorce, Family therapy, Grandmothers)

Insomnia

For long-term sufferers, there is nothing more infuriating than the person you meet at a party who tells you that as soon as their head hits the pillow they sleep for an uninterrupted eight hours and then in the same breath goes on to recommend an alternative practitioner who will sell you an expensive but useless cure.

Rather like Persephone and/or Count Dracula, insomniacs live part of their life in a silent, dark, disorientating and often isolating world. The condition is, of course, self-fulfilling: the more you don't sleep the more you don't sleep. Reams and reams have been written about insomnia, its causes and possible solutions. However, there is no doubt that worry, stress, grief, depression, a disastrous love-life or troublesome teenagers can all contribute to this condition, so addressing and dealing with these factors, rather than simply 'coping' with them, can be enormously helpful. Top tips for 'through thick and thin' insomniacs are as follows:

1. Establish a strict bedtime routine.
2. Only use your bed for sex and sleeping.

3. Cut out alcohol (although a counter-intuitive suggestion from a contributor is to drink a glass of chilled white port at three in the morning, which, of course, we rather approve of).

4. See the glossary for suggested reading.

5. If you are really desperate, go and see your doctor: there are some finely tuned meds available that will nudge you towards 'the land of nod'.

Two final reassuring thoughts. Prior to the Industrial Revolution it was commonplace in the summer for people to rise at three or four o'clock in the morning and eat, work or play and then go back for a snooze before getting up to face the day. Some mystics believe that three a.m. is the holiest time of the day. It's known as the 'The Waking Hour.'
(v: Catnapping, Depression, Grief, Meds, Persephone, Sunglasses)

Instinct

Sometimes we just KNOW someone is not to be trusted, or that a particular flat or house will make us happy for the next 20 years.

Feminine instincts are women's natural way of knowing. In a male-dominated work world, they are often perceived as inferior or too subjective. But we should listen to that gut feeling that something is totally right – or wrong. Thinking too much can actually lead you to make the wrong decision. Like a computer, the rational brain has limitations. It can handle a certain amount of information at any given moment, but if you give it more than that you can overwhelm it.
(v: female logic)

It turns out that in what scientists call 'our internal supercomputer', emotions that emerge from our unconscious minds tend to reflect more information than our rational minds.

The best time to trust your emotional, intuitive thought process is in situations in which you've had a lot of experience, such as buying a car or getting married.

Listening to your heart doesn't involve doing more, but doing less – so set your mind free.

Insurance
You can insure anything. If you are finalising a divorce, it is interesting to know that you can insure your soon-to-be-ex-husband's maintenance payments in the event of his death. Think about it.
(v: Cars, I don't, Money matters, Things that make your life easier)

Intensify the pleasure
Deferring gratification is seen as a marker of positive adult behaviour, but it also intensifies the pleasure. So whether you're deferring sex or a cup of tea it gives you time to think about the choice you make and whether it's the right one.
(v: Deferment of pleasure, Mercy fuck)

Intimacy
Intimacy isn't always easy. Many of us fear being swallowed up by another person and losing our unique selves. Don't let your relationship problems – which are normal – dictate your behaviour or wreck the relationship itself. Conscious emotional availability takes work.
(v: Commitment phobia)

It's a gift

Although we live in modern times there is, particularly as you get older, quite a strongly disapproving clique who say one-night stands are bad for morale. This may be the case and nobody respects a man who simply takes advantage but, very occasionally, if an offer comes your way, think about taking it. If you have just come out of a long-term relationship it may help you to break the spell, if you just want some fun and a bit of companionship what is so bad about that? So ignore the moral majority, ensure you use effective contraception and don't harbour long-term expectations, after all is said and done it's a gift.

(v: Committed bachelors, Orgasms, Think like a man, Twice is polite)

It's a girl

'One day ... the girl and the woman shall exist with her name no longer contrasted to the masculine; it shall have a meaning in itself. It shall not bring to mind complement or limitation – only life and being: the feminine human being.'
– *Letters to a Young Poet*, RAINER MARIA RILKE

Girls may be the new boys. Gender disappointment is not formally recognised in its own right and is mostly treated as a feature of postnatal depression. Most of those affected long for daughters and seize eagerly on natural methods to sway gender. These include sleeping with a lime-soaked tampon (to increase vaginal acidity); eating plenty of dairy products (a high calcium intake is anecdotally linked to having girls) and carefully timing intercourse for just before or just after ovulation (i.e. outside peak fertility, to favour slower, more resilient female sperm over live-fast, die-young male sperm). The fun aspect of this is to have lots of good sex in the week running up to ovulation and a few days post-ovulation. The great step forward is that the western world is a fabulous place to be born a girl. Let's make it so for the other half of the world's population.

(v: Babies, Fertility, Godmothers, Raising Girls)

Introducing people

'Do you know so and so?' Introducing friends to one another who you think might get on is a very generous thing to do, and everybody knows it. Introducing people at a party should be second nature, though it can be a teeny bit annoying if you are on the prowl and have just started chatting someone up to be interrupted mid-flow and forced to smile politely at somebody new. So if you are a long-term 'introducer' be sensitive to the social context. However, it's a pretty straightforward skill to acquire. 'Do you know such and such? Do you two know each other?' Conversation will easily follow and the world will somehow be a better place thanks to you.

(v: Hospitality, Reading groups)

It seemed like a good idea at the time

Well, if it seemed like a good idea at the time, it probably was. We all need to kick off our killer heels from time to time and letting off steam can be good for the mind, body and spirit, but if it results in sleeping with your best friend's boyfriend, betting your holiday money on a horse in the Grand National at odds of 250 to 1, or setting fire to your boss's desk in a moment of frustration, you may have some letters of apology to write and some further thinking to do.

(v: Benders, Drunk-dialling, Regrets)

It's not all about you

We can all get paranoid about other people's motives. But so often, it's not actually about us. The boss is in a bad mood because his/her baby didn't sleep last night. Your friend 'ignored' you at the party because an awkward situation arose with her husband. Instead of rushing to get upset about a perceived slight, try and look coolly at the situation. Or even ignore it altogether until you get a proper explanation. It can be a relief not to be the focus of everyone's attention. Most people are too busy worrying about their own personal problems to notice yours. In our desire to be sensitive and 'fit in', we can make ourselves rather more important than we actually are. Time to stop playing the drama queen.

(v: Self-pity)

It's okay to watch TV

Don't knock it. TV is a great resource. It's educational, informative and entertaining and a shared love of a particular programme is a way of connecting with your tribe. It's great if you just need to chill out and relax; brilliant if you are getting over a love-affair … there's nothing like a costume drama or three to take your mind off it, and good for infinite vistas if your budget and your mindset won't let you leave your armchair. However, don't veg out on a 24/7 basis. That's the definition of depression.

(v: Be well informed, Grief, Good stuff that's free)

ᕲᕲ

Jealousy
A really insidious and destructive emotion. Nothing good can come of it. If it rears its ugly snake-shaped head consider immediately, with some degree of compassion, why you feel jealous in the first place.
(v: Frenemies, Schadenfreude)

Jewellery for fat days
Whether it's a vintage silk floral corsage or a fabulous bit of bling, brooches are a form of personal symbolism. Each tells a story of its own – and they're great ice-breakers at parties. You can dress up an inexpensive outfit. Or hide behind them on a down day. Whether it's a vintage silk floral corsage, a fabulous bracelet, or Coco Chanel's double rope of pearls, jewellery is the best form of armour. Who cares if you're wearing the black tent dress again?
(v: Ballooning weight, Pearls)

Joy
'We should all do what, in the long run, gives us joy, even if it is only picking grapes or sorting the laundry.'
– E. B. WHITE

Jumping off
'If we listened to our intellect, we'd never have a love affair. We'd never have a friendship. We'd never go into business, because we'd be cynical. Well, that's nonsense. You've got to jump off cliffs all the time and grow your wings on the way down.'
– RAY BRADBURY (1920–2012)

Jung
'Even a happy life cannot be without a measure of darkness, and the word happy would lose its meaning if it were not balanced by sadness. It is far better to take things as they come along with patience and equanimity.'
– CARL GUSTAV JUNG

If Freud is for the first half of your life, Jung is for the second. His interpretations of archetypes, myths and symbols are rich, informative and filled with non-judgemental insight into the stories of our lives.
(v: Be well informed, Depression, Dreams, Freud)

Karma

What goes round comes round. Karma is the cosmic realignment of good and evil in the universe.
(v: Charitable giving, Hospitality)

Keep your diary full

Plan ahead and make sure you've got a week to look forward to. Call the friend who makes you howl with laughter. Invite out the most promising contact you've made in the last seven days – buy two tickets for a film or play, or invite them for a simple supper. Don't turn down a promising invitation – especially if you have just been dumped, rejected or fired. There are plenty more fish in the sea.
(v: Hospitality)

Keepsakes and talismans

Little treasures. Engraved with dates and messages. Mementos or stones or charms that are pertinent only to you. String them on thin chains to make dainty necklaces and exquisite bracelets. You can carry these with you for good luck and/or pass them on to people you love.
(v: Sentimentality, Tattoos)

THE GUIDE TO MODERN LIFE

Kick-ass female heroes

At last Hollywood is starting to wake up to a new cinema-going demographic. *True Grit*, *The Hunger Games*, *Twilight*, *Brave* all feature strong, complex female heroines for the under-18s. But these aren't girlie-girls. Instead of the sparkly pink world of Disney princesses, we are seeing savvy and occasionally foul-mouthed but brave protagonists – who just happen to be female. Surely young girls benefit from seeing characters whose gender plays no part in their success or failure. It's never been more fun to kick ass.

(v: Film Club, It's a girl, Pink)

Killing with kindness

Is such an underused tool of torture. Slyly turning your bile into kindness is so incredibly disarming and confusing, which is why it is so darned effective. Start by giving a fabulous present to someone you despise, so much so they think you made a mistake. Buy that person a drink and make it a double. Before you know it you have achieved the dubious situation of both burying the hatchet and making a new friend that you didn't particularly want.

(v: Bury the hatchet)

Kind mirrors

Your ego is only as good as your last mirror. Find your favourite one and stick with it.

(v: Necessary vanity)

Kindness

'Kindness is the greatest form of Wisdom.'
– the TALMUD

It expands the soul. And it's the best anti-ageing beauty tip we can give!
(v: Good stuff that's free, Karma)

Kirby grip

When you're feeling at your most dreary, never under-estimate the transformative power of the kirby grip. It can make you look and feel ten years younger and its slightly retro style makes it perfect if you are wearing vintage.
(v: Vintage)

Knees

Cycling, walking, going on the Power Plate, cross-training or swimming.

You've got to do everything you can to look after these babies as they are the utter lynchpins of your skeleton. cf. 'the hip bone's connected to the thigh bone, the thigh bone's connected to the knee bone' and so on and so forth. The key is to keep the supporting muscles strong, to keep the kneecap in place, and able to remain supple and agile. Slinky knees can be yours. When in doubt, take up tap-dancing.
(v: Bones, Cycling, Outdoor exercise, Riding, Tap-dancing, Wild swimming)

✑

Laser surgery
Really helpful for bad eyesight, scarred skin and painful veins.
(v: Skin, Veins)

Late love
(v: Accepting invitations, Little black book, Open mind, Salad days)

Late starters, In praise of
The very thing that holds us back as a teenager and blights our life (shyness, problem hair, fear of intimacy) can become our USP in later life. Or rather, it gives you something important to write, campaign and blog about! It's important to break those taboos. Yes, we live in a youth-dominated society, but some people mature at different rates. As author Daniel Coyle observes in *The Little Book of Talent*, 'don't fall for the prodigy myth'.

We presume that the surest sign of talent is early, instant, effortless success. And the British have a fantastic tradition of triumphing late in life – just look at Brenda Blethyn,

Mary Wesley, Diana Athill, or even Winston Churchill and Charles Darwin.

Don't despair if it takes a while to blossom. Treat your early efforts as experiments, not as verdicts. It's not over until it's over.

(v: Confidence, Mentors)

Lateness

'Punctuality is the politeness of kings.'
– LOUIS XVIII

There's nothing grown-up about unpunctuality. It wastes other people's time and goodwill. To the very punctual your lateness is basically a mark of arrogance, i.e. my day is more important than yours. To your therapist, lateness is a sign that you are surreptitiously stealing time from other people thus testing their love. But punctuality freaks need to be flexible, too – no one should be bullied into a deadline they can't possibly meet. If you are the punctual type, use the extra time to catch up on other things or maybe just dream a little.

(v: Kindness)

Lateral thinking

When all else fails, when the shit has hit the fan and you cannot, however hard you try, fit a peg into that round hole, the last but not least resort is lateral thinking. This is thinking 'outside the box'. It will deliver, in its own particular way, a completely different solution. That's why it is used in many professions where people simply aren't allowed to say 'can't'.

(v: Can't, Crisis, Emergency exits)

Laughter

'The appreciative laughter of a girl, however charming, is not to be compared to the deep pleasurable laughter in which a woman of intelligence can envelop a man.'
– *Daily Mail*, 25 January 2010, HOWARD JACOBSON

The good news is 100–200 belly laughs a day will burn off 500 calories and tone your stomach. Laughter is a natural painkiller and inspires the immune system to create white T-cells, commonly called 'happy cells'. It's especially good for controlling Type A personalities!
(v: Female comedians)

Lawyers

Don't ring your divorce lawyer until you've stopped crying.
(v: Divorce, Money matters)

Lazy maths girl

'Computers are like Old Testament gods; lots of rules and no mercy.'
– JOSEPH CAMPBELL

Apparently the average punter only uses, at best, about two per cent of her computer's capacity, but that is predicated on the fact that you understand computer technology at all. Essentially, if you dream of becoming a web-maiden you need to understand and acquire a system of logic, which is frankly easier said than done if you were a lazy maths girl at school – and most of us were. Essentially, we were all too busy fantasising about Lord Byron to bother with basic algebra (unlike his daughter Ada Lovelace, co-inventor of

he computer). In recent times it has been pointed out
:hat this is not necessarily our fault. Had the mathematical
:onundrums been invested with psychological importance,
e.g. 'If your sister's female cousin has five siblings, three of
:hem girls, how many daughters does your aunt have?', as
opposed to, 'There are three men laying a railway track . . .',
we might have got somewhere. As it is we have to rely on
the kindness of work colleagues, teenagers and godchildren
to get us through.

(v: Relativity, Technology)

Le gadget

Princess Di's code name for her vibrator was *le gadget*.
According to her biographers she often had it delivered
incognito in front of foreign ambassadors.

Once upon a time 'marital' aids were embarrassing and
unaesthetic. But the days of 12-inch phallic-shaped vibra-
tors brought out with sniggers at hen nights are defiantly
over. From cones, pebbles and balls, to rabbits and scor-
pions, you don't have to hide them away in your drawer.
Some are solo toys, others are to share with a partner. Cool
furniture designers Tom Dixon and Marc Newson have
designed beautifully shaped, vibrating sculptures. Having a
vibrator doesn't mean you're sad and lonely. They're just
as likely to be given as gifts between girlfriends, couples
and even as wedding presents – the new scented candle, if
you like. The good thing about the 'new openness' is vibra-
tors no longer threaten men, who have come to see them as
helpful. It's also fine if you have no interest in acquiring one
whatsoever.

Learning to love yourself
'Nobody can make you feel inferior without your consent.'
– ELEANOR ROOSEVELT

(v: Accepting compliments, Confidence)

Leaving the party
I used to think,
Loving life so greatly,
That to die would be
Like leaving the party
Before the end.
Now I know that the party
Is really happening
Somewhere else.
– 'Leaving the Party', ANONYMOUS

Leaving the party is hard to do. The only grain of comfort is that a billion people have done it before you, so you can too.
(v: Cancer buddy, Hair loss, Making a will, Memory boxes, Ward wear)

Legs (get them out)
Yours are beautiful. No matter how short, wide or gangly. Whether they're standing, walking, jumping, running or kicking arse, legs are freedom. So love your legs, they're your best friends and the surest escape hatch. Any room, any situation that's not up to muster, just walk out. Elegantly, defiantly, surely. Stand up, give your legs a little shake and glide away.
(v: Emergency exit, Exercise, Legs)

Lesbian bed death

When it comes to forming a healthy, sustaining, emotionally intelligent relationship it might seem like the answer to one's prayers finally to fall in love with another woman. However, one tiny word of warning, once the excitement of discovering a different aspect to one's sexuality has worn off you may discover that you are not a lesbian after all.

(v: Baby dykes)

Let it go

'The heart gives, the fingers just let it go.'

- NIGERIAN PROVERB

Libraries

Are worth fighting for. They offer timeless knowledge, nurture our chance to reflect on life and are free to use, providing books for everyone. They are also a neutral space, a refuge in a busy world and, in the roaringly acquisitive 'globalmarket' in which we live, they are a symbol of civic pride and representation of the antiquated, but vitally important, belief in learning and education for learning and education's sake.

(v: Be well informed, Good stuff that's free)

Lioness mother

As the late Victoria Ingrams said of someone who had insulted her son Richard, 'Never forget that if you insult my son, there is a lioness in the background waiting to pounce.'

(v. Under-parenting)

Lipstick

'The red badge of courage.'
– MAN RAY

At the turn of the century cosmetics were often sold 'under the counter'. Selfridges was the first department store to openly sell powder and rouge, thus transforming the social acceptability of make-up. During the 1910s, many women in the suffragette movement wore bright red lipstick as a symbol of their defiance. Suffragette leaders like Elizabeth Cady Stanton and Charlotte Perkins Gilman argued that wearing lip rouge was an emblem of women's emancipation. Nowadays lipstick is the ultimate credit-crunch indicator. Economists believe that during hard times people forgo extravagant purchases, such as cars and holidays, and spend their money on small luxuries. During the Second World War it was considered women's patriotic duty to wear lipstick. Nowadays you may not have to chain yourself to the railings to get your point across but please wear your Mac Russian Red with pride.
(v: Art of make-up, Mascara)

(A) little bit of what you fancy does you good

Whether it's the occasional cigarette, a Crunchie or sloping off to the cinema in the afternoon, honour these small and entirely harmless whims and fancies. Nobody else is going to do it for you.
(v: Variety is the spice of life)

Little black book

We've all got one of these, but we need to dust it down and freshen it up a little from time to time. If necessary, swap

ntries with a friend. Remember, however, to pay the price
of a bottle of champagne or a finder's fee of £50 for a fella,
specially one who turns out to be good husband material.
Come on ladies. Share and share alike.
v: Good husband material)

Little white lie

Sometimes truth is a luxury that you can't afford. If you are
intending to lie only tell 97% of the truth.
v: I can't afford to buy cheap, Kindness)

Living in the moment

v: Flow, Instinct)

Lodgers

Very useful they are too in times of financial trouble.
However, you do need to set some ground rules. You are
not there to be a cleaner or to run a cheap hotel. Give them
their own cupboards in the kitchen and bathroom. Provide
bed linen if you wish, but shared use of the washing machine
can be annoying. Three golden rules: ask them to clean up
after themselves and request payment on time and in cash,
and you'll be fine.
v: I don't, Money matters)

Long-haul travel

Comfortable knickers are vital.
v: Adventure, Camiknickers)

Losing things

'The art of losing isn't hard to master; so many things seem
filled with the intent to be lost.'
– ELIZABETH BISHOP

Losing things may be one of your special skills. If it is, you
probably drive your nearest and dearest mad with your
obsessive search for lost reading glasses, keys, theatre
tickets, pearls, scarves and designer sunglasses ... The
phrase, 'I know I put it somewhere safe', will have a hollow
ring even to you, but losing things as a character trait may
signify deeper concerns. In particular, if we have lost a
parent or sibling at a very young age we may set up a
repetitive losing and finding psychodrama that allows us to
sustain the belief that one day we will find that person again.
Whatever the underlying causes for your forgetfulness, with
a little bit of effort, you can put some basic strategies in
place that will make your life easier. Sadly, experience tells
us that however strict you are about putting your ultra-cool
sunglasses back in their case and back into your bag you
will eventually lose them. This is the strange universal law
of very expensive sunglasses.
(v: Pearls, Sunglasses)

Loss

'"But I think she would have been happy with Fabrice,"
I said. "He was the great love of her life you know." "Oh,
dulling," said my mother sadly. "One always thinks that.
Every, every time."'
– *The Pursuit of Love*, NANCY MITFORD

(v: Age of bereavement, Grief, Insomnia)

Love

'Love conquers all; let us also yield to love.'
– VIRGIL

'At the touch of love, everyone becomes a poet.'
– PLATO

'Love is the extremely difficult realisation that something other than oneself is real.'
– IRIS MURDOCH

'Love letters'

'Where will all the love letters go
When cyber space gobbles them up?
Can you stand tall beside that risky email
When it is reduced to nothing at all.
Give me sly notes to add
To that knicker drawer cache
Give me secret love behaviour, on some paper I can keep.
Leaving marks of blistering rendez vous,
The sight which makes me weep.'
– SARAH-JANE LOVETT

(v: Handwritten letters, Overuse of the Internet, Technology)

Lovers

'Alice: I don't love you anymore. Goodbye.
Dan: Since when?
Alice: Since now. Just now.'
– *Closer*, PATRICK MARBER

(v: Affairs, Arrangement, Cinq à sept)

Lumley, Joanna [icon]

'I don't think men are that attracted by glamour. I think women are attracted by glamour. I think men are attracted by a sense of friendship.'

Lymphatic drainage massage

Lymphatic drainage is a key to removing toxins and maintaining healthy skin. Rolling with a Yuroll brings oxygen to the skin and stops areas of the face suffering from 'stagnation' which is when the circulation is not running smoothly. It's a way of ironing out the wrinkles as well as boosting natural collagen and promoting a youthful bloom. Key lymph areas are sited across the forehead, behind the ear, under the chin, along the jaw line and also down the neck to the collarbone. The legendarily beautiful Catherine Deneuve is a great ambassador for lymphatic drainage.

Mad women

Men very often like to describe women as 'mad'. It has long been the ultimate stick to beat a woman with. It is dismissive, pejorative, cruel and manipulative. It is a way of making a woman doubt her own faculties and it is also a clever way of fuelling rumour mills and helping a boyfriend or husband to pursue his own agenda. It is a prognosis that should not be trusted and can be very damaging, not just to the individual but also to children and extended family too. History, literature, opera and the psychiatric couch are littered with perfectly sane women who have had an adverse reaction to the male world and are being punished accordingly. The ultimate weapon of the patriarchy? 'She is mad because I say so.' Beware.

(v: I don't, Opera, female logic)

Magic spells

Whether you are seeking love, happiness or just some extra cash, they can sometimes work. The best days for magic spells are at full moon or at the summer or winter solstice. Essential ingredients are candles, scent, fresh herbs, salt and an elegant glass of something alcoholic. Be creative!

You are the one who knows what you are trying to achieve. Lay everything out on a dinner plate and add extras such as love hearts, special ornaments, treasured letters – or, if you are feeling financially squeezed, a large cheque made out to yourself! If you are making a spell to help somebody else, take a photograph of it with your mobile and send it to the person in question. Two rules: let the candles burn out before you go to bed and don't take it too seriously.
(v: Candles)

Magical thinking

Magical thinking is human thinking sometimes, it's successful thinking and it's an elegant way to marshal obsessions and compulsions around a good cause. Most of us go through life fuelled by dreams, hopes and wishes – something that the cleverest computer will never be able to do for us. If we hitch our tics to a dream, or simply a magical paradigm, we beat that bus to the corner; we don't step on the cracks; we salute every number 7, we focus our minds on a positive outcome. And the more frequently we call an outcome to mind, the more circumstance rallies behind it. It really does. Touch wood.
(v: Grief)

Maisonette

Halfway between an apartment and a house, the maisonette is the answer for a woman on a 'realistic' budget. You get all the pleasure of running up and down stairs – plus your own front door – without the stigma of the dreaded bedsit. Basically, it's a chic 'microhouse' where the cats can hold their heads up high.
(v: Cats)

Make do and mend

Get a lovely little sewing kit and jazz it up by filling it with silks and hooks and eyes, press studs and thimbles. We are all recycling now. Dyeing clothes, adding buttons and bows, taking hems up or down, will make you glow with self worth. Stick clothes in the deep freeze to destroy moths' eggs before fixing little holes with silk thread. Lady Ottoline Morrell, famed hostess of Garsington Manor, kept a fine multicoloured sewing box on the go at all times. She found that sewing was incredibly soothing. We say, give it a go.
(v: Being green, Embroidery, Flow, Hemlines)

Make the most of it (*carpe diem*)

'But at my back I always hear
Time's winged chariot hurrying near'
– 'To his Coy Mistress', ANDREW MARVELL

Make your own knickers

It's surprisingly easy to make comfortable, elegant and sexy knickers. There are easy-to-follow patterns on the Internet and you can use fancy fabrics or even old shirts for the ultimate in recycling. There's something deeply rewarding in doing so, though your partner may be in for a shock when you turn his newest Paul Smith shirt into a pair of stylish French knickers.
(v: camiknickers)

Making a will

It is hard for people to make a will, particularly if you have a life-threatening illness, because it means facing up to your own mortality, but it's essential that you do, otherwise the government will just swipe the lion's share. If you have extensive assets it's probably best to get some good legal advice as how to best share out the loot. However, if you are on a tight budget just get a form from WH Smith and fill it in. You will need two friends or acquaintances to witness it. If you have particular wishes about the way you want your funeral to be conducted, it is a good idea to write a letter of intent, which can be kept alongside your will. However don't make your funeral arrangements too elaborate. It's really good for those you have left behind to think through what best reflects you and organise accordingly. It helps take their mind off sad things. Most important of all, if you have children under the age of 18 think carefully about who you would wish to be their legal guardians.

(v: Grasping the nettle, Insurance, Leaving the party, Money matters)

Making impossible demands on yourself

The omnipresence of digital technology has made slaves of us all. Pity the poor dame who, if she is not zipping around assuring one and all of her efficiency in the meeting place, is on call to pick up everybody's else's kids from school, have an emergency conference call with the board of governors, while fundraising for environmentally challenged frogs in Micronesia via the Internet or googling to check rates for a yogatasic mini-break-cum-hen night for the bride-to-be and 25 of her closest friends. A tool that was meant to bring freedom to all now seems to leave even less time for covering yourself in biscuit mix and getting your boots muddy. Unplugging your technology or leaving the grid altogether (which has been tried by the enviably hardy few with varying degrees of success) as yet remains unpunishable in law.

(v: Catnapping)

Mammogram

These are X-rays of the breast to screen for breast cancer in women who have no signs or symptoms. Two images are generally taken of each breast to check there are no tumours. Mammograms often take place at a portable breast screening unit (which frequently have no loos!) and are offered to women in their fifties and above. To be repeated every one or two years, minimum. Don't delay.

A diagnostic mammogram is used to do a second check after a lump or sign or symptom has been diagnosed. This testing usually takes longer.
(v: Cancer buddy, Hair loss)

Manifesting a man

'I wrote a list which was very precise, included in that list was his ability to be kind, generous, financially solvent, noble, strong, quick to laugh and slow to anger. A man that respected women and loves his mother. Someone who would accept me for who I am and what I am.

I used a new moon, as symbolic of a new beginning.

I ran a bath and added rose, jasmine and rosemary. I put a big piece of Rose quartz in the tub and began to visualise my husband.

I also made a commitment to the universe that I would become much more flexible; flexibility bends rigidity. I stayed in the bath for about a half an hour, got out and went to sleep with rosemary sprigs under my pillow. I met my husband the next day.'
– JOHNNIE FIORI

(v: Good husband material, Magic spells, Top table)

Manners
(v: Accepting a compliment)

Mantel, Hilary [icon]
'I think for a woman to say that "I'm not a feminist" is [like] a lamb joining the slaughterers' guild. It's just empty-headed and stupid.'

Mantras (things to help you live a good life)
It is useful to have a few calming and insightful sayings to hand to get you through irritating, stressful or tough moments. Sometimes even a boring platitude will do.

Man up
A little note to self on a daily basis. To not whimper or blub. Take yourself to task and think like a land girl. We have it easy. Do not let men and awkward situations get the better of you. Simply man up. You will feel better for it in the long run.

Map reading
Map reading was designed for men but the goddess of serenity has now designed and sent us the satnav. So no more rowing in the car. No more sweaty palms as you summon up the courage to admit that yet again you have directed the designated driver to take the wrong exit from the motorway resulting in an extra hour and a half on a 200-mile round trip. We repeat: the emancipation; the liberty; the joy. So, 'at the next exit take the first turning on the left.' We most certainly shall.

Martinis

'I like to have a martini,
Two at the very most.
After three I'm under the table,
After four I'm under my host.'
— DOROTHY PARKER

The Vesper Martini:
'Three measures of Gordon's, one of vodka, half a measure
of Kina Lillet. Shake it very well until it's ice-cold, then
add a large thin slice of lemon peel. Got it?'
— *Casino Royale*, IAN FLEMING

(v: Alcohol, Benders, Booty-calls, Drunk-dialling, Mercy fuck)

Mascara

You'd be silly not to.
(v: Allure)

Massage (any form)

Whether you're tired, lovelorn or simply out of touch with
your body, there's something incredibly soothing about
neutral touch from another human being. We all want to
feel the warmth of a hand on our shoulder after a long
day; a gentle stroke on our head in moments of difficulty.
Massage allows you to switch off that nagging inner voice,
unwind and breathe deeply and slowly. You will emerge
blinking into the daylight but as languorous as a cat.
(v: Intimacy)

Matchbooks

Why the demise of the matchbook? So small, neat and often
covered with brilliant designs. They may be archaic and

time-consuming, wasting those precious seconds of your cigarette break out in the cold of the bar façade, but surely romance isn't dead? So many memories can be garnered by a mere glimpse at old ones kept. They are the postcards that you send yourself. Bring them back.

Material girl

We all know women who are only motivated by money. They're great fun, keen to party, and quite like taking you along with them – particularly if they don't feel that you are a sexual threat. In their company you get the best restaurant table, slip past the velvet rope into the VIP lounge, and that can feel great for a limited period of time. But the truth is they are simply not to be trusted. In the end it's all about them and their upward trajectory, cf. Becky Sharp in *Vanity Fair*. They've always got their eye over your shoulder for richer pickings. And, funnily enough, you'll more often than not find yourself bankrolling them, in your role as the substitute man. It's boring that they don't see the point of earning their own living or that ultimately they give women a bad name.

(v: Frenemies)

Mating in captivity

Can you continue to have great sex in a long-term relationship? Does good intimacy always make for great orgasms? And why do couples who care for each other very much often end up in a sexual desert? For psychotherapist Esther Perel (author of *Mating in Captivity*), the paradox of modern love is that the very forces that bind us – trust, mutuality, friendship – can kill our sex lives stone dead. Erotic desire is complex, messy and very often non-PC.

The trick – to paraphrase Jerry Hall – is to see the bedroom and kitchen as very different places. Forget endlessly talking everything through and shared bathrooms. We need more distance, novelty and spontaneity. Be selfish, lustful. Create tension.

(v: Affairs, Divorce parties, Have you got the kit?)

Maturity

'The moment someone comes across as real and unstaged and comfortable, it has so much more power.'
– WOLFGANG TILLMANS, artist

McArthur, Ellen [icon]

'You don't fear for your life in the middle of a storm, you can't really afford to.'

Meditation

Through simple relaxation techniques we can learn to step off the treadmill. It only takes ten minutes a day and it doesn't matter if you don't have spiritual faith. Meditation is a free tool for stress relief. You don't need to chant or lie down; you can meditate on the Tube – it's a good way to beat commuter stress. And the beauty is that it is both inexpensive and portable and scientifically proven to be a powerful defense against stress and anxiety.

Remember, if you are busy allow for one hour's meditation a day. If you are rushed off your feet allow for two!

1. Sit on a comfortable chair, close your eyes and take five deep breaths.
2. Let your mind have free rein. Don't feel guilt if you

find yourself thinking about food, shopping – or sex.

3. Scan through your body and notice which parts feel comfortable and which feel tense. Each time your mind wanders bring it back to your breathing pattern. Simply be aware of your feelings, that way you can provide a framework for them to arise and fall away.

4. Focus on being at ease with whatever is happening in your mind. Open your eyes after ten minutes (it's worth setting a timer) and you should feel like you've had a great catnap.

(v: Flow)

Meds

'The art of medicine consists of amusing the patient while nature cures the disease.'
– VOLTAIRE

There are plenty of useful meds for different ailments ... and if you have to pop a pill once in a while, it doesn't mean that you will turn into an addled Stepford wife. For many a gal, Valium – or just call them calm pills – are useful for a fear of flying. You have to take half a pill for Europe and a whole one for a longer haul. It makes the flight very short indeed. A sympathetic doctor will give you these to help with the anxiety.

There are also pills to lose weight. Psychologically, battling on with battling the bulge can become a tad trying. A month of something speedy to give your regime a quick blast will set you back on track and you'll see real results.

Some use beta blockers or a tiny nibble of a sedative when having to speak to the old ex-hubby. A gin and tonic and a chaise longue can also help with this fairly gruesome task.

(v: Diets, Drugs, (the) Ex, Pain)

Meeting the in-laws

Guess who's coming to dinner?

(v: Courtesy, Exquisite listening, Grace, In-laws)

Members' club

Traditionally a male preserve. If you have some spare funds it's a very good idea to join one. In particular, a members' club is a great way to meet friends, to entertain and amuse Americans, to stay over in town occasionally, to sit by yourself and write that novel. Take your mum, your lover or, if you need to impress a new business contact or work colleague ever so slightly, a members' club is also a great place for old-fashioned grown-up business meetings where you want to make a good impression.

(v: Infinite vistas, Mentors)

Memory boxes

Shoe boxes are wizard for this. Fill it with all your treasures, love letters, old passports and the crappy tape your first boyfriend made for you and a whole host of other stuff that only has meaning for you. If the long-term prognosis isn't great, start making these for your children.

(v: Cancer buddy, Emergency exit, Hair loss, Leaving the party, Making a will)

Men

Just make them think it is all their idea! A perfect example of counter-intuitive feminism.

(v: Counter-intuitive feminism)

Mentors

We all need an elder sister-cum-fairy godmother. Someone who can help us take creative risks, move up the work ladder or offer a cool head when we're raging about injustice at work. The key is to think of someone who has complementary skills to yours. If you are feeling adventurous set up your own networking group. Whether it's exchanging career tips, address book secrets or after-school coaching for the kids, there are lots of ways to peer-monitor.

(v: Members' club)

Mercy fuck

Urban myth has it that this term, now in everyday use, was coined by an episode of *Sex and the City*. But wherever it came from, to request a 'mercy fuck' from somebody is not the action of a tragic woman, but of somebody who recognises sexual attraction and thinks of themselves as an equal. Ask and you will be rewarded. But do remember that at some point the favour may need to be reciprocated.

(v: Bachelors, Booty-calls)

Mess

(v: Muddling through)

Metabolism

(v: Cider vinegar, Diets, Eat your greens, Super-foods)

Micro-finance

'. . . these millions of small people with their millions of small pursuits can add up to create the biggest development wonder.'
– PROFESSOR MUHAMMAD YUNUS, managing director of Grameen Bank

Micro-finance is a way of making financial resources available to the poorest people and a brilliant way in which you can help a woman in the developing world set up a business and support her family. Check it out.
(v: Charitable giving, Karma)

Middle-aged male novelist

'The sense of the middle years as a period of life whose task is to grapple from the hostile void of time some evidence of reality, some permanence, some tangible proof of having existed, became a rich source of inspiration to male novelists of the twentieth and early twenty-first centuries; from John Updike to Martin Amis, they roamed the labyrinth of the male psyche, recording the wonders they found there.'
– *The Stranger in the Mirror*, JANE SHILLING
(v: Gynocrats)

Middlescents

Once upon a time MAWs (middle-aged women) wore woolly hats and sensible wellingtons. But middlescents aren't letting go of the boyfriend jeans and sequins just yet. Middlescence is officially the years when you are in-between your promising twenties and the grey wastelands of middle age.

Middlescents know that they are no longer young, and that they can't party to 4 a.m. without a gargantuan hangover, but they still dress and behave as if their hipster years aren't over and they always act as if they are having fun. Poster girls for middlescence include Helena Bonham Carter – who seems never happier than when she is wandering around in a bonkers dress with tousled hair and always looks like she's having a good time.

Middlescents do 'casual' and 'eccentric', but never scruffy. They know you have to choose your face or arse, but they have proper haircuts and a beautician on call to keep skin in good nick. They also like the occasional pedicure and may have experimented with false eyelashes. As far as families and career go, it's anything to convert boredom into fresh energy.

(v: Comfort zone, Portfolio careers)

Mid-life crisis

Generally associated with the male of the species – but women are increasingly subject to mid-life crises too. Whether it's because your children are leaving home, your once vibrant partner won't leave the house without an umbrella or you have just bought yourself a Harley-Davidson, you may find yourself challenged in the middle of life's journey. Depression, lack of purpose, ballooning weight or developing a massive crush on the barista in the local Starbucks are common symptoms. It will pass but it's a day at a time.

Minogue, Kylie [icon]

'Having had cancer, one important thing to know is you're still the same person at the end. You're stripped down to

near zero. But most people come out the other end feeling more like themselves than ever before.'
(v: Cancer buddy, Hair loss, Leaving the party, Memory boxes, Visualisation)

Mirren, Helen [icon]
'The trick in life is learning how to deal with it.'

It's a bit mean of Helen Mirren to get even more beautiful as she gets older, but it's also inspiring. Why not try it?
(v: Childfree, Jealousy, Waist)

Missed opportunities
Gosh. It's hard to bump into the man at the Christmas pantomime with his lovely young wife and three tiny tots and realise that he was the 'one'.
(v: The man I should have married)

Misogyny
When you feel this sliding around you like an anaconda, get away quick. When you find yourself having to tolerate hideous slippery anti-female nonsense slam it down, cut it off, nip it in the bud. It's no longer acceptable in any way, shape or form.
(v: complete wankers)

Mistresses
'Marrying your mistress creates a vacancy.'
– JAMES GOLDSMITH

You might know one, your husband might have one or you might be one.
(v: Affairs, An arrangement)

Modern families
(v: I don't, In Bluebeard's castle, Teenagers, Stepchildren)

Mojo
It's still there, we promise, even if your house looks like a pigsty.
(v: Mid-life crisis)

Moles
Are gorgeous, provocative and divine, cf. *The Wicked Lady* or Cindy Crawford. But if for any reason they begin to enlarge, become raised or itchy, please go to your doctor and get them checked out.

Money matters
Women's much misunderstood relationship with money is explained by the fact that consumer spending throughout history was one of the few ways women could exert their power, influence and choice, even if they didn't have the vote. The financial services sector is only beginning to wake up to the fact that women in the modern world are earning a living and may, in some cases, have considerable spending power but little experience or knowledge about pensions, insurance, savings or investments. Amazingly, recent research shows that most women rely on their male partner for advice and unbelievably in some cases on their ex-partner. This is insane. There is no excuse. Seek independent financial advice at all times and if your financial advisor is a woman, so much the better.
(v: Debt, Grasping the nettle, I don't, Insurance, Opening brown envelopes)

Mood lighting
One quick way to sex up your life.
(v: Candles, Kindness)

(The) Moon
We usually think of the moon as a grey, sterile and unchanging world – untouchable and far away. Yet its close synchronicity with the earth determines the rhythms of our worlds more than we might think. Its gravitational influence guides the ocean tides and the minutes of the day, and its phases and cycles structure our own seasons – both physical and emotional.

The movements of the moon have been a source of wonder since ancient times, and have influenced the language, literature, art and music of our cultural landscape.

The association between the moon and the rhythms of women's lives traces back to the ancient world (the word *Lunar* comes from the feminine Latin *Luna*). The stages of the moon's cycle – the waxing, full and waning – have also been used as a metaphor for the female's development from virgin to creator then crone. Perhaps most popular is the close association between the moon and women's monthly menstrual cycle.

In fact, nurses at Queen Charlotte's Hospital assured us that the labour wards are busier on the night of the full moon than other times in the month, and let's not forget it's not called 'labour' for nothing. It is a long-held belief, particularly in boarding schools, that there is huge synchronicity with women and their periods, and a lunar pull bringing them together. McLintock's recent study states, 'Social interaction amongst women and body compounds can change the way the ovary functions.'

Moral high ground
Don't take it. Ever. It's deeply unattractive.
(v: Grace)

Mortality
'You only live once, but if you do it right, once is enough.'
— MAE WEST

'It's no use reminding yourself daily that you are mortal: it will be brought home to you soon enough.'
— ALBERT CAMUS

Mothers
It is probably not until you actually experience or witness what it is to be a mother that you begin to realise what they do and go through. Whatever your mother is like, or was like if she is no longer with you, the chances are that she tried to do her best for her babies, as all mothers do. Her maternal instinct would have compelled her to walk through fire, take the food from her own mouth, sleep on sacking and know no fear in order to feed and clothe her children. The concern that a mother has for her young is monumental. She only wants the best for you.

So now it's your turn – buy the chocs, bring the flowers and pick up any clothes and books you think might suit her. Be thoughtful and call with news. She's probably even got a mobile phone and is into texting and emailing in a sort of Morse code. Good for her and lovely for the grandchildren. Invite her to stay, it's your turn to take her out now. Try and work out how many hours you can rub along for without going into meltdown on both sides. Remember all the squillion selfless things she's done for you, and try to make her happy.

(v: Daughters, Family therapy, Sisters, Sons)

Motivation

'I am not a has-been. I am a will be.'
— LAUREN BACALL

'. . . never give up then, for that is just the place and time that the tide will turn.'
— HARRIET BEECHER STOWE

Know yourself and go for it.

Muddling through

If you are feeling totally overwhelmed and your sense of self-worth is at an all-time low, try the 'five things mantra'. Simply write down five things you need to do every day, and do them. You'll find that life begins to take shape again. You may not find a cure for cancer, but if you take this rule to heart you will knock 25 things off your dreary-things-to-do list in a working week. That's a result! Then you can give yourself a well-earned drink or treat yourself to a jasmine tea truffle.

(v: Chocolate, Feminism, Flow, Self-pity)

Mummy bores

You were not the first and you won't be the last, so ladies take a deep breath and put a sock in it. Motherhood is not supposed to be a competition and you will not win an Olympic Mummy Medal if your children are only allowed to eat hummus and wear socks made out of hemp. Your only achievement will be people yawning behind your back at parents' evening and giving you a wide berth at parties. It is a real turn-off with men, all of whom have had the kind of Mother who tended just to get on with it.

(v: Babies, Self-obsession)

Mummy porn or 'Fifty Shades of Not That Much That's New'

Mummy porn has been sweeping the country, and the sale of batteries has risen accordingly, but dig just a little beneath the surface and we discover that these so-called enticing stories of bondage and desire are really the fairy tales of our childhood: *Cinderella* with added handcuffs.

Do they help perpetuate a harmless fantasy or do they set up unrealistic expectations and desires that can never be fulfilled? Will they damage our relationships or are we going to see a seismic shift in women's sexual habits?

Tales of the so-called sordid and indecent have in fact been gracing our shelves for years, from Lawrence's *Lady Chatterley's Lover* to Edith Templeton's brazen memoir of psycho-sexual entanglement, *Gordon*. And it's often women who are the writers.

Mumtrepreneur

From making cupcakes to running a graphic design company from the kitchen table, many women are driven to set up their own companies after having children in order that they can take charge of their live/work balance. Mumtrepreneurs are the ultimate networkers. Just think about how many parents you know through your children's classmates, play dates, and other social activities but if you are about to embark on a kitchen-top start-up company do make sure you treat your co-workers fairly and pay them

the minimum wage. It can be irritating for the lazier amongst us when cupcake making is not just turned into a competitive sport but a million-pound business, but the answer is to be inspired rather than overwhelmed.
(v: portfolio career)

Music

With apologies to Shakespeare, but 'If music be the food of love, play on', and on and on and on. Everyone has a song that has changed their lives and most people have the soundtrack of their life cf. Desert Island Discs, which will evoke all sorts of perfect or not so perfect times. Share it around. No matter what the device, wind up or digital, tinny speakers or surround-sound, turn it on, turn it up, and let the good times roll. Your life simply wouldn't be as much fun without it.

Name-dropping

'David Bowie told me I should never name-drop.'
– KATE MORRIS

Narcissus

You will have come across one or two of these on your travels. It's worth recognising the type when faced with him or her. Though, interestingly, it's usually a him. A Narcissus will tell you that he has been in love '20 times' but when push comes to shove, it turns out he has never been in a meaningful relationship. A Narcissus is often in a surface relationship instead with his good looks. The women in his life have no real form and shape and can only echo what he says back to him because he is unable to allow anybody a separate, unique identity. So the good news is that while you may feel very badly treated by a Narcissus, don't take it personally, he is far too busy looking at his own reflection in the mirror to worry about your feelings. He has no ill intention.

(v: Committed bachelors, Complete wankers)

Necessary vanity

Newspapers and magazines seem to swing like a pendulum on the subject of vanity and, of course, it's a very convenient way of frightening, punishing and then advertising to women. At one level, everybody is excoriated for even considering Botox and facelifts, yet on another, the pressure to look younger, more beautiful and to sip at the spring of eternal life has never been greater. It was recently reported that teenagers are beginning to have Botox. This is a tragedy.

However, if we take it as a given that nobody really wants to walk down the road in a pair of mismatched gym shoes, smelling of pee with a jumper on inside out, let us accept that necessary vanity should be equated with a sense of self-worth and secret confidence. Why shouldn't one look one's best at whatever age?

There are all sorts of health and beauty treatments that are non-invasive, life-enhancing and well worth investing in. As with so many things, the French have got it right: a good skin routine is worth its weight in gold, doesn't have to cost a fortune and reaps rewards over the years. The phrase '… because I'm worth it' has become something of a joke in recent years, but actually, you are.
(v: Bien dans ta peau, *Moisturiser, Secret confidence)*

Networking
(v: Dating, Get out of a rut and get involved, Instinct, Members' club, Mentors)

Neurosis
(v: Exercise, Freud, Jung)

Never turn down promising encounters
We don't need to expand on this. Just don't. Life is short.
(v: It's a gift, Safety)

(The) New financial intimacy
Women can be the worst sort of money martyrs. Too polite
to complain when we realise we have been short-changed,
we obsess about it all the way home. The problem is women
are socialised to look after others. We think, as good girls,
we shouldn't let anyone down. From mortgages to mobile-
phone contracts we are often reluctant to switch providers –
or renegotiate deals on contracts.

Many of us self-sabotage around money – whether it's
an overwhelming need to be liked ('Don't worry, I'll pay
for it'); fear of confrontation ('Don't worry, I'll pay for it');
being uncomfortable with the concept of success ('I'm not
worth it. I'll pay for it'); even a sense of false pride that we
can manage on less. But actually it's a broader political
issue. No one knows what anyone else is earning (women
are more likely to be made redundant in a recession). We
owe it to each other to be more straightforward. Whether
it's admitting 'I'm pretty broke at the moment' or 'I had a
wallet-busting month, so we are taking the cheaper seats.'

It's fabulous now that it's fashionable to be frugal –
whether collecting restaurant vouchers, bringing round
home-made dessert or getting austerity tips from your
granny.

We need to share financial intimacies. Start by men-
tioning the M-word to friends and family. Forget the idea
that money is 'taboo' or 'private' – if we can talk about
a friend's sex life we can discuss their net take-home pay
or how much 'play money' they have left at the end of

the month after bills. That way we can genuinely tell who is having a tough time and learn more about money management.

(v: Sheconomics, Opening brown envelopes (the bills),
Holidaying with girlfriends: pleasures and pitfalls)

New people

Every six months or so the old address book needs oxygenating and new people need to be brought in. New people will keep you on your toes by offering fresh insights and unlikely experiences. Sharing your friends, however, is a very generous thing to do, so go steady on this so you don't have your nose put out of joint if your best friend makes friends with your other best friend and you are no longer invited to the party. Breezing new people into your life from all walks of life and from all nationalities is a great way to keep young, open-minded and full of zip.

(v: Little black book)

The new sexual frankness

Once upon a time, 'vagina' was a taboo word. Today, young female artists and craftspeople are making representations of the vulva – reclaiming the female body in all its 3D glory. The aim is to be out and proud about a neglected area of the body. Much of the new fanny art also stems from direct action. Shoreditch Sisters WI made a quilt comprised of beautiful hand-sewn applique vaginas to support a campaign against female genital mutilation, with more than 100 patches contributed from as far as France and the US.

In many ways it's a reaction against the tyranny of waxing and 'vajazzling' – porn-chic culture where young men surfing the Internet see only hairless models and are therefore surprised to discover that young women have pubic hair.

Of course, there's an honourable tradition of representing female genitalia in art through mixed media – from Georgia O'Keeffe's calla lily paintings to Judy Chicago's art exhibit, *The Dinner Party*. In the 1970s, Chicago created 39 place-settings for famous female guests – including Sappho, Emily Dickinson and Virginia Woolf – with labias rising up out of the plates themselves.

Hurrah for the new spirit of frankness in popular culture. Just don't ask anyone to accept the word 'clunge' (cf. TV show *The Inbetweeners*).

(v: Hairiness, Pornification, Cunt, Galleries)

New Year's Eve

Can be brilliant or it can be awful and there is often no rhyme or reason why.

(v: Self-pity)

Nifty 50

Twenty-one used to be the age of adulthood. But now that today's stressed-out graduates can't afford to buy flats (the average age of a first-time house buyer is now 38), marry, have children or start a business . . . As a result, 50 is looking pretty damn youthful and middle-age starts at 55. It's official.

No sex before marriage

'Abstinence is easier than temperance.'

– SENECA

According to the Greek author Homer, Hera, Zeus's much vexed wife, renewed her virginity each year in the spring

Kanathos. In doing so she put aside the troubles of her marriage (Zeus was a renowned philanderer) and found sexual fulfillment again. In the twenty-first century 'becoming a virgin again' has a slightly different connotation. But essentially it is a path chosen by young women who feel that in our over-sexualised world the female sex has become objectified and undermined. They believe that by returning to the traditions of no sex before marriage one creates a space where it is possible to establish a relationship with a man, which is based on friendship, like-mindedness, respect and soul. They hope that out of this balanced and spiritual connection a true and long-lasting love will grow. This may well be the path for some of us but not necessarily all of us.
(v: Chastity, Entering a convent, Self-discipline)

No strings attached

If you haven't had sex for a long time and somebody offers it to you, why not accept? No strings attached. It's a gift not a life-long attachment.

Northern racism

'It's grim up North' or 'The worst thing about it is it's full of Northerners'. So this slightly toxic banter continues and though they can stand up for themselves right enough this is really not right on. If these kind of comments were addressed to Somalians or Ethiopians there would be trouble afoot. Charlotte Brontë, Kes, The Arctic Monkeys and David Peace all hail from the North and although they do things differently there they are nevertheless part of our culture and our constitution.

Not safe in taxis

If a friend's husband offers you a lift home, then proceeds to tell you she doesn't understand him, and lands a hand on your thigh there is only one course of action. You must blacklist him immediately and tell all your friends. The code is NSIT (Not Safe in Taxis) or MTF (Must Touch Flesh).

(v: Complete wankers)

Not that friendly but actually quite nice

Weirdly, the man who appears a little bit diffident and not very good at parties may actually turn out to have a heart of gold and be honest and proper and true, cf. Darcy in *Pride and Prejudice*. Don't rush him and don't dismiss him.

(v: Good husband material, Top table)

❧

Office wife

It's quite flattering. A gorgeous man in the office who is happily married turns his attentions to you. Soon you are telling each other everything, going for lunch every other day and gossiping about work colleagues. All fine and dandy, but rest assured that he doesn't talk about you at home. Make sure you are still socially available.

(v: Cinq à sept)

Oily fish

Has got to be consumed on a regular basis to keep you clever, cheerful, slim and your skin healthy.

(v: Eat your greens, Menopause, Skin)

Old-fashioned Italian restaurants

From the red and white tablecloths and raffia-clad Chianti bottles to the flirtatious patron straight from central casting who loves a woman who eats dessert, they're a great port in a storm. Gourmets may rhapsodise about crab and ground-squash ravioli, but OFIRs are guaranteed not to break the bank, are ideal for tricky dates or impromptu work parties.

We've eaten in OFIRs from Berlin to Thailand – and, guess what? They never disappoint.

(v. Ballooning weight, Carbohydrates, Gelati)

Old flames

Don't go there. If you are still referring to them as an old flame, they are still secretly a live passion. However much you may think you have moved on, part of you is still hoping something will rekindle. We tend to revisit old flames out of boredom, pique, to make someone else jealous or to prove to ourselves how 'over' it we are. (If we were genuinely over it, they would have become our good friends 20 years ago.) There's nothing worse than sitting in the cinema with an OF thinking: 'We'll never be in the dark, just the two of us, again.' Or noticing a new item in their wardrobe that the new lover picked out. Yes, revenge can be a dish best served cold: 'Heavens, now he's bald/bisexual/bankrupt.' But that just makes you realise how much time you wasted. Reigniting sex with the ex is a dangerous game and you may get your fingers burnt.

(v: Complete wankers, (the) Ex)

Old ladyish behaviour

Being trapped in an unbendable routine and doing particularly pedantic things with tea are quite old ladyish and should be avoided. As should over-application of lipstick without a liner, and having to wear glasses while attempting to take drugs. Endless rooting around at the bottom of vast bags (looking for glasses, phone or keys) and not being able to use the remote control are quite OL-ish and should be guarded against. The cure? Smaller handbags, skydiving or a road-trip through Italy.

(v: Adventure, Climacteric, Handbags, Losing things)

Omnishambles

Just the most glorious word to describe 'a situation which is shambolic from every possible angle' – whether it's a disastrous Budget or a one-night stand. First coined by BBC political satire *The Thick of It*, it was named *Oxford English Dictionary* Word of the Year in 2012.

(v: Abbreviations and neologisms)

One step at a time

It's a cliché, but sometimes life is so overwhelming that one small step after the other is the only way forward. Like the Alcoholics Anonymous slogan 'One Day at a Time', it may be slow, but is less discombobulating.

One-night stands

(v: It's a gift, It seemed like a good idea at the time, Mercy fuck, On the rebound, Twice is polite)

On the rebound

'To be rejected is the beginning of being free.'

– GERMAINE GREER

Don't bounce off the furniture too much or get married within the year but do what you need to do.

(v: Agony, Bachelors, Mercy fuck)

Online snooping

In the old days, if we wanted to make contact with an ex-lover we had to phone them or arrange to see them in person. Now, thanks to Facebook, Twitter and other social sites, it's easier than ever before to keep tabs on past loves quite anonymously.

Part of the problem is defining what exactly constitutes stalking. When we first start to date a new partner, we often look them up online to find out more about their job and friends we have in common. It's the thrill of flirtation. Later on, we 'friend' each other on social-networking sites and feel flattered if they invite us to read their blog or look at photos of their family.

But 21st-century digital courtship can be a minefield. One savvy nineteen-year-old deletes her Facebook from time to time, expressly so she is not tempted to see what the guy she has just dumped is up to, thus clouding her judgement. 'I find I can move forward much more quickly without the constant awareness of possible contact,' she wisely says.

We may convince ourselves online 'stalking' doesn't hurt anyone. But isn't it the same as cold-calling someone's ex, or going to a dinner party and spending the whole evening asking around for unkind gossip? The key is to look honestly at the quality of our experiences and what they're doing to us.

Also, the absolute delight of getting to know someone, and finding things out about them face to face – like the peeling off of the layers of an onion – is in severe danger of being lost. We must beware.

Open mind (keeping one)

Keeping an open mind is an important philosophy. This is not an excuse for putting up with bores and boars. Sometimes your gut instinct is right. But it's healthy not to make snap decisions, or over-plan. Just see what happens.
(v: Down the rabbit hole, Not that friendly but quite nice)

Opening brown envelopes (the bills)

God, it's boring isn't it? Some of us would rather walk up Snowdon backwards carrying a 100-pound backpack in the sheeting rain rather than open a brown envelope, but it has to be done. Facing up to managing your financial affairs is essential for a happy life. Household bills, credit card statements and tax bills have to dealt with and the sooner you deal with them, the better. If you are self-employed, ensure that you have a good accountant on hand and if you are desperate put the bills in the post to them.

(v: Finances, Grasping the nettle, Insurance, Making a will, Money matters, Pensions)

Opera

And the undoing of women. With a few honourable exceptions, notably *The Merry Widow*, women tend to get a raw deal in opera. Whether it's Lucia di Lammermoor going mad in her tower, Camille in *La Traviata* dying beautifully of consumption (though all things considered in pretty good voice) or those poor nuns in Poulenc's *Dialogues of the Carmelites*, it's not looking good for the female sex. Many of the women in opera are archetypes: their stories encapsulate a history of women who have offered resistance to the male of the species, often with dire consequences. However, if you like the combination of exquisite music and high drama going to the opera is the ultimate TREAT. Everything is on a grand scale: the set, the cast, the music, the emotions and sometimes even the people. Unless you are extremely unlucky you cannot fail to come out moved, transported and perhaps irrevocably changed by the experience. And no excuses about the expense. Every opera house offers the most amazing deals if you put the time in and

opera is often broadcast through cinemas and occasionally is free.
(v: Entering a convent, Film club)

Opportunity
Knocks.
(v: I won't, It's a gift, Middlescents, Never turn down promising encounters)

Optimism
You can fake it. Even pretending to be optimistic and outgoing can make a difference – it only takes 21 days to create a new habit pathway in the brain. It's a better way to spend your time than waiting for your credit card bill. And certainly cheaper than trying to lift your spirits through alcohol or drug abuse.
(v: Opportunity)

Oprah [icon]
'You CAN have it all. You just can't have it all at once.'

Orbach, Susie [icon]
'Fat is a social disease, and fat is a feminist issue.'

'The Body Beautiful is so distressing because it is an assault on mothers, particularly the mothers of the generation that tried to change the world and make it a better place for women. The assault on them to get smaller and smaller and smaller. We were trying to get bigger and take up more space economically, politically and intellectually and every which way. One of the tragedies nowadays is that young

women have no experience of being okay in their bodies.'
cf. *The Beauty Myth* by Naomi Wolf.

Orgasms (the power of)

This is self-evident but not just because it's a glorious feeling. A woman's right to enjoy pleasure during sex was a cornerstone of the Sixties sexual revolution and it continues to be your right. It's about time it was enshrined in the constitution.

(v: Booty-call, It's a gift, Le gadget, Mercy fuck)

Orthopaedic footwear

We're in love with orthopaedic footwear. From nurses' shoes to FitFlops. From Birkenstocks to MBT (Masai Barefoot Technology) trainers. The first designs weren't very aesthetic, but now you can get glittery sandals, jellies, boots and trainers. Men loathe 'wellness footwear', of course – too practical. Not enough arch of the leg, no erotic tension. Sorry boys, get with the programme: it means we can walk for miles!

(v: High heels, Legs)

Outdoor exercise

(v: Adventure, Comfort zone, Handstand revolution, Trampolining, Wild swimming)

Overspending

(v: Debt, Money matters)

Overuse of the Internet

It's not where you are.

(v: Technology)

Oysters

Six of the best! Oysters used to be the food of the masses. Nowadays, while not quite at the level of a can of beans, oysters are an occasional affordable treat. Creamy and salty, served with lemon, Tabasco or chopped onion in vinegar, you have to down them in one. Alternatively, fry half a dozen and serve in a baguette for a Southern-style po'boy. You either love them or hate them, but if you are lucky enough to fall into the former category they are filled with zinc (more per serving than any other food) reportedly incredibly good for your sex life and are carbohydrate-free.

(v: Diet)

Pain
'Pain is life – the sharper the pain the more evidence of life.'
– CHARLES LAMB

(v: Age of bereavement, Agony)

Parks
The park is the great democratic space. Everyone deserves an expanse of green, a place to lie in the sun, read a novel, have a leisurely lunch. It gives you a chance to expand your world view, look at sculptures and historical monuments, chat to strangers, enjoy local gossip. Even if you want complete peace, you're out of doors sitting alongside your community. Human beings need to feel the grass beneath their feet.
(v: Green living)

Parton, Dolly [icon]
'If I ain't done it, I'm capable of it or I just ain't got round to doing it yet.'

Passing stuff on
That is, the good stuff. The favours, the rides, the dinners,
the frocks, and in some cases, the man. It's very green too.
(v: Bombshells, Karma)

Passion
'Love is a fire. But whether it is going to warm your hearth
or burn down your house, you can never tell.'
– JOAN CRAWFORD

'Love without passion is dreary; passion without love is
horrific.'
– LORD BYRON

We all need passion in our lives. The highs and lows are
what tell us we are alive. Great emotion makes us write
poetry and music, take risks, climb mountains, scale con-
tinents, find cities. There's nothing more thrilling than being
the object of another person's passion. It's like being the
heroine of your own private film.
(v: Film club, Music, Quests)

Patience
'I am extraordinarily patient, provided I get my own way
in the end.'
– MARGARET THATCHER

(v: Counter-intuitive feminism, Deferment of pleasure)

Pearls
'Pearls lie not on the seashore. If thou desirest one thou
must dive for it.'
– ORIENTAL PROVERB

'Perle, plesaunte to prynces paye
To clanly clos in golde so clere;
Oute of oryent? I hardyly saye.
Ne proved I never her precios pere.'
— UNKNOWN AUTHOR

'Pearl' is one of the greatest literary works of the Middle Ages. Scholars still don't fully understand the coded symbolism of this eponymous poem, but what we do know is that this is an elegy written to the poet's daughter.

The qualities that the poet associated with his 'Perle' some 750 years ago remain true for pearls today. They are singular, virginal, beautiful, luminous and secretive and they reflect the essence of the soul. Pearls grow when a grain of sand embeds itself inside an oyster shell. Once harvested, they tend to go cloudy and dull if left unworn for any length of time but quickly begin to glow again once worn against human skin. Don't hold back! Real pearls are never vulgar and if you are fretting because gentlemen prefer blondes, all you need to remember is that pearls look much, much lovelier on brunettes, cf. Elizabeth Taylor.
(v: Godmothers, I can't afford to buy cheap, Oysters, Playing it cool, Secret confidence)

Pears

Everything's gone pear-shaped, we apologise. Especially those of us with a petite top half and heavier bottom. But actually can't we rehabilitate the pear shape? Think luscious ripe green fruit, a tapering vase, or the curvaceous body of a cello, cf. Botticelli's *The Birth of Venus*.
(v: Shapes)

Pelvic floor

There's nothing more irritating after a 36-hour labour than the physiotherapist, usually with a figure like a whippet, who bounces onto the ward to encourage you to start doing your pelvic floor exercises. However, she's right. Think of it as an internal workout. You don't need any special equipment. You can do them sitting, standing or lying down or at the bus-stop. There are plenty of discreet ways to tone and strengthen your pelvic floor muscles. Think of it as an upward and inward contraction. Hold the muscles tight for ten seconds. Repeat up to ten times. As relationships expert Tracey Cox reminds us: 'Use it, or lose it.' It makes a huge difference to your sex life and can help prevent old lady incontinence and other gruesome age-related liabilities.

(v: Trampolining)

Pensions

Back in the day there was a notion that we would retire at sixty and live on a pension. Unless you work for the government forget it! You will have to work into your seventies and possibly beyond. The upside is that you will stave off Alzheimers and be generally far more fun to be around and live longer. That's a pretty good upside.

(v: Accounting, Grasping the nettle, Money matters)

Pep talk from a fiery redhead

We all need one of these occasionally. Maybe it's a useless lover, something not quite right at work or maybe you are just in the doldrums, but the fiery redhead knows that the only way forward for you is a to-the-point, five-minute-long, pep talk. It smarts a little at first but the wounds will

heal quickly and 24 hours later you'll be raring to go back on the razzle with aforementioned fiery redhead.
(v: Bachelors, Cocktails)

Perfect put-down

'I never forget a face, but in your case I'll make an exception.'
– GROUCHO MARX

Nancy Astor said, 'If you were my husband, I'd put poison in your coffee', Churchill said, 'If I were your husband I'd drink it.' You cannot store up perfect put-downs. They come unbidden.

Perfect Martini
(v: Martinis)

Perfect mayonnaise

2 organic egg yolks
1 heaped teaspoon of Colman's dry mustard powder
Maldon sea salt
ground pepper
2 crushed garlic cloves

Mix these together with a whisk and then add:

400mls of groundnut oil
followed by 400mls of light olive oil

For the first batch of oil add it drip by drip (hard on the arms so try to get a friend to help) and increase slightly but steadily to a trickle. If the mayonnaise looks as though it is getting thin or separated just add a teaspoon of boiled water and stir like mad and you will have your mayo back to where you want it.

When you have finished adding the oil, finish off with white wine vinegar and lemon juice. Steady as you go – you can always add more if it is under done but when you have put too much in you are screwed.

(v: Cooking, Hospitality, Picnics)

Perfectionism
'Well, nobody's perfect.'
– *Some Like it Hot*, BILLY WILDER

(v: Perfect mayonnaise)

Persephone
Persephone's abduction and subsequent journey into the underworld and her mother Demeter's desperate search for her reveals, in a many-layered way, how we all have the potential to abduct from within. Part of growing up is to be drawn to the darker side of life. By 'abducting from within' we take a course of action, consciously or unconsciously – in Persephone's case, eating a pomegranate that symbolises knowledge and sexuality – which may appear to be against our best interests. By entering the metaphorical underworld we are forced to explore a much more complex path. The story of Persephone resonates down the ages and touches on many themes in women's lives including mother/daughter relationships, fertility, rebirth, growing up, marriage, youth versus experience, male control, abduction and rape, depression, grief and loss and the symbolic and symbiotic relationship that women have with the natural world.

(v: Affairs, Benders, Drugs, It seemed like a good idea at the time, Jung, Self-sabotage)

Personal code of conduct

When you grow up it is important to develop a personal code of conduct. You don't have to boast about it or use it to shame other people. You just have to stick to it.
(v: Courtesy, Good behaviour, Grace, Mistress, Philosophy)

Petticoats

What is this retro item and why the hell do I need it? The answer – because your frock or your skirt will sit so much better on your hips if you are wearing one. Truly, your looks can hinge on this much misunderstood undergarment. An added advantage is that it's much easier to wear a scanty pair of knickers underneath. Many a blip can be concealed with a slip. That is a petticoat's purpose in life. Look out for a beautiful bias cut, made of vintage satin or silk and make sure the material drops rather than clings to you. Full petticoats with gorgeous thin straps are very enticing in a Fellini-esque way. We suggest that you will need several as, unless you are incredibly well organised, they tend to be hard to find in the morning when you are running out the door.
(v: Allure, Have you got the kit?, Vintage)

Philosophy

The central tenet of philosophy – how to live a good life – applies to us all. Studying philosophy teaches you how to approach problems, view arguments from multiple perspectives and think around situations. It refines your ability to communicate clearly with others and articulate your thoughts in a meaningful way. It might even make episodes of *The Simpsons* easier to understand! It's never too late to distinguish between your Descartes and your Wittgenstein.
(v: Keeping an open mind, Personal code of conduct)

Phone etiquette

There is a button on the mobile telephone called 'off' and unless you don't mind being taken for a teenage boy game addict we suggest you use it. There is nothing more dispiriting when going out for cocktails with a friend than to watch them scrolling through their messages while you try to make polite conversation. Always turn your phone off before entering churches, theatres, cinemas and concert halls. Copy your SIM card, or get someone else to (probably a teenager or maybe a godchild), otherwise when all your contacts are accidentally wiped out while wild swimming you will go into deep mourning.

(v: Courtesy, Godmothers, Technology, Wild swimming)

Photo albums

'A good snapshot stops a moment from running away.'
– EUDORA WELTY

These days we're just as likely to record birthdays and weddings on laptops and mobile phones. But don't forget the humble photo album. For over 100 years it has narrated our individual and collective stories and contained our most precious memories. It offers a permanent record of family history – what we wore, what we ate, where we went on holiday. A photo album gives us back our younger selves and children and grandchildren love them.

(v: Memory boxes)

Pick-up artist

You only have to read Neil Strauss's *The Game* to understand the murky world of male pick-up artists. Strauss's most insidious weapon is 'the neg' – a back-handed compliment calculated to lower momentarily a woman's self-confidence. ('Nice nails. Are they real? No? Oh, they look nice anyway.') There are two schools of thought on this. One is that it is undermining and makes women with low self-esteem miserable. The other is that it's a silly little game and anybody who tries to play it is a bit of a git. Neil Strauss sort of comes to this conclusion at the end of his own book too, which is why we secretly like him.

Picnics
Cold chicken or salmon. Pain Baynard, cf. Elizabeth David. Box of Vietnamese salad. Hummus. Perfect mayonnaise. Baguette. A cheese. Berries and cherries. Chilled water. Chilled rosé. A tartan blanket.
(v: Cooking, Hospitality, Perfect mayonnaise)

Piercing
Sorry, no can do. Earrings are fine. But nipples, navels, genitals, they're a body part too far. The most common emotion is regret. A permanent hole as a reminder of something we've changed our minds about. Think what you were wearing five years ago. Would you be seen dead in it now? NB Also watch out for mullets and men wearing slogan T-shirts.
(v: Regrets, Tattoos)

Pilates
It's all about 'the core' although most of us are blissfully unaware that we have one. It's all too easy to slump in a chair, letting our stomach muscles collapse, or lean forward so we get that tell-tale 'old lady' curve of the spine, which also results in back pain and rounded shoulders.
(v: Yoga)

Pilates Bands

Roll them up and put them in your handbag. These highly transportable latex bands are very effective at keeping muscles toned and stretched. Super for arm muscle definition and handy for resistance exercises for legs. Top choice for physiotherapists and injuries and the sure fire way to grab a little 'work out time' wherever you happen to be.

OK, they look a little *Fifty Shades of* Grey if draped around your boudoir, but a quick look on YouTube will teach you a bundle of exercises to follow and ensure good skeletal alignment and a degree of bounciness.

Pink

'The navy of India.'
– DIANA VREELAND

Germaine Greer hates it (pink denotes all things girlie and fey, she insists). Parents rightly worry about the 'pinkification' of little girls – their clothes, their bedrooms, their toys. The PinkStinks campaign was launched to challenge unacceptable gender stereotyping, from earliest childhood.

But one thing's clear, pink has always had a reference to secret, inner parts. *Surrender the Pink* (the title of a Carrie Fisher novel) is slang for male sexual advances to a female, but while we deplore manufacturers who think making a product pink (vodka, notepaper, novels) will automatically make us buy it, there's something marvellous about wearing a dash of Schiaperelli's shocking pink, whether it's lipstick, a pair of tights or the colour of your shiny new handbag.

According to psychologists, pink helps create a feeling of harmony and balance, with the passion and power of red, restrained by the introspection and quiet energy of blue/

purple and pink painted walls reflect back a soft warm light and can be extremely flattering.

Men of course experience a violent body swerve at the sight of pink, but to this day, the male rowing teams at Westminster School wear a fondant-fancy coloured kit; legend has it that they had to beat their arch-rivals Eton in a race in 1837 for the privilege of wearing this enduring and fashionable colour.

(v: Allure, Body management, Colour, Navy blue, Pornification)

Placing a bet

Consciously or unconsciously, we are placing bets every day of our lives. A bet is the inverse of insurance, but the mathematical equation is the same: essentially it is chance against probability.

Placing a bet may be a quick way to boost a flagging income, but unless you're a mathematical genius (cf. Dustin Hoffman in *Rainman*) it shouldn't become a habitual part of saving your life.

We don't only place bets on horses, dogs and in poker games – we place bets on lovers, friends and our children. We gamble with our emotions just as much as we do with money. And as we all know, it may be a gratifying thrill to see the outsider 100–1 horse gallop home, but as on the racetrack, in our own lives, it's a rare outcome.

Play

'We don't stop playing because we grow old; we grow old because we stop playing.'

– GEORGE BERNARD SHAW

Players (how to spot them)

Would-be players spend a great deal of time casually dropping the names of rich people, the names of artists who rich people think are cool, the names of expensive holiday destinations that rich people go to and the sums of money they have recently spent acquiring 'art'. It's incredibly boring but because you are well brought up you have to appear to listen with interest. True players just get on with it.

(v: Bores, Emergency exits)

Playing it cool

'Cool' – according to the rulebooks, you either have it, or you don't. At 20 you will not totally understand what cool really stands for ... by the time you are 50 it's a mass of infinitesimal incremental changes in the way you think about life.

The appearance of a calm exterior, poise and a sense of self-confidence, even while your stomach is churning, will garner you respect and admiration from all around. Remember, sometimes you have to act it to become it.

(v: Allure, Elegance)

Pleasure of work

'Work is much more fun than fun.'
– NOËL COWARD

'Choose a job you love and you will never have to work a day in your life.'
– CONFUCIUS

We spend most of our lives at work – so the difference

between getting it right and wrong is life-changing. This is just as true for those engaged in unpaid work, such as caring for children or elderly relatives. A satisfying job can bring structure and meaning to life, along with mental and emotional stimulation. Ideally, we should choose work that lets us use the qualities we value every day; that fits with our 'Big Idea' of ourselves. Put simply, the best career advice is to find out what you like doing best and get someone to pay you for doing it.

(v: Money matters, Portfolio careers)

Pleb

Derogative term used by snooty blue bloods to dismiss the lower order (see also 'chav' and 'grockle'). Short for plebian, the latin word for the common people. Use sparingly, if at all. Apart from anything else it feels weirdly out of date. As former Tory cabinet minister Andrew Mitchell found with 'Plebgate', it can also get you into a lot of hot water.

Pledging parties

Pledging parties are the latest way to raise funds for new book, film, music projects. They are a natural extension of crowd sourcing websites – such as Kickstarter, Pledge-Music, Unbound (the online platform where authors pitch their book ideas directly to readers) and Hugh Fearnley-Whittingstall's ethical funding site Peoplefund.it

Hosting your own party can be as simple as asking people to pay £10 on the door. You could hold an auction, a reading or a musical performance. Just remember to lay on delicious food and drink – and the opportunity for superior flirting. People like to feel connected and they get to vote with their feet for projects and charities they admire.

Not every pledging party is about money. Sometimes they're an 'auction of favours'. In return for a fabulous evening, guests are asked to pledge not money but tweets.

Crowd-sourcing isn't new. Back in the 18th century, Samuel Johnson funded publication of his famous dictionary by holding subscription salons to raise money in advance.

(v: Be well-informed, Comfort zone, Salons)

Poetry

If in doubt forget sex and discover poetry. Keep a slim volume of verse in your handbag at all times. Useful for queues, bus journeys and doctors' waiting rooms. But if you absolutely insist on fiddling with your mobile instead, install Shakespeare sonnets as an app.

(v: Queuing)

Poker

Traditionally a male preserve but women are proving themselves to be extremely good at this game, cf. Victoria Coren. Not least because of the psychological double-bluffing required. Old-fashioned maths helps too and, even if advanced algebra escapes them, most women are secretly good at adding 2+2. If you have a proclivity for card games (a childhood grounding in Pelmanism and Strip Jack Naked helps) seek out a poker course near you. You will form a whole new bunch of eclectic friends, more than likely set up a regular poker night and have enormous fun. Poker skills are also translatable to other walks of life and will come in useful if you are on a bender and down to your last 20p. Weirdly, having had slightly too much to drink may enhance your poker skills rather than lessen them. However, set yourself realistic financial limits and quit while you're ahead.

(v: Benders, Cheating, Counter-intuitive feminism, Lazy maths girl)

Politics

The vote was hard won. Women in the UK finally got the vote in 1928 (essentially we have been a democracy for less than 100 years) and it is the duty of every woman to care about who is running their country. You may disagree with all of them (including the women) and elect not to vote, but then become a conscientious objector and spoil your vote. It will still be counted.

(v: Demonstrations, Lipstick, Very public inconvenience)

Pornification

Has become increasingly hardcore and accessible and this needs addressing. The extreme objectification of porn stars and prostitutes is relatively new and it is a gruesome by-product of the Internet, and one of the unpleasant aspects of the liberal agenda. At the extreme end pornography endorses submission and violence towards women through brutal and often depraved acts, which are totally unacceptable.

Porn stars often have drastic surgery to enhance breasts, reduce waists and slim thighs. In addition, the uniformity of the Brazilian means that these women are often totally hair-free. The kind of body paradigm this sets up is a sad male fantasy and one of the knock-on effects of exposure to online pornography is that boys and men have completely unrealistic expectations when it comes to a real-life woman.

Most worryingly, we've heard disturbing stories of young men surfing the Internet for porn, who see only hairless models and are therefore surprised to discover that young women have pubic hair. This is reminiscent of John Ruskin, who was reportedly so shocked by his wife's body hair on their wedding night that the marriage was never consummated and subsequently annulled. At the moment porn is totally orientated towards male dominance and male pleasure, but how would we feel about it, if it was the reverse?

(v: Hairiness, Pornography)

Pornography

'Porn is not sex but in fact a very elaborate form of avant garde performance art.'

– BIDISHA

Our advice is never allow yourself to be filmed.

Portfolio careers

Many of us will work for life because we just can't afford to quit our jobs. Or we're just plain rubbish with money (preferring jam today and every day!). The good news: we stay engaged and active and society benefits from our experience. The bad news: no sunloungers in the Mediterranean. Which is why it's so important to set in place now the building blocks for a late career we can actually bear (not necessarily office-based). Maybe a two to three days a week consultancy, or a mix of PR, retailing, writing, entertaining, etc. Ask yourself what gives you pleasure, then how you can persuade someone to pay you for that. By definition, we'll be pitching to competitive, younger

people – but actually everyone likes reliable colleagues who aren't after their job!
(v: Freelance, Grasping the nettle, Pensions, Pleasure of work)

Posh pants
(v: Adventure, Camiknickers)

Possession
We can be possessed by the strangest of things. Lovers, shoes, bags, gardens, cats, diamonds, you name it. It's great to have a driving force that pushes us through life. Part of the fun is that you shift your life balance slightly to adjust it to your current enthusiasm – when your passion tips into an obsession warning bells start ringing.

Maybe we were going through a barren patch in our life, but if the love object appears to be Jeffrey from accounts, maybe it's a wake-up call. Alternatively, maybe it's just a temporary excuse to forget about our health and/or about our finances. Think of it as a holiday – with a return ticket.
(v: Mid-life crisis, Passion, Quests)

Postnatal depression
You may have had the easiest of childbirths and you may love your baby to bits but you can still succumb to postnatal depression. The symptoms of extreme tiredness, weepiness and loss of self-confidence often come post-childbirth and can tip into postnatal depression, which is a chemical malfunction exacerbated by hormonal changes and extreme fatigue. The healthcare system is extremely good at offering support to new mothers. Seek their help.
(v: Blues, Childbirth, Depression, Meds)

Power
(v: Deferment of pleasure, Orgasms, Power of prayer, Power of weeping on the sofa, Secret confidence)

(The) Power of now
'The eternal present is the space within which your whole life unfolds, the one factor that remains constant. Life is now. There was never a time when your life was not now, nor will there ever be.'
– *The Power of Now*, ECKHART TOLLE

(The) Power of prayer
'The function of prayer is not to influence God, but rather to change the nature of the one who prays.'
– SØREN KIERKEGAARD

The power of prayer is the power of hope over negativity. Just be calm in the knowledge that a little prayer will make you a sweeter person and could mean a great deal to someone else. To quote soul diva Aretha Franklin, 'The moment I wake up. Before I put on my make up. I say a little prayer for you'. Well, maybe after a strong cup of coffee.
(v: Cancer buddy, Hope)

(The) Power of weeping on the sofa
Sometimes we don't have to buck up and deal with all that life throws at us. Lying crying on the sofa is exactly what's required. You can indulge yourself completely for a day or two – and get the whole damn thing out of your system. Forget a stiff upper lip or keeping busy. Take time off work: allow yourself compassionate leave. Life

has dealt you an unfair blow. If you re-enter the world too soon, you'll regret it. Like a wounded animal, it's good to lie down somewhere quiet, to grieve. Allow yourself any vice that helps – violet creams, bad TV, and the occasional whisky (for shock). Gradually, through the gloom, you'll be able to think about things properly and eventually re-engage with the world.
(v: Crisis, Divorce, Grief)

Power Plate

A miraculous machine and the physio aspect of it is easily as beneficial as acupuncture. True, it does reduce cellulite, but more importantly it keeps your knees working, dammit.
(v: Diet)

Poverty

'Who, being loved, is poor?'
– *A Woman of No Importance*, OSCAR WILDE

(v: Debt, Money matters)

Pregnancy

(v: Breastfeeding, Contraception, Childbirth, Childfree, Fertility, Mummy bores, Termination)

Present drawer

You need to keep a present drawer stocked with bottles of scent, luxurious knickers, vintage china and general knick-knackery to give as tokens of your esteem to family and friends throughout the year. You like to receive. We all like to receive, but giving is even better and very fashionably twenty-first century.

Pre-threaded needles
Extraordinarily useful.
(v: Department stores, Make do and mend)

Privacy
(v: Boundaries, Beach huts, Bolt-holes, Co-dependency)

Problem-solving
'... tomorrow is another day.'
– *Gone with the Wind*, MARGARET MITCHELL

Things always look far worse at 3 a.m. Give yourself permission to go back to sleep, 'It is the middle of the night, I can't solve it now', and tackle it in the morning. If you can put the problem to one side, instead of gnawing at it like a dog with a bone, a solution may come to you unbidden.
(v: Crisis, Lateral thinking, Power of weeping on the sofa)

Prophets
We are all drawn to charismatic teachers and leaders but remember even prophets can have feet of clay. You friend's hot new guru/ meditation master/psychotherapist may well be bearded Dave from Essex. Beware of false promises. If something seems too good to be true, it probably is.
(v: Astrology)

Prostitution (male and female)
Anyone buying sex reduces another human being to a commodity. We all understand loneliness, frustration, the desire to separate sex from love. Clients may tell themselves it's a pretend girlfriend or boyfriend, a casual date, not business-like or mechanical. But prostitution is about money – and

control – over another (usually vulnerable) person. The pro-prostitution lobby may argue that a woman/man selling sex is just selling labour (paying the rent) like any other worker, but we should not pretend it is a career choice. Violence in the 'workplace' is a daily issue for many prostitutes, not the extraordinary event it is for others. Of course sex workers deserve to be safe. Pushing the sex trade further underground is counterproductive: forcing women to work alone makes the legal activity of selling sex a much more dangerous business. But buying another human being – paying someone to act out your fantasy – is capitalism at its ugliest. For every high-end call girl, such as Belle de Jour, making a good living, there's a trafficked woman from Eastern Europe living in fear. In the end there's only one question: would you be happy for your daughter/son/sister/brother to do it?

(v: It seemed like a good idea at the time)

Protect your core
(v: Boxing, Pilates, Trampolining, Yoga)

Pros and cons of animal husbandry

It only needed the opening ceremony of the London 2012 Olympics to remind us that England has a long history of pastoral life. Therefore, it is hardly surprising that we should fancy ourselves as shepherdesses. The vision of tending to our very own organic farmyard of ponies, donkeys, sheep and goats is a wonderful antidote to the pressures of 21st-century life, it's a modern-day version of Marie Antoinette's *Petit Trianon*, but would probably prove too much for most of us. It may seem wildly romantic to taste the honey from your very own bees, but do you really want to endure the sting that comes with being a bee keeper? One Kent-based shepherdess friend left an office job to move and work in the countryside. Little did she realise that RSI, the bane of keyboard users everywhere, is just as likely to happen on the farm in the hectic lambing season as it is in the office.

Public displays of affection
It can be extremely irritating to be forced to watch people oblivious to the external world exchanging bodily fluids six inches away from your nose. You probably long to shout 'Get a room!'. The rule of thumb is that hand-holding, hugging and general loving closeness is okay – anything else is too much but you *must* forgive first-time Romeo and Juliets everything.
(*v: Affairs*)

Pudenda
Sadly, *pudenda* is the Latin word for 'that which is shameful'. However, times have changed, be proud of yours.
(*v: Hairiness*)

Punctuality
Is the politeness of kings.
(*v: Lateness*)

(The) Pursuit of love
'If thou remember'st not the slightest folly.
That ever love did make thee run into, thou hast not loved."
– *As You Like It*, II. iv., WILLIAM SHAKESPEARE

(v: Affairs, Booty-calls, Cinque à sept, *It seemed like a good idea at the time, On the rebound)*

Putting out fires

From the unauthorised overdraft to the meeting that never got rescheduled, we need to put out fires before they spread. Everyone takes their eye off the ball occasionally – it's only human – but it's important to stay solution-orientated, rather than just wallowing in the problem.

(v: Grasping the nettle, Opening brown envelopes)

(The) Queen [icon]

Is without vanity, loves corgis and horse racing and has a personal code of conduct, which we only have glimpses of but is impressively old school. She has fully accepted her destiny. We can say that very few others have.

(v: Icons, Personal code of conduct, Tweed)

Quests (this has nothing to do with laser swords)

'Come on. We're all on one.'

— JOSEPH CAMPBELL

Whether we are in search of a man/woman/job/car/ higher spiritual plain, most of us have usually got at least three quests on the go. They feel like a cross between a crush and a prayer. It's personal and intense. Perhaps your quest is to have kids – or if you have them, maybe it's to look after them as well as you can. Or, maybe it's achieving something such as staying off the booze or perhaps it's keeping your herbaceous borders bushy (as it were). But whatever they are, and however many you have got, we implore you to embrace them. Your inner quests are the motor within. Quests are what drive us and keep us going. They are the sign that we remain ready for adventure and what could be more life-changing than that?

(v: Adventure, Crushes)

Queuing

You will have to do this and it is always a drag but it is also our continued ability to queue that makes us proud to be British. Carry a slim volume of verse or a short but perfectly formed novel (*The Turn of the Screw, The Great Gatsby, To the Lighthouse*) with you at all times. This will ease the pain and distract you from the melee.

(v: Poetry)

ഏ

Rain

'Millions long for immortality who do not know what to
do with themselves on a rainy afternoon.'
– *Anger in the Sky*, SUSAN ERTZ

Do not to be afraid to go out in the rain. Rain will not
poison you and nor will it shrink you (sadly!). It is claimed
that the beautiful bloom of the classic English complexion
is enhanced by rain. There is no need to make a song and
dance about rain. Just get outside. If you have children, the
school run still goes on. If you have a dog, he needs to
ramble. So scarves on, put your gloves in your pocket,
brollies at the ready! Life goes on.
(v: Blues, Depression, Self-pity)

Raising boys on your own

It's a challenge but above all you mustn't continue the battle
of the sexes that was initiated with their father with them.
Try and be empathetic, however difficult that may seem.
Do not quash their innate masculinity even if you find it
baffling at times and encourage conversation even if you
only get a series of grunts in return. Encourage as much

sport as possible and, if their school is less than enterprising, check out what local football and cricket clubs have to offer. Boys need to be run ragged as it gives them less time to get up to mischief.

Check pockets regularly and if you find anything untoward, i.e. drugs or knives, discuss it openly, preferably with backup. Finally, if the father is truly absent, call on a godfather (or significant male presence) for help. Now is the time for them to really help out. Encourage cooking and other household chores, there are plenty of male role models in that department, and this will ensure that your boys can look after themselves properly as they grow older and not become a burden to their girlfriends. The rule of thumb is that if they are old enough to have sex they are perfectly capable of putting their jeans in the washing machine. Don't worry if their rooms are ridiculously untidy. They have to live with the mess, you can just shut the door on it. Litter the flat or house with newspapers and inspiring reading material – if boys can keep the reading habit going through the early teens then they will be readers for life. Once they are properly in their teens encourage discussion and debate about setting boundaries, timekeeping, attending meals, getting up for school and being courteous to women. After all they live in a democracy so prepare them for it. Most important of all, prepare to battle it out with them if they display sexist behaviour towards anybody, but most of all you. Good luck.

(v: Brothers, Family therapy)

Raising Girls

We seem to be doing a good job.

Ranting

You don't find your topic, it finds you. One day in the middle of discussing real fur/natural childbirth/private education/the e-book versus print, you realise you've been declaiming wildly for the past ten minutes. Ranting is great fun: it shows you're engaged, that you care. People enjoy watching someone in full flow. The topic can be as highbrow or trivial as you like. The whole point is to look eccentric. It's perfectly fine to punctuate your flow of words with, 'Sorry, I'm ranting' and just carry on. But do watch that you're not becoming an adult bore. If your friend's grin is starting to look a little fixed, stop.

(v: Bores, Old ladyish behaviour)

Rap

Partly responsible for dragging feminism back, probably by the hair and wearing a teeny-weeny bikini encrusted with diamonds, into the Dark Ages. Boys who are raised on this bilge and play no sport to boot will become like caged dogs. It's not hard to work out why. It's sad to see a procession of beautiful young women playing dumb in support of this nonsense. It's not funny or clever, and it's no example to impressionable girls.

(v: Bitches and hos)

Rape

Is not about sex. It is about power and it is usually per-petrated by men who feel powerless or who wish to exert power over women regardless of their feelings, wants, desires or needs, in order to feel that they are in control.

Raves
We miss them. Can somebody bring them back?
(v: Dancing, Tap-dancing)

Reading groups
There is often more than a whiff of competition about being part of a book group, although recent evidence claims that joining a group brings the same level of happiness as a pay rise. You may well discover that your readers are far too busy checking out your chintz, your wine rack and everyone else in the room to deign to discuss *Madame Bovary*. That said, it really is an excellent incentive to get books read and, if you are a passionate reader, to share your enthusiasm with others. If in doubt, start your own but pick fellow members carefully. Ban all conversation about partners, children, schools, holidays, houses or money and if your time and money are under pressure stick to white wine and sausages.
(v: Film clubs)

Regrets
We've had a few.
(v: Benders, Drunk-dialling, It seemed like a good idea at the time)

Rejection
There are no two ways of looking at this. It is extremely hard to be dumped by a lover or sacked by your boss. It's a shock. It's painful. It can evoke long-held memories of grief and loss. The natural impulse is to seek revenge and then, once we have calmed down, justice. What we really need to do is learn from rejection.
(v: Crisis, Power of weeping on the sofa)

Relations
(v: Brothers, Extended families, Daughters, Family, In-laws, Mothers, Sisters, Sons, Stepmothers, Teenagers)

Relativity
'When you sit with a nice girl for two hours, it seems like two minutes. When you sit on a hot stove for two minutes, it seems like two hours. That's relativity.'
– ALBERT EINSTEIN

Oh. Ok. We get it.
(v: Lazy maths girl, Philosophy)

Retirement
Because the world is financially fucked very few of us are going to be able to retire. But we can still rejoice as we will remain connected to the world, live much longer and still be able to take taxis, cf. Diana Athill [icon].
(v: Deferment of pleasure, Money matters, Pensions)

Revenge
'I was born to dominate your sex and avenge mine.'
– CHODERLOS DE LACLOS, *Les Liaisons Dangereuses*

Rewards
Rewards come when you least expect them. You're trying to keep faith in the darkest hour. Nothing. Still nothing. Then suddenly bang – the universe sends you an email offering you the chance of a new job/holiday/assignment. Good fortune is mercurial. But it nearly always comes from taking a risk and breaking your everyday patterns –

befriending someone, going that extra mile – without any thought of recompense.

(v: Karma, Where's my fucking pony?)

Riding

The English have tended to choose dogs over horses, something that the Arab world finds hard to understand, but who hasn't fallen secretly or not so secretly in love with a horse? The Greeks understood it and mythologised accordingly. We are only just beginning to understand our evolutionary and personal relationship with horses.

(v: Outdoor exercise, Pelvic floor, Where's my fucking pony?)

Rise of Albion (Queen, Corgis, Jubilee)

Who could have imagined it would be so cool to be British? Once characterised as a chippy uptight nation with wonky teeth and inclement weather, Team GB is looking pretty hot. Thanks to Danny Boyle's quirky, multi-cultural take on Britishness for the Olympic Opening Ceremony, Albion is something to be proud of again.

Finally, we can enjoy the red, white and blue of the Union Jack without wincing. The Queen revealed her secret sense of humour (skydiving with James Bond, indeed). And thanks to the Diamond Jubilee celebrations, the corgi has seen a leap in popularity. The stumpy-legged dog with a big bark has become a major fashion icon.

The old images of traditionalism and noblesse oblige are being updated. Yes, it will still rain through the summer. Yes, foreigners still think we live in big houses like Downton Abbey. But the summer of 2012 looked like the start of a new chapter in the 'British' story.

Which only goes to prove that patriotism, i.e. taking

pride in your country, is a far more interesting beast than blinkered nationalism.

(v: Rain, Ranting, Picnics; Public displays of affection, (The) Queen (icon), Sconesseurs, Tweed)

Rise of the shoffice

If you work from home, the shoffice, a shed-like structure in the garden, which has Internet, phone and coffee-making facilities, is extremely useful. It eliminates the two-hour commute to work and the dress code is pyjamas, unless the accountant is popping by.

(v: Bolt-hole, Personal space, Portfolio careers)

Rising above it

When everybody else is behaving badly it's good to rise above it and continue on your way.

(v: Grace)

Role models

(v: Angelou, Maya; Blaize, Immodesty; Del Conte, Anna; Lumley, Joanna; Mantel, Hilary; McArthur, Ellen; Minogue, Kylie; Mirren, Helen; Parton, Dolly; Queen, the; Rowling, JK; Smith, Patti; Streep, Meryl; Suu Kyi, Aung San; Swinton, Tilda; Thompson, Emma; Vitti, Monica; Westwood, Dame Vivienne)

Roots (Touch up)

According to Voguette Plum Sykes it only takes 15 days until you need to touch up your roots. The hairdresser can always do an energising T-section before you need to do a full head of highlights. Hair mascara, naturally, is a massively useful tool when you are too busy to make an appointment, or simply too cash poor.

Rowling, JK [icon]

'When you dream, you can do what you like.'

❦

SAD

Though unattractively titled Seasonal Affective Disorder, this form of misery due to long dark winters can be banished by a cheery, disco-tastic, super invigorating lightbox. Away joint pain, over-eating, lethargy and carbohydrate dependency. At the flick of a switch, hello bouncy, fizzy invigorated individuals with boosted levels of seratonin and melatonin, which are stimulated through light. Every home will have one soon.
(v: Carbohydrates, Diet)

Safe sex

(v: Contraception, Safety)

Safety

It's horrible to stop a woman doing anything, walking anywhere, suggesting limits on her freedom. But the number one rule is to stay safe. Always wait for the bus or train in a well-lit place near other people if possible. Walk the route you know best and stick to well-lit, busy streets. Look confident. If you think you are being followed, take action. You may feel a little silly at the

time, but so what? The most important thing is you get to do what you want to – when you want to – without letting an idiot ruin your day.
(v: Adventures, Comfort zone, Dating sites, Long-haul travel, Strenuous exercise)

Salad days

'... my salad days,
When I was green in judgement, cold in blood.'
– *Antony and Cleopatra*, I. v., WILLIAM SHAKESPEARE

We are all allowed three great loves in the space of one lifetime. Despite the knowledge that our salad days are over and despite the onset of wrinkles and widening hips, late love offers us the chance of romantic fulfillment one last time. Late love has its own particular bloom and depth.
(v: Accepting invitations, Late love, Little black book, Open mind)

Salary

At your annual review always ask for a minimum of a ten per cent rise.
(v: Accounting, Money matters, Pensions, Portfolio careers)

Satisficers (don't be too perfect)

'Satisficers' enjoy the pursuit of pleasure – but they know when to call a halt, or discreetly compromise – when everybody is getting exhausted. Far better to opt for the third restaurant you see ('This is good enough – it will do for me') than trail everyone around for hours. After all, the point is to see your friends and relax over a glass of wine.

The direct opposite of the 'Satisficer' is the 'Maximiser', perfectionist and driven, they are doomed to misery and regret, continually haunted as they are by all the choices that weren't made.

(v: Co-dependency, Perfectionism)

Saucy seaside postcard

Appreciation of the physical form could soon actually be condemned by parliament and we might perhaps be staging citizen's arrests for inappropriate comments towards members of the opposite sex. The Sixties and Seventies seem so dreamy now compared to the terrifyingly judge-mental and bossy nature of the Noughties.

(v: Wolf-whistling)

Saunas, Turkish baths and spas

Spas are crash courses in major relaxation. They should be available on the NHS for a calm, collected life.

(v: Grief, Massage, Skin)

Saving money

If you can, save ten per cent of your salary every month and then diversify your investments through property, stocks and shares, and tax-free saving schemes. However small your investment, seek advice from an independent accredited financial advisor.

(v: Debt, Money matters, Pensions)

Scarfology

From shawls and wraps to pashminas and bandanas – there's a scarf for every occasion. Pack one for holidays and it can double as blanket, coat, belt, halter top, headpiece, even as a sarong. Guaranteed instantly to transform a dull outfit and rescue you on a bad hair day. Add a sparkly rhinestone pin or brooch to make a statement. There really is an art to tying scarves with elan. Think Bette Davis, Joan Crawford or Grace Kelly – who used an Hermès scarf as a sling for her broken arm.

(v: Animal prints, Jewellery for fat days)

Scent

A great scent is the final link in the chain of your signature style. Seek out the classics. You will know when you have found the right one for you because everybody will tell you how wonderful you smell. Once you have found it, stick with it.

(v: Allure, Elegance, Luxury, Necessary vanity, Style)

Schadenfreude

A German word that distills the feeling of satisfaction we sometimes experience at someone else's misfortune. It's not pretty, in fact, it's up there with jealousy and selfishness as one of the most ignoble feelings we may have about another human being, but it is a universal feeling and what's weird is it comes with a momentary sense of pleasure. Luckily, if you can put a name to it you'll find you can push it back into the box swiftly and no harm done.

(v: BF, Frenemies, Freud, Jealousy, Jung)

Sconnoisseurs

Lemon and White Chocolate. Bramley and Apple Crumble. Pesto and Chorizo ... Bespoke scone flavours are the latest foodie trend. On websites such as Sconquest and scone-advizor.com, 'Sconnoisseurs' share their experiences with

other scone fanciers. There are even underground afternoon tea clubs. You can put it down to the 'We love the
Queen' factor (the scone made a come-back during the
Jubilee festivities and street parties) as well as the national
obsession with baking. Yes they are often perceived as part
of the anachronistic ritual of blue bloods – afternoon tea –
but scones, like pasties and sandwiches that could be par-
celled up as lunch for working men, are essentially a
working-class food.

(*v: A little bit of what you fancy does you good*)

(The) Seaside
(*v: Beach huts, Bolt-holes, Infinite vistas, Picnics, Water*)

Second marriages
Are commonplace. Enjoy them, celebrate them, but do try
to ensure that you are not repeating the patterns of the first
one.

(*v: Good husband material, I don't*)

Secret armour
(*v: Elegance, Enigma, Personal code of conduct*)

Secret confidence
Some of us are naturally more confident than others but we
all need to work on building up our confidence. The steady
or quiet accruing of compliments, fulfillment through
family and/or work, age and experience all help.

(*v: Accepting a compliment, Camiknickers, Necessary vanity,
Pleasure of work*)

Secrets

'If you reveal your secrets to the wind you should not blame the wind for revealing them to the trees.'

– KAHLIL GIBRAN

Some secrets are fun, some are exciting and some are a downright burden. One person's secret is another's whopping piece of pernicious gossip. If you are the holder of a full hand of secrets, guard them closely, and do NOT place them in an email. Very often you will be in possession of the equivalent of a little hand grenade, which you don't want igniting on your watch. Guard them carefully.

(v: Benders, BF, Dancing with the devil, Gossip, Regrets)

Self-acceptance

'The most terrifying thing is to accept oneself completely.'

– CARL GUSTAV JUNG

(v: Bien dans ta peau, Learning to love yourself, You've got to do it)

Self-deprecation

Don't do yourself down. It's pointless and can become embarrassing and irritating for those around you. As much as you put yourself down they will politely feel the need to build you up and frankly that's not their responsibility.

(v: Accepting a compliment, You're the bomb!)

Self-discipline

Is unfashionable but worthwhile.

(v: Diet, Quests)

Self-doubt

However great we think we are feeling about ourselves self-doubt seems to have an insidious ability to creep in and change the way we see things. It is like a worm gnawing an apple. It burrows deep and can be very damaging. It is not to be confused with useful self-examination or insight. Guard against it.

(v: Accepting a compliment)

Self-obsession

Rather like being a bore (and the two are closely related), you are probably the last person to realise that you are becoming increasingly self-obsessed. Knock it on the head immediately. The signs are:

1. You are beginning to dominate conversations.
2. You repeat the same stories again and again, always about yourself.
3. You don't really listen to or take in what other people say.
4. You always somehow manage to bring the conversation back to yourself.

It takes a brave sibling or friend to point this fault out to you, whether in conversation or during a row. Your immediate response will be to feel cruelly hurt but please take this criticism on board and make some changes, otherwise you will end your days as a lonely old lady.

(v: Bores, Exquisite listening, Old ladyish behaviour)

Self-pity

It is fun to wallow in self-pity once in a while, but if it extends for longer than a day or two it can become self-defeating for you and boring for other people. However, you do need to take self-pity slightly seriously as it can develop into depression. So in the first instance: count your blessings and make a gratitude list, i.e. write down the ten things you are grateful for in your life. Do some gardening (even if all you are doing is replacing the plants or herbs in your window box) – a connection with the soil and the earth is apparently particularly therapeutic for women. Volunteer for some kind of community service. But, most of all, be easy on yourself. So, early nights, easy TV watching, woolly socks, etc. And, at the end of each day, think of two or three things large or small that you have achieved in the day, such as being nice to your neighbour's cat. If, after a week or two, you are still waking up in tears and/or none of your friends will return your calls, make an appointment to see your doctor.

(v: Container gardens, Depression, Gardens, Power of weeping on the sofa, Therapy)

Self-righteousness

A really unattractive quality. 'He who casts the first stone . . .' and all that. It smacks of smugness, preachiness and boring self-obsession and if you continue down this road you will lose friends and alienate people.

(v: Bores)

Self-sabotage

(v: Persephone)

Self-sacrifice

Is not to be confused with being unselfish. Self-sacrifice has connotations of unnecessary nineteenth-century female victimhood. Your daily martyrdom – insulting to those who really do put themselves on the line – is boring for family and friends and probably ultimately pointless. Life may one day throw you an extraordinary calling, cf. Joan of Arc, The Fukushima 50, but until then take a balanced view of your needs versus other people's.

Sense of self
'With stammering lips and insufficient sound I strive and struggle to deliver right that music of my nature.'
– 'The Soul's Expression', ELIZABETH BARRETT BROWNING

(v: Bien dans ta peau, Secret confidence, Self-acceptance)

Sentimentality
Has its place but don't major in it.
(v: Keepsakes and talismans, Memory boxes, Tattoos)

Separate Spaces
Demanding, advocating or perhaps preferring a space of one's own is allowed. Not so much radical feminist theory, though heck, there could be a tincture of that, but more the feeling that it can be liberating to not have to share everything with fellas around. Hence the burgeoning women's only cafes, clubs, spas and gyms. Men already have gazillions of them.

The aristo habit of women withdrawing from dinner to leave the men to their port and cigars used to feel antiquated and old-fashioned but now it is beginning to look like a brilliant escape into a separate space.
(v: A room of one's own)

Sex
'Sex is not a noun like coffee.'
– SYBILLE BEDFORD

(v: Affairs, Bachelors, Benders, Cinque à sept, Contraception, Exercise, Have you got the kit?, Instinct, No sex before marriage, Orgasms)

Sexual abuse
(v: Daddy damage)

Sexual harassment
An age-old male device for oversexualising and undermining women, usually in the workplace, cf. *Mad Men*. Nowadays, there are very strict rules against it. Know your rights.
(v: Bullying, Politics)

Shapes
As an apple shape, you store your excess fat predominantly on your mid-section and bust. Unfortunately for you, this kind of fat storage is known as 'android obesity'. It makes 'apple' the most dangerous of all body shapes, putting you at higher risk of hypertension, type 2 diabetes, coronary artery disease and premature death (compared to individuals with a pear shape, or 'gynoid obesity', where fat is deposited on the hip area).

An interesting, and often shocking fact is that a waist measurement of over 35 inches for a woman puts her at high risk of all of the above diseases – so get your tape measure out! (You might want to check out any men in your life too – the waist measurement for men should be 40 inches or less). The good news is that apple shapes normally respond well to exercise and diet and you can very quickly see the results.

(v: Pears, Waist)

Shapewear

Once upon a time curvy girls were laced into hideous Fifties foundation garments, but today's figure-enhancing shapewear – tanks, bodices, T-shirts, dresses – is smart enough to wear as outerwear. The painless way to enhance cleavage, smooth out love handles and find that waist, which was last glimpsed in 1983.

(v: Ballooning weight, Necessary vanity, Waist)

Sheconomics

Just because you're a woman there's no excuse to be in debt. Be aware of how your emotions affect the way you behave with money. If you insist to yourself and others that you are bad with money, you probably will be. If you think you deserve to be comfortably off, that's half the battle won. Once you've worked out what's standing in your way, you can start to change your behaviour – and attitude – towards money. A very important note to self is that your bank manager is not your father.

(v: Grasping the nettle, Money matters, Opening brown envelopes, Pensions, Something for a rainy day)

Shoes

'The shoes, the shoes,
Won't change your life dear,
Your feet, or the shape of your legs dear,
Twinking away life like big Easter eggs

In the shiny shop window
Not for walking in you see.
Just wearing to a party.'
— SARAH-JANE LOVETT

(v: Feet, Flats, High heels, Orthopaedic footwear)

Shipwreck scenario
The shipwreck scenario is quite a useful tool. If you find yourself high on life, whether it's a lover, a new job or a risky enterprise, focus a little on the possible downsides. A reality check is rarely wasted.
(v: Affairs, Crisis, Divorce, Househusband, I don't, Self-pity)

Sideburns
Bradley Wiggins, we salute you, one and all. In one bound the Tour de France-winning Olympic cyclist has put extravagant facial hair on the map. For years the clean-shaven look dominated and sideburns were the preserve of swingers and San Francisco's gay club scene. But now it seems the hirsute male is back – everyone wants to date a man with mutton chops! It denotes muscularity, independence of thought and an eccentric fashion sense. As 'Le Gentleman' Wiggins observed himself: 'Sideburns have not been as popular since Noddy Holder.'

On the plus side the new trend may free up some more bathroom time for us, with less razoring for the gents. Though we do draw the line at goatees or chin curtains.
(v: Bien dans ta peau)

Single supplement (well worth it)
Yes, it's aggravating to be charged extra for single occupancy. Twin rooms are cheaper if you don't mind bunking up with a friend. But we'd argue it's well worth paying for bathroom privacy – and that vital hour alone to recharge before cocktails.
(v: Holidaying with girlfriends)

Sisters
'Whatever you do they will love you; even if they don't love you they are connected to you till you die. You can be boring and tedious with sisters, whereas you have to put on a good face with friends.'
– DEBORAH MOGGACH

'For there is no friend like a sister, in calm or stormy weather, to cheer one on the tedious way, to fetch one if one goes astray, to lift one if one totters down, to strengthen whilst one stands.'
– CHRISTINA G. ROSSETTI

No relationship is more complicated, more deeply tangled with highly charged emotion. The bond sisters share is dark and light, simple and dangerously complex. Constant yet ever evolving: sisterhood is a baffling incomprehensibility to those outside of it. And no matter whether it's taut and buzzing with daily contact, or slack and dusty from years of neglect, it's a bond that's always there.

The relationship you have with your sister is likely to be the longest of your life. Probably the most rewarding: she is a piece of your childhood that's never lost and the person most likely to stick with you in the future. So even if times

are troubled, unless she's run off with your husband or bumped off your rabbit, best to forgive and forget. You are, after all, singing from the same songsheet.
(v: Brothers, Family therapy)

Skin
'Eat an apple every day,
Get to bed by three,
Oh, take good care of yourself,
You belong to me!'
– 'Button Up Your Overcoat', DESYLVA, BROWN AND HENDERSON

Current thinking suggests that by eating an anti-inflammatory diet your skin will be kept in super-fine fettle. Well, what the hell is that we hear you cry? It means high protein and low-glycaemic carbohydrates, i.e. not too much refined white breadstuffs and loads of fruit and vegetables. And lots of water, naturally.
(v: Diets, Eat your greens, Facial acupuncture, Super-foods, Vitamins, Water)

Skinny
As the distinctly odd Wallis Simpson declared, 'You can never be too rich or too thin'. Well, on some levels that may be true but it's not necessarily a question of choice ... There are many women who are naturally very thin. This may be incredibly galling for those battling the bulge, but this is just the way it is. It is rude to go around endlessly commenting on people's skinniness and making them feel awkward and embarrassed.
(v: Diet)

Sleep

We spend a third of our lives sleeping. It's a uniquely private experience even if we share a bed. The sensuality, the pure surrender (when we get it) is a wonderful thing. It's the brain's way of wiping the computer and re-booting. Sometimes creative problems solve themselves overnight. As actress Penelope Cruz insists: 'Sleep is the best way to happiness and beauty. Once, my sister slept for three days straight. My record is 18 hours.'

Sleep can be a great refuge from difficult life events. Tell yourself not to reply to an upsetting email or make a decision about a bad patch in a relationship for at least 48 hours. Instead go to bed.

Sleep makes us brainier (it helps maintain normal cognitive skills, like speech and memory). It helps regulate our weight (sleep deprivation lowers the amount of leptin the body produces, which leads to increased appetite). It's the fastest – and cheapest – boost you can give yourself.

Many high-fliers regard it as a waste of time and have accumulated a chronic sleep debt. But, like a bank account, make sure you pay in extra at weekends, or days off.
(v: Beds, Insomnia, Skin)

Sloe gin

Should be in everybody's cocktail cabinet. Sweet and dry and a deep purple. It can be a secret ingredient in all sorts of jellies, trifles and fruit salads. It's brilliant with prosecco, known as a sloegasm, delicious with tonic or perfect as an after-dinner alternative to port. Or in the deep dark heart of winter sit around a fire and sip slowly, with pleasure.
(v: Booze, Dipsomania, Grappa, Hospitality)

Slut-shaming

Slut-shaming, refers to the act of making a young woman feel guilt or humiliation for participating in certain sexual practices, such as having multiple sexual partners. Worryingly it's considered funny by some teenage girls to mock and thus ostracise their 'promiscuous' peers on social media sites. To protect young women from bullying we all have a duty to explain the difference between sexual exploration and exploitation. We've all made mistakes.

Small talk

Why do so many clever, high-minded people think they're too good for gossip? Scientists tell us it is fundamental to being human. It makes us healthier, boosts levels of progesterone (a hormone which reduces anxiety), and fosters trust and co-operation. And, in times gone by, gossip proved vital to survival, with the trading of titbits helping cavemen catch thieves and democrats elect leaders.

Gossip is a completely different thing from bitching. It's when – over red wine or at the school gates – we begin to discuss how hard it must be if one person is more successful in a relationship. Or whether you expect sexual fidelity. Yes, we may mention a celebrity or two, but only to get everything fired up. You need to be interested in the minutiae of other people's lives, otherwise friendship or a romantic date can feel like a maths A level with more drinking. There's no let-up. The big questions are lobbed over the net: 'Who do you think should inherit Pinter's library?', 'Did you read the new essay on Dorian Gray?' Bang, bang. Until you're pleading for mercy.

No one can be that interesting or that well informed. If you want to become a great gossiper, you must:

1. Feign ambivalence.
2. Appear unimpressed upon receipt of gossip from other people.

To be blasé, in other words, is key. Be very Wikileaks about your gossip but never ever commit gossip to email.
(v: Conversation)

Smith, Patti [icon]
'Never let go of that fiery sadness called desire.'

Smoking
The 1950s ad campaign ran, 'You're Never Alone With a Strand', and how right they were. The supremely comforting ciggie is a wonder for so many, many reasons: for calming your nerves; accessorising your outfit; giving you something to fiddle with that is a million times more enigmatic than a phone; making you part of a gang; making new friends; it is the perfect accompaniment for a drink. In fact, let's face it, it's not just a cigarette, it's a poem.

For obvious, scientifically researched reasons it's bad to smoke, but then it's bad to do lots of things including eating tar and throwing cats at walls. So, as long as you manage to do it in moderation, and if possible after 6 p.m., it is something to treasure. Hide spares around the place and in the car, and if you live in the country have a stash of spare tobacco and achingly gorgeous liquorice papers. You never know when you might get to stock up again.
(v: A little bit of what you fancy does you good)

Snobs

Snobs endlessly waste their time on genealogy and reassuring signs of aristocratic breeding. A disappointing and rather soul-destructive trait that is still surprisingly prevalent – although extremely unfashionable. It is to be hoped that a snob will be hoist on their own super-smart petard.

Snoring

Let's get one thing straight, the fairer sex never snores. It's biologically impossible . . . unless, of course, it's a side-effect of hay fever, feather pillows, dining late or hard liquor. That aside, snoring can be the great divisive issue in relationships. We all need sleep (anything less than six hours is dangerous). There are plenty of whizzy sprays and remedies on the market: surgery is a last resort. But whether it's your partner, best friend or you who's disturbing the peace, it's helpful to talk about it – and out the taboo. There's nothing wrong with separate bedrooms. You can read late and watch films on the laptop – and it can be damn sexy to visit each other's sleeping space.
(v: Ballooning weight, Grappa, Holidaying with girlfriends, Insomnia, Single supplement, Staying the night)

Snow

'I sought my lover at twilight
Snow fell at daybreak . . .
Secret or not
No matter.
Footprints have been left in the snow.'
– from *The Turquoise Bee: The lovesongs of the sixth Dalai Lama*

Soapbox

If you want to air your opinions, just do it. We've all got issues and how good it is to spread them around. Do beware, however, that you don't become a grade A bore.

(v: Bores, Demonstrations, Heckling, Politics, Ranting)

Sobriety

It is good to flex the sobriety muscle from time to time, even if this means going, 'Negroni? Water? Negroni? Water? Negroni? Water? Yes, please. A large double water, with a liver-boosting slice of lime too, please Mister'!

January is traditionally the time when everybody gives up the bottle but it can feel rather glum if you and everybody else you know is drinking elderflower water round the kitchen table in the freezing cold. February has the virtue of being a short month. Lent is a good time for super sobriety, it has proper religious clout and, when you get to the pearly gates, St Peter will have noted it down on your report card. Whatever your religious views, sobriety is a good way of keeping an eye on your drinking and calmly reminding yourself you can go for a week or two without. But, hey, everything in moderation. Including maybe this.

(v: Alcohol, Dipsomania, Quests)

Soirées

Are spreading through the country like wildfire. The formula is based on a perfectly mixed cocktail, a little music, a dash of poetry, a soupçon of a novel and some lovely drinks and canapés. Have an interval so people can smoke and chat, and a flat fee of ten pounds on the door should cover expenses.

(v: Cocktails, Film clubs, Music, Poetry, Reading groups)

Something for a rainy day

Try and stash ten per cent of your monthly salary in a savings account. That cash will be there for you should the worst happen and you lose your job. It will repair the roof, see off the tax man, rescue your teeth, put you through a short college course/work placement. It just gives you that extra bit of secret confidence and it's your running-away fund, if something terrible – or wonderful happens.

(v: Money matters, Pensions, Taxis)

Soothsayers

Are kind of fun once in a while, but dangerous if you become co-dependent. By all means read your stars, make your spells, magic your thinking, but don't spend too much time with a soothsayer as they can be awful drags and at the end of the day ruinously expensive – and we don't just mean financially.

(v: Astrology, Prophets)

(The) Soul

Weighs 21-grams and is one of the cornerstones of religious belief, although its existence is generally denied by fundamentalist scientists. It's an amalgamation of genetics, circumstance, nature and nurture and the individual response to destiny helps to constitute this illusive core of our being. Friends and relatives often have a profound sense of a soul leaving the body at the moment of death.

Soulmates

Civil partnerships require you to become your lover's best friend and modern social mores suggest that this is a 'good thing'. But is this strictly necessary with your hubbie or your

fella? Isn't it best to keep soul sharing for the girlfriends?
(v: BF, Good husband material, Top table)

Spending your way out of a depression
Who'd have thought it? The Keynesian theory of economics
suggests that we buy our way out of a depression. Now you
have a proper excuse to spend your way through your blues.
It's slightly unfashionable at the moment as we try and slash
trillions off the national debt but like all good ideas it won't
go away for long and, if your husband gets hold of your
unfeasibly large credit card bill, just explain quietly and
firmly that you are helping restore your country's economic
fortunes.
(v: Money matters)

Sperm
(v: Babies, Contraception, Skin, Termination)

Spinnies
'Don't laugh at the spinsters, dear girls, for often very
tender, tragic romances are hidden away in the hearts that
beat so quietly under the sober gowns, and many silent
sacrifices of youth, health, ambition, love itself, make the
faded faces beautiful in God's sight.'
– *Little Women*, LOUISA MAY ALCOTT

The single woman is everyone's favourite caricature –
whether demonised as home-wreckers and ball breakers
(and that's just the good stuff), or patronised as a controlling
career woman secretly frustrated because they don't have a
home life. But these days, singlehood is a state of mind.
Sometimes you're in relationships, sometimes not.

Lots of 'singles' have grown-up children. People don't have to stay in bad relationships any more, and women are relishing their new economic independence. No wonder the US grassroots movement Quirkyalone promotes the idea that it's better to be single than settle.

And being a spinny has a noble pedigree. The first 'spinsters' appeared in thirteenth-century France as spinners and weavers of cotton and wool. The term denoted respectable employment, as unwed girls, orphans and widows forged a life outside the family home. In Victorian times, many middle-class spinsters enjoyed a life of 'single blessedness' (among them Florence Nightingale and Louisa May Alcott). Some taught, others set up all-female households. These special friendships would be regarded as loosely lesbian today, but no one worried much about female crushes back then.

(v: Cocktails, Friendship, Maisonette, Urban tribes)

Spitting
'Stop it please now', and spread the word, not the germs.

Split the bill?
We're inevitably 50/50 on this. Yes, of course, it's important to assert your individuality, your economic separateness, your right to have sex with no sense of debt. But how wonderful, lovely and moving it is when a bloke says, 'I insist'.

(v: Courtesy)

Spring
The moment when the sap rises and a long, dull winter is finally over. We love spring because soon the fields will be

green. The leaves will return to the trees, violets and jonquils will bloom and seeds will be sown. It is a time of new beginnings. Of triumphant rebirth after hibernation and symbolic grief. Pagans decorate their altars with a light green cloth and candles, flowers, a bowl of soil, a wand, a large seed, flowers, parchment and a pen. But if you want to you can celebrate your vernal equinox ritual with a cactus and a large gin. Just don't waste the first day of spring.

(v: Candles, Hope, Magic spells)

Staff

Behind every reasonably successful career woman are probably some staff. Don't exploit them. Pay them properly and recognise their worth.

(v: Alpha females)

Statistics

Tell you everything and nothing. The interesting thing about statistics is that they present themselves as fact but are usually governed by human motivation but without much insight. Distrust them as far as you are able.

(v: Spending your way out of a depression)

Status anxiety

'Envy should motivate not paralyse. As for keeping up with the Joneses, while we can't altogether suppress status awareness, we can largely control whom we compare ourselves to. If we make social comparisons by gazing upwards, we are bound to be unhappy. But compare downwards, and we feel sane again.'

– *Status Anxiety*, ALAIN DE BOTTON

(v: Sense of self)

Staying the night

It's easy to get old ladyish about this, let's face it everyone loves their own bed. But it's good for us to mix things up. By all means travel prepared – toothbrush, lenses – it makes the appearance of spontaneity so much easier. Friends will supply the rest. Of course, if you're staying overnight for the first time, there are a few things to establish. Where's the bathroom? Are there flatmates? Does anyone have to get up early next day? You might road-test your underwear first. Ditto the condoms. But do try to relax, you're not planning to invade a small country.

(v: Contraception, Elegance, It's a gift, STDs)

STDs

If you can't get pregnant and/or are over 50 it doesn't mean you can abandon contraception. STDs are not just on the rise but in a mad rush to get to the party, particularly in the latter demographic.

(v: Condoms, Contraception, Safety, Sex)

Stepchildren

It is unimaginably hard bringing up a stepchild, but however revolting they are being to you, try and put yourself in their shoes.

(v: Divorce, Family therapy, Modern families, Teenager)

Stepmothers

Traditionally stepmothers in fiction and throughout history have generally had a notoriously bad press with a few exceptions, cf. the second Mrs Dombey, Isabel Archer and Katherine Parr.

Stepmothers are at the dark heart of many a fairytale,

myth or legend and even the word 'stepmother' can still send a chill through a lovely summer garden party, cf. Snow White and the seven dwarves. However, perhaps it is time to reassess the stepmother. The truth is that in the world of ever-extending families you may well have one, be one or be about to become one. The definitive book on the role of the stepmother has yet to be written so, in the meantime, it is worth understanding that this is a delicate and difficult role.

If you are about to become a stepmother you need to believe that you can be an entirely positive force in your new stepchildren's lives, while facing up to the fact that you are entering into a very complex dynamic. Your step-children may well be traumatised by events in the past and may unconsciously believe that the only reason you have power and influence in their lives is that you are sleeping with their father (which is sort of true) and that will feel very unfair to them.

You need to find love in your heart when there may be none; you need to create strong boundaries while being flexible too; you will need to accept openly your mistakes and, more importantly, that you are going to make a lot of mistakes. There will probably be rows and you are going to have to learn how to make the peace. You will need to be scrupulously fair about money and in particular wills and, although it may seem counter-intuitive, it is wise to encourage your husband to have as constructive a relationship with his ex-wife as possible. If your new husband is a widower do encourage open and loving and ongoing conversations about his first wife with the children. It may feel like a dagger in your heart, because stepmothers can begin to love their stepchildren very much, but this must be done with a loving smile on your face.

It sounds gruesome doesn't it, but don't wrench your engagement ring from your fourth digit just yet. Please, please believe us that being a stepmother can ultimately be an extremely rewarding experience and if you haven't had children of your own, stepchildren can really be a gift from God.
(v: Childfree, Divorce, Family therapy, Modern families, Teenager)

Sticking with it
Don't give up too easily.

Straight talking
Instead of fuming and festering, why not speak your mind? And then be a grown-up and let it all blow over.

Streep, Meryl [icon]
'It is well that the earth is round and we don't see too far ahead.'

Studio
'Women, then, have not had a dog's chance of writing poetry. That is why I have laid so much stress on money and a room of one's own.'
– *A Room of One's Own*, VIRGINIA WOOLF
(v: Bolt-hole, Infinite vistas, Personal space)

Style
(v: Elegance, Instinct, Suits)

Suffering
(v: Agony, Aloneness, Freud, Grief, Jung, Self-pity, Therapy)

Suicide
To borrow from Nietzsche, the contemplation of suicide can help one get through a long night. However, don't do it. It is essentially self-murder and is devastating for friends and family.
(v: Crisis, Leaving the party)

Suits (men and women)
In the 1980s women had to wear power suits to prove they were the equals of men. Dresses were considered suspect. The suit said: 'Listen to me, give me your money and your votes.' It also said: 'I am an honorary man.'

Women's business attire has changed significantly since those Thatcherite times, becoming more relaxed and more 'feminine'. It's perfectly acceptable to 'mismatch' separates. The skirt suit can have a girlish dirndl or slick pencil skirt. Vivienne Westwood gives a suit a Lauren Bacall twist. Of course a great suit or tux, cf. Tilda Swinton or Carla Bruni, gives you confidence, skims curves and takes you effortlessly from day to evening. A string of pearls helps.
(v: Alpha females, Angry birds, Frocks, Pearls, Style, Whither feminism?, Work wear)

Sunday nights
Have a particular kind of melancholy.
(v: Grasping the nettle)

Sunglasses

It is rather like being inside a limo – you can hide tears of joy and pain, late nights and dark shadows. Whether you prefer classic Jackie Os or huge bug-eyed lenses, sunglasses play a game between concealment and display. Plus we are the lucky generation that's got prescription lenses. Just don't wear them indoors unless you're Anna Wintour.

(v: Elegance, SAD, Style)

Sunshine

'Keep your face always toward the sunshine – and shadows will fall behind you.'

– WALT WHITMAN

Get as much of this good stuff as you can. It keeps you happy, healthy and pretty. A sunny day can take all your cares away and it definitely takes your mind off shopping.

(v: Eat your greens, SAD, Vitamins)

Super-foods

(v: Blueberries, Eat your greens)

Suspenders and stockings

(v: Affairs, Cinq à sept, Have you got the kit?, Twice is polite)

Suu Kyi, Aung San [icon]

'Peace as a goal is an ideal which will not be contested by any government or nation, not even the most belligerent.'

Swinging

The modern-day equivalent of the Dionysian orgy but without the attendance of the gods and it is once more back in vogue, cf. Killing Kittens. The phrase smacks of Seventies-style sexual liberalism and a pre-Aids age of innocence. It conjures up images of pampas grass and German porn but take stock, before you throw your car keys onto the table, are you prepared to face the consequences on the school run in the morning? Perhaps best left to the realm of fantasy.

(v: Affairs, Divorce, Tie me up, tie me down)

Swinton, Tilda [icon]

'Face slapped, fingers through the hair. Never look in the mirror, and never ask anybody how you look.'

Taboos
(v: Boundaries, Swinging, Tie me up, Tie me down)

Tailoring

The nip and the tuck. The hip and the bosom. Sliding your shoulders into a perfectly sized jacket with the damn fine ratio to your perfection will save you top dollar. You will put it on endlessly. You can get it copied. You will feel a bit of a hottie when you wear it and a bit of a babe. You could find your tailor in any street and take what material you want to be made to your specifications. Hold on to threadbare vintage suits and get those copied. You certainly won't look back.

Take the weight off your sling-backs

We live in a society that is constantly stepping up the pace and stealing our time, expecting us to be everywhere and anywhere all at once. The idea of taking regular breaks seems to remain just that: an idea. But literally lying on the sofa or sitting in an armchair with your feet on a stool, even for five to ten minutes, can be just the tonic to soothe the strains of everyday life. The disco nap might not always be possible, but we shouldn't underestimate the importance of taking the weight off your sling-backs – it's an easy and free way to revivify the body and the brain.

Talent shows
Avoid them.

Talks
Are the new gigs. Forget dusty lecturers coughing through three-hour papers. Many of today's talks have the wit and energy of stand-up comedy. Not only do you get to meet intellectual titans, it's a clever way to check out a new dating partner without any of the embarrassment. Debates are happening all over the place but check out events hosted by Intelligence Squared, the Royal Geographical Society, the Tate and the ICA. London's The School of Life offers secular sermons, pilgrimages and courses on love, work and family. Or look up the website TED online (www.ted.com) – and crunch through a 20-minute talk on architecture, or on how Internet pornography is ruining relationships, without leaving your armchair.
(v: Be well informed, Good stuff that's free, Libraries)

Tango
(v: Dance, Exercise, Flow, Passion)

Tap-dancing
Everybody loves it, but fewer people are doing it. Excellent for thighs, knees and ankles. Or, if you are feeling lazy, dig out some old Fred Astaire films and just sit back and marvel.
(v: Dance, Exercise, Flow, Passion)

Tattoos

Tattoos were once the preserve of sailors, fat ladies in the circus and the occasional aristo but now everybody has got one or is talking about getting one. Tattoos radically divide people and men tend to love them or hate them on women, they rarely take a neutral view. However, once again it's your choice and they can be a brilliant way of marking important moments in your life.

(v: It seemed like a good idea at the time, Keepsakes and talismans, Sentimentality)

Taxis

Never, ever, regret money spent on taxis. They can save you time, rescue your hair/wardrobe/shoes – or all three on a rainy day – and provide an important psychological breathing space in a stressful day.

(v: Safety)

Tears

Yes, they are occasionally embarrassing and a bore on the make-up front. When we cry the body releases toxins – such as the stress hormone cortisol – so you always feel better afterwards. Tears can melt the sternest of hearts and they can even incite an unexpected crush. True, it's hard for most of us to cry and remain photogenic. Lucky people can shed a single, graceful glistening tear while their already perfect bone structure is heightened by a becoming flush but most of us are chaotic, 33-hankies-a-day sorts, cf. Juliet Stevenson's fabulous portrait of snotty raw grief in *Truly Madly Deeply*.

As a rule of thumb try to avoid crying at work, unless in exceptional circumstances. Dig your nails in your palms.

Take deep breaths. Walk around the park – or have secret convulsions on the stairs.

When you witness a fellow weeper – never more than five feet away in a big city – be compassionate. We've all sat on night buses next to a stranger sobbing (bad date, bad boss, bad everything), and felt anguished that we didn't intervene. Pat them kindly on the shoulder. Reassure them it's okay to have big, messy emotions and hand over some tissues. We all need to have a really good cry from time to time.

(v: Foundation, Grief, Kindness, Power of weeping on the sofa)

Technology

Is there an app for this stuff? Of course it's horrible, annoying and complicated but this is why teenagers were invented, yours or other people's, and jolly useful they are too. All those hours of downloading and poking and Facebooking and whatever else they get up to, finally comes into its own when they apply their skills (unpaid, naturally) to your problems and needs. Teenagers love technology and are happy to help, mainly because it's much more interesting than tidying their room or taking out the bin bags. It is second nature to them. They can whizz things around the Internet faster than the speed of light: it's a bit like watching Jamie Oliver cook pasta alla puttanesca. If you have to learn some basic technological skills, borrow the aforementioned teenager for a few hours. If you are really stuck, it's worth coughing up for some proper lessons from a trained adult. However, if you have fulfilled your godmotherly duties you may find your god-children will be kind and help you out.

(v: Godmothers, Teenagers)

Teenagers

Teenagers can be ghastly but the truth is 99% of the time, as the result of the rush of hormones into the body they really can't help it. Don't enforce ridiculous punishments, i.e. cancelling pocket-money for two and a half years in a row, or prolong arguments because you are feeling hormonal and/or liverish. Once they get going teenagers do not have a turn-off switch. You do, so use it. Re: drugs, getting home late, sexual health and overdue homework reassure them it is your concern for their health and safety that motivates you, not wanting to be a member of the moral majority. Re: untidy rooms, just shut the door and let them get on with it.

(v: Daughters, Divorce, Godmothers, Sons, Stepchildren, Stepmothers, Tears, Technology)

Teeth

Time to invest in your mouth: it's never too late to rescue your teeth. And we're not just talking about fillings and gum disease. Smiling boosts your immune system, lowers blood pressure and releases endorphins (natural painkillers) and serotonin. It is a truth universally acknowledged that people with fabulous smiles are perceived to be more attractive, more intelligent, wealthier and younger.

Top tips:

1. Use an electric toothbrush. It's like cleaning the floor with a vacuum compared to a brush and pan.
2. Flossing (the 'f-word') is vital. Bacteria are clever creatures and they can hide in gaps between your teeth and multiply.

3. Use a straw. Fizzy drinks are bad for your teeth because they attack the teeth's protective enamel.
4. If you having a boozy meal, opt for cheese as dessert – it neutralises the acid from alcohol.
5. If you know you will be drinking wine, brush your teeth before your first tipple. This removes the plaque which attracts the wine.
6. Eat sugar (sweets) all in one go. It takes an hour for your mouth to neutralise a sugar attack.
7. Grazing ruins your teeth.

(v: Necessary vanity, Secret confidence)

Ten thousand hours

'Researchers have settled on what they believe is the magic number for true expertise: ten thousand hours.'
– *Outliers: The Story of Success*, MALCOLM GLADWELL

Termination

It's a sad fact that, despite the widespread availability of contraception and the morning-after pill, the UK has the highest abortion rate in the western world. Confusingly, very premature babies, born at 24 weeks, which is the current limit for abortion, have been known to survive. The moral and legal lines blur at this moment.

A termination is a relatively minor medical procedure but it can leave long-lasting emotional scars. If it is something you are contemplating, do seek professional counselling. If you are single and pregnant and in your late thirties – and you have always wanted children – we do advise you to keep your baby, even it means rearranging your life.

(v: Contraception, It's a gift, Sperm)

That's the way I always do it
Well, why not change it? There is nothing more boring than doing the same thing, in the same way, over and over again.
(v: Bores, Old ladyish behaviour)

Therapy
Take your pick.
(v: Freud, Jung)

Things not to do in public
Picking your nose, clipping your nails, French kissing on the Tube, shagging people on the escalators.
(v: Bad habits)

Things that make your life easier
(v: Bras, Cars, Contraception, Dishwashers, Family therapy, Friends, Frocks, Handyman, Lipstick, Lovers, Money matters)

Think like a man
'I would have been perfect as a man.'
– ANNIE LENNOX

Research shows that men and women think differently but perhaps not as differently as you might think. So instead of wasting time on *The Rules* (frigid with a hint of peevishness), and who'd want to end up with the kind of man who goes for that type of woman anyway, or agonising over *He's Just Not That Into You*, just think about it from the male perspective – whether it's food, sex, companionship, responsibilities or chores – and liberate yourself accordingly.
(v: Big babies, Complete wankers, Female logic, Manning-up)

(The) Third sex

With the rise of female athletes we're seeing a new female body – lean, muscular, healthy. A far cry from fashion's obsession with size zero.

These are women who are proud to look powerful, and who aren't afraid to sweat and pant their way to a gold medal.

Some male commentators find this threatening, of course. Should women really be boxing or playing football. Isn't it unfeminine or worse, proof of gender abnormality? Sex testing of female athletes such as Caster Semenya, the world-champion runner from South Africa strikes us as bad manners and intrusive, and rightly there was a huge outcry at the time.

However, we're unstoppable: the exploits of athletes such as Jessica Ennis, Nicola Adams and Laura Trott during the Games have ignited the desire and determination of women of all ages to take up sport. Hurrah for powerful roles models who don't just marry footballers or take their clothes off (cf. Kim Kardashian).

(v:Androgyny)

(The) Third space

Isn't to be found between your eyebrows, though pressing down with your thumb on this acupuncture point can help you ease tension on a busy day.

(v: Beach-huts, Bolt-holes, Libraries)

Thompson, Emma [icon]

'It's unfortunate and I really wish I wouldn't have to say this, but I really like human beings who have suffered. They're kinder.'

Threesomes

These sound a lot more exciting than they actually are and one person tends to get left out and usually starts crying. But obviously you should try everything twice. Back in the day threesomes were symbolic of sexual liberation, but increasingly they have become the preserve of overpaid footballers and kiss and tell 'glamour models' and as a result, dare we say it, have become rather humdrum.

(v: Swinging, Taboos, Tie me up, tie me down, Twice is polite)

Tie me up, tie me down

Once upon a time people thought bondage was quite daring, but nowadays as a leitmotif it's everywhere, whether it's advertising ice cream or a family car. A little 'vanilla sex' as the euphemism goes, such as being tied to the bedpost with a pair of silk stockings is one thing, but it can get more addictive and extreme and before you know it you are in your own hand-luggage. Bleugh!

Time

'You don't have time, you make time.'
– ANONYMOUS

Top girls

Alpha females burst through the glass ceiling for us – just to prove we can. They lead by example and rewrite the rules. They have changed the world by their determination and hard work, and they have made an impact by the way they live, or have lived, their lives. In general, they are self-created. But being an alpha female is not an excuse for bullying or machismo or hostility towards other women (or beta males). A truly assertive woman is great fun to be around. You flourish in her company and enjoy the ride (however bumpy) and because she is confident enough of her skills, her philosophy is that others should be too.

(v: Househusbands, Staff)

Top table

In the heat of the moment it can be quite hard to judge whether a man is truly worthy of your attention and love. Our suggestion is that you make a list of the men whom you would invite to sit at your imaginary 'top table'. They may be friends, lovers, husbands, fathers, godfathers, a bloke from the office, straight or gay. The key point is that although you may fancy them that is not the reason why they are welcome at your top table. Maybe it's for their moral values, maybe their intelligence, maybe their kindness or their courage in adversity, maybe it's for their genuine love and respect for women, children and dogs, whatever, but an unexpected outcome of this exercise is that you will remind yourself how many lovely men you know. Seat a minimum of six at your table and then ask yourself is there room for your prospective fella? You will be surprised at how quickly you come to a decision.

(v: Committed bachelors, David Attenborough, Good husband material)

Totes amaze – abbreviations and neologisms

The penchant for truncating words (WTF, OMG) and making up clever portmanteau phrases and neologisms (glamping, blegging, intexticated) is part of our new boredom threshold. We're multitasking and we want everything now – faster, sharper, more abbreviated than ever.

Yes, we can blame the perma-tanned stars of reality TV shows such as *The Only Way Is Essex* (TOWIE) for jettisoning any attempt at grammar. But actually it's rather good fun. Colourful new phrases such as 'wine flu' (drunk) and 'celebutante' (a young woman who achieves fame through her inherited wealth) add to the gaiety of the lingo. English is a fluid, evolving language – and Shakespeare himself was the king of cut and paste.

Just as long as we remember in the long run it's no replacement for the Petrarchan Sonnet.

(v: Cheating, Be well informed, Poetry)

Toy boys

'How absurd and delicious it is to be in love with somebody younger than yourself. Everybody should try it.'

– BARBARA PYM

Up to a point. You should be aware that there is nothing more grim to the young than a woman of a certain age trotting about with someone who looks like a nephew or a male au pair. Yes, we hear you cry. Men can do it so what the hell? True. But more often than not these guys are trophy buffers or tax-dodging exiles from their country of origin, signing very large cheques for pneumatic women who have to fake orgasm. And pity the doll who is caught with the fella who looks like her son's best friend. The likelihood is that in the short term it may put the va back into your va-va-voom. But the upkeep is exhausting and suggests a battleship-load of maintenance just to keep yourself in the frame. In the long run, it's all a bit of regional soap opera as opposed to *Tender is the Night*.

Trains

Hours of novel reading, great scenery, no rows or traffic jams. The sheer joy of surrendering to a train journey can't be overstated. As a car-obsessed nation, rail travellers are often regarded as second-class citizens but there's a huge romance to trains, whether you're embarking on the Orient Express or going home to see your mother. Book ahead and you'll get great bargains (two singles often cheaper than a return). Then spend the money you've saved on a swanky picnic or glass of champagne. The best bit – no one can boss you around or be a back-seat driver – you're in charge.
(v: Poetry, Holidaying with girlfriends, Meditation, Never turn down promising encounters, Picnics)

Trampolining

Bored of the gym? Hate jogging? We are here to tell you that bouncing is far more fun. Trampolining helps you shape up and reduces cholesterol levels. It's the most effective aerobic and cardiovascular exercise for the whole body (a ten-minute session provides benefits equivalent to a half-hour run).

A word of caution: do watch drink-bouncing. Trampolines are for sober days. Most accidents on a trampoline occur when over-enthusiastic adults come back from the pub and think: 'Ooh, let's try the trampoline!' Hours, if not days, in A&E can follow.
(v: Flow, Handstand revolution, Pelvic floor)

Travel

There is a new kind of snobbery along the lines of: 'Look how little I can travel with, aren't I marvellous?' When flying by plane, all this hand-luggage stuff is fine and worthy, until you are freezing your ya-yas off in Dublin and your friend is trying to shove her MBTs into your restricted luggage. Our view is that it's worth paying extra to be able to take your luggage on holiday. If you are going abroad, you will want to take skincare essentials, plus sun lotion and aftersun, and you will also want to buy stuff and bring it back. Yes. You will.

(v: Adventure, Balcony holidays, Orthopaedic footwear)

Trust yourself
(v: Instinct)

Truth
'. . . to thine own self be true.'
– *Hamlet*, I. iii., WILLIAM SHAKESPEARE

'And ye shall know the truth, and the truth shall set you free.'
– JOHN 8:32

(v: Guilt, Little white lies)

Trysts
We all know that lovely phase before a relationship becomes carnal – and you're still conducting the courtship out of doors. At this age it's important to have a list of trysting places. Chic, safe, low-key (preferably with excellent seating and shelter if it rains on your blow-dry), where you won't scare passing teens by holding hands.

The whole point of an assignation is there is a frisson of danger. You might decide to wear a splendid hat. But don't let things get too gothic or self-conscious. Never take a new

suitor to a place associated with memories of an old lover, it's just asking for trouble.
(v: Affairs)

Tummy tuck

For many women when they hit middle age or beyond some form of cosmetic surgery is now the absolute norm, but surely ageing is not an illness – it's a fact of life? The emphasis should be about feeling great within yourself not pleasing other people. Medical science is changing so many aspects of our lives and also extending our lives way beyond the expectations of even a decade ago. Many women feel that cosmetic surgery is simply an extension of the opportunities opening up to them and therefore entirely a matter of choice. Interestingly, the men we canvassed on the subject were at worst indifferent to the notion of cosmetic surgery for women, at best quite anti it. So, in theory, it is up to you but we do recommend that you do your research, cf. *The Beauty Myth* by Naomi Wolf, before taking the plunge.
(v: Facial exercises)

Tweeds

The subtle, beautiful blend of colours that make a perfect tweed. It's one of the things that make us proud to be English, well actually mainly Scottish although there are many English estate tweeds, and Welsh tweeds too ... ho hum and thereby hangs a tale. But if you haven't got your own personal crag, highland, course of river, stretch of gorse or patch of heather, a beautifully cut tweed jacket gets you close.
(v: Suits, Vintage)

Twice is polite

Since the arrival of the Pill in 1963, casual sex has become part of modern life. Part of the fun is that in the heat of the moment there are no rules: the downside is that by the cold light of day, well, there are no rules. This can leave both parties floundering, uncertain and embarrassed and may, in the days to follow, lead to self-doubt and self-castigation. This is unnecessary. If we could all agree that 'twice is polite', i.e. once to do it and then once to get it right, the world would be a happier place. Alongside an agreement that this is not going to develop into a long-term relationship, this common courtesy denotes mutual respect and appreciation. It also adds an air of 'sweet sorrow' to the second goodbye. It could also be the basis for a long-term friendship instead (although we would suggest a bit of a break before contacting the relevant person again) and what could be nicer than that?

(v: Bachelors, It's a gift, One-night stands)

Two cures for love

1. Don't see him. Don't phone or write a letter.
2. The easy way: get to know him better.

– *Two Cures For Love*, WENDY COPE

(v: Drunk-dialling)

Two-thirty

Make 2.30 p.m. the time of day to make all your challenging or difficult calls. Whether it's to ask somebody out on a date, make an apology or ask your bank manager to extend your overdraft, it's the hour of non-refusal. It's post-lunch so the person has got through the worst of the morning's tasks and their blood sugar levels are reasonably high. You will, of course, still be mightily relieved if their phone goes straight to voicemail.

(v: Apologising, Grasping the nettle, Opening brown envelopes, Will you marry me?)

Two for two

If you see something and buy it and love it, if you have the cash buy two. That way, when the beloved garment, shoe, pen, jacket, rips, breaks or wears out and when they don't make them anymore, Hey Presto, you will already have another tucked away in your second drawer. Bliss.

(v: Style)

❧

(The) Underbrag or Humblebrag
The underbrag is when someone manages to show off wildly while simultaneously couching it in terms of self-deprecation – i.e. 'I'm so hopeless I don't know why they commissioned me to write the lead article' or 'I can't believe it's 20 years since I graduated from Oxford'. Yes faux modesty is understandable: in the most competitive job market in recent memory, the pressure to portray yourself, albeit slyly, as better than everyone else is intense. Facebook and Twitter status updates are dangerous territory, ditto the dreaded round-robin Christmas 'Dear all ...' letter. Unfortunately, some people can't seem to tell the difference between sharing positive information that others might actually want to know and flat-out boasting. We've become so accustomed to other people showing off that we don't even realise we're doing it ourselves. A return to genuine honesty is required.
(v: Name dropping, Narcissists)

Under parenting
'How to begin to educate a child. First rule: leave him alone.

Second rule: leave him alone. Third rule: leave him alone. That is the whole beginning.'
– D.H. LAWRENCE

Forget helicopter parents, who insist on little Jacinta eating gluten-free ice-cream, and Chinese Tiger Mothers who want their offspring learning Latin at three, there's a growing backlash against overparenting.

Slow parenting argues that less is more; hovering is dangerous; failure is fruitful. You really want your children to succeed? Learn when to leave them alone.

Children need time and space to motivate themselves and surprise surprise they learn to be resourceful when thrown back on their own resources.

The slow parenting movement insists there is no reason why a generation of parents who grew up walking to school, or taking public transport should be forbidding their kids to do the same.

Scientists tell us that play is the way to practice for adulthood, to build leadership, sociability, flexibility, resilience. To gain confidence in the world we need to make our own discoveries.

When we assume our children need more help than they actually do, we are undermining their abilities and hurting their self-esteem. Offering empty praise can also be unhelpful (kids tend to see through it). Too many afterschool activities can bombard children with choices way before their ability to handle them.

Autonomy – being your own companion – is a valuable life lesson. No one wants to go back to the Victorian days where children were 'seen and not heard', but sometimes it's nice to go to bed early with an apple and a book.

(v: Aloneness (as opposed to Loneliness), Big babies, Confidence, Expanding universe)

Undying love/ *Coup de foudre*

Is it a bird, is it a plane? No. It's Superman. If you can't eat, your knickers are a little bit slack and your heart feels like it's on beta blockers, don't call the doctor. You've fallen for him. That's all.

Urban tribes

For many of us, friends are often our most significant kinship group. As we delay pairing off, end long marriages or strive to stay independent adults for longer, we crave the depth of knowledge of people who know 'the real' us: people who reinforce our sense of self rather than try to change us.

American writer Ethan Watters has dubbed the phenomenon 'Urban Tribes', an intricate community of people who live and work together in various combinations, perform regular rituals and provide the same kind of support as families used to do. Good examples of urban tribes are shown in TV programmes such as *Sex and the City* and *Friends*, which show groups of friends who are always available for each other, a constant in each other's lives. One of the pleasures of living in the city is being able to see so many different tribes of friends, for the different parts of our jigsaw lives – from the school gate to sports chums to Friday-night cocktail friends. (All tribe members must be aware of the farcical elements of the others' lives.)

Every tribe needs a naughtier-than-thou friend – whose life is more rackety than your own. They might drink more, have affairs or stay out later. Whatever the vice, it's a pleasant reminder of your less well-behaved days, while impart-

ing a modest sense that you really are quite responsible now. And, of course, we all have the high-powered friend – always running in heels, dashing back from somewhere exotic and on the way to somewhere you haven't been invited. The advantage: you feel connected to a different world. The downside: as soon as she's gone you feel like howling: 'Where did I go wrong?'
(v: Friends, Spinnies)

Urban walking

You don't need specialist equipment – just lightweight trainers you can throw in your bag. Building 'active travel' into your day is far easier than going to the gym or the pool. You can do it in an art gallery, the park or while shopping. Or rather like the Grand Old Duke of York and his 10,000 men, you can march yourself to the top of the hill and march yourself down again.
(v: Ballooning weight, Comfort zone, Green exercise)

USP

We've all got one. Find out what yours is and make the most of it.
(v: You're the bomb)

⟆

Vagina monologues

'My teeth, my car, my vagina, my business.'

– KELLY OSBOURNE

(v: Cunt, Pelvic floor)

Variety is the spice of life

(v: Mojo)

(The) Veil

The vision of the veil, in whatever shape or form, can be a fairly discombobulating experience and, in the vexing international political landscape of the 21st century, raises complex issues. Many young women take to the veil for cultural and religious reasons, but responses to wearing the veil can be extreme. Joan Smith was recently taken to task for questioning what many see as sheer audacity: what the veil represents in Muslim culture. The Koran states 'Men have authority over women because God made the one superior over the other. Good women are obedient.' For Smith, the covering of the face and body was a feminist issue. She argues that 'It establishes women as sexual property of individual men- fathers, husbands and sons who are the only ones supposed to see them uncovered.' Others see it as a matter of individual choice set within a cultural context, like wearing a bra or having a facelift.

What is true is that the wearing of a veil or burka challenges many core aspects of what a liberal society purports to be. One of our number has worn a burka for research purposes and can report back that aside from being difficult to drive while wearing one as it hampers your peripheral vision, it is very, very hot indeed.

Veins

No one wants to talk about this, but veins are not your fault. Weight has nothing to do with them, nor does standing for long periods of time, and neither are they a direct result of pregnancy. 'Veins' run in families. A little-known fact is that men are more likely to suffer problems with veins, although women are more likely to ask for treatment.

You don't need to suffer in silence. Forget the idea that it's an old lady's ailment. Surgeons say we develop faulty valves in our leg veins at an alarmingly young age. One in twenty eleven-year-old schoolgirls has already lost her valves, and one in nine has by the age of eighteen. The problem starts when the valves in your veins fail and thus allow blood to go back the wrong way down your leg, which causes the vein to start dilating. It is believed that it is the stretching of this muscle coat that accounts for the painful symptoms such as tender veins and apparent bruising. In the old days, treatment was brutal: veins were removed by stripping under general anaesthetic, which caused bruising and required two to three weeks off work. In 80% of cases, they grew back within five years. The good news is we now have 'keyhole surgery' for veins. You can be in and out of hospital the same day and the recovery time is about two weeks.

(v: Legs, Necessary vanity)

Vermin

Pesky rats or jumping fleas, whatever it is it makes you feel a dirty Chaucerian slut from a back alley. A little bit like herpes. Not something you share. Tons of people have fleas, rats and mice hidden around their homes. Once in, get them straight out.

Damp, mild weather promotes furious breeding amongst these pesky beats. Make sure crumbs and food are not lying around (plates, please) and always wipe the surfaces. If you have pets, make sure you have them under strict flea control.

(A) Very public inconvenience

When Gordon Selfridge opened his eponymous store in 1909, one of its biggest selling points was the 'Ladies Room', which women would visit for its own sake. The creation of these toilets was a bellwether for women's rights and the fight for sexual equality. A lack of public toilets was an effective way to ensure that women stayed in or close to their homes. The arrival of the public convenience (how canny was Mr Selfridge?) acted as a nexus for a variety of things that helped women achieve equality, such as being able to ride a bicycle, a change in underwear and a relaxation of dress codes. The department store, in particular, benefited from the latter two developments.

(v: Lipstick, Politics)

Viagra

Let's not get into the gory details but if you want to have a satisfying sex life into your fifties and sixties it may be that your partner will need to neck some Viagra from time to time. It has been said that it is like making love to a diving board, but we suppose there are worse things. However, if you want a slightly more all-round good feeling, why not try Cialis?

(v: Salad days)

Vintage

Wear a 1920's tea dress or edgy retro jacket and you have that dash of untraceable cool. No danger of bumping into someone in the same thing. Each piece has its own secret history.

Back in the day families passed on cast-offs to relatives, not because it was chic – or even green – but because they were poor. As a result wearing hand-me-downs was humiliating. Punk changed everything, thank God, and suddenly it is cool to recycle, but the essential rule of thumb is don't dress in vintage head to foot, you may look too Miss Marple – but tweedy two-piece suits can be fashion gold. The trick is not to wear the librarian-worthy skirt and jacket together or if you insist make sure you are wearing fishnets too.

Buying vintage means you can be more ethical while enjoying your individuality. Second-hand has soul. In fact the new euphemism for used clothing is 'gently used' or 'love worn'. No longer a badge of shame – it's a badge of honour.

(v: Kirby grip, Tweed)

Violence against women

Can never be tolerated. If you find yourself a victim of abuse take stock now. It is ugly, unpleasant and frightening and contrary to popular opinion it's not defined by class and money. At a profound level it makes women feel ashamed and the men involved almost universally claim that women bring violence upon themselves. Be very clear it is not your fault. It is also a truly ghastly reference point for your children if you have them. Love has got nothing to do with it, in fact, love may be contributing to the problem. If you are the victim of domestic violence talk to a friend, seek help, set your boundaries. It may not be the end of your relationship but something absolutely has to change.
(v: Boundaries, Rape)

Visualisation

By using the power of your imagination you can relieve symptoms of illness, manage problems, or simply learn to relax in stressful situations. Important in every stage of life but never more so than when confronted by illness.
(v: Cancer buddy, CBT)

Vitamins

We all love stockpiling dinky bottles full of beta-carotene and selenium, but really we would be better off obtaining antioxidants and vitamins from fruit and vegetables.
(v: Eat your greens, Metabolism, Skin)

Vitti, Monica [icon]

Is Monica Vitti the sexiest woman on the planet? It's no surprise that Vitti's look – tousled hair, heavy kohled eyes, fabulous Roman nose – is still so seductive. Best known in the early 1960s for the films of Michelangelo Antonioni, her lover at that time, she embodied ambivalence and complexity and she also proved that blondes can do arthouse.

If you want to find your inner femme fatale, join LOVE-FiLM (www.lovefilm.com) and get out DVDs of Vitti in *La notte*, *L'eclisse*, *Il deserto rosso* and *L'avventura*, where she plays a chic, but emotionally detached woman drifting into a relationship with the lover of her missing girlfriend – it was billed as featuring 'the most provocative kiss ever filmed'.

You'll also know that Vitti started as the enigmatic refugee in Joseph Losey's spy-spoof *Modesty Blaise* alongside Terence Stamp. Today she lives quietly in her native Italy but remains the great no-age film star of the twentieth century.

(v: David Attenborough, Film club)

Volunteering

Is a brilliant way of getting over yourself and making a contribution to the world around you.

(v: Christmas, Get out of a rut and get involved, Self-pity)

❁

Waist (expanding)

If you are fashionably and boyishly slender don't bother to read this entry. If like most of us you are curvy of shape, looking after your waist is vital. Forget about dieting, forget about weighing yourself and just concentrate on fine-tuning your waist. A waist gives you shape, a graceful line and is for most men irresistibly sexy. All you have to do is find the clothes to match: nothing looks more gorgeous than a beautifully made corset on a woman with a proper waist. Looking after your waist also has some unexpected health benefits too. If you keep your waist trim you will, in due course, fend off dreary age-related medical conditions such as heart disease and diabetes.

(v: Ballooning weight, Boxing, Helen Mirren, Necessary vanity, Petticoats, Secret confidence, Vintage, Wear black wisely)

Walking away

Sometimes this is the only thing to do if a situation has become truly untenable.

(v: Almost date, Bores, Emergency exit)

War paint
Is just that. Remember that ladies. Go forth.
(v: Lipstick)

Ward wear
Looking and feeling good is vital to getting you on the road to recovery, so bring on the ward wear. Gone are the days when a pair of slippers and quilted dressing gown would suffice. No girls, now you require an eye-popping capsule wardrobe of ward wear. If you are thinking aeroplane garb, along with socks (cashmere socks are ruinously expensive but if someone offers go for it), a throw to snuggle up in and some comfortable pants, if you are allowed to wear them, you are on the right track. You need something that you can both pad about in (stitches permitting) and lounge about in while you are recuperating, as you always need to be slightly on guard in case that sexy doctor (or nurse) pops by to see you.

1. Eye masks are good for sleeping during the day.
2. An iPod will get you through pain, boredom and hospital insomnia. If you haven't got one of your own, borrow one, and if a kind friend asks if there is anything they can do to help, then downloading a selection of soothing and soul-calming music is a useful task you can ask of them.
3. Reading. We suggest some volumes of poetry. Anthologies are good: *Staying Alive*, published by Bloodaxe may have a particular resonance. Poems are easy to read in short bursts, particularly after an anaesthetic when concentration can be affected.

4. A Yuroll, to de-puff your face and help lymphatic drainage.
5. Writing paper is essential. Now is the chance to catch up on your thank-you letters.
6. Don't forget scent and mascara. And definitely dry shampoo.

Ward wear is the last thing you will be thinking about as the dreaded day dawns, but actually once you are out of your scratchy paper gown it's important to look and feel as good as you can; you never know who might visit, so go for comfy, loose-fitting linen trousers.
(v: Cancer, Childbirth, Hospital etiquette, Leaving the party, Necessary vanity, Secret confidence)

Walkers
Every woman over 40 needs a charismatic man she can take to parties who will laugh at her jokes and remember which cocktail she likes. You don't automatically sleep together (many of the best walkers are gay) but it might be quite nice if you did. Why shouldn't women who are between relationships make the same pragmatic decisions as men?
(v: Think like a man)

Water
Water is everything and we abuse it at our peril for it is vital for all forms of life. It represents physical freedom, purity, cleanliness. In 1810 Lord Byron, despite his club foot, found his ultimate freedom and challenge in swimming the choppy 4.8-kilometre stretch of the Hellespont, where the Black Sea flows to the Aegean, and Asia almost kisses Europe.

Water comes with bubbles, or still: through waterfalls, via rivers, showers, seas and rain. It can pound you and quench you, drown you and save you, and you cannot exist without it. Drink it in throughout the day to keep healthy, stealthy and wise.

It can baptise you and anoint you. And as many a fair maiden knows, there is simply nothing like it for simply washing that man right out of your hair. Literally. Rumour is, it works.

(v: Rain, Seaside, Skin, Wild swimming)

Wear black wisely

Particularly when you are older. You don't want to look like a Greek granny, an ageing Left Bank student or a backing singer for Iron Maiden. Think Fellini, then think pencil skirts and sling-backs, maybe topped off with a little cardigan, and you're away. So Anita Eckberg. Whatever you do don't bedeck yourself in black day in, day out. It's an easy trap because it feels failsafe. Try to think of black as a colour and then treat it with the appropriate respect.

The little black dress should be just that – little. Beautifully tailored hunting jackets are a good look with skirts or capri pants. As are cashmere wraps. Charcoal greys and deep dark purples are a little more forgiving on the crow's feet but a black pencil skirt gives you the perfect silhouette, so if it takes a pair of iron knickers or 'grippers' to pull it off, so be it.

(v: Colour me beautiful)

Wearing white dresses

It's rare for somebody to remain a virgin until they get married so nowadays the wearing of a white wedding dress is a symbolic gesture rather than a reflection of a reality. Back in the day if you were marrying for a second time a pretty dress or sensible suit was appropriate. Nowadays you can go to town. Again.

(v: Catching the bouquet, Wedding cakes, Will you marry me?)

Wedding cakes

What is fabulous about the way we live now is that we can still respect tradition but we can reinterpret it and bend it to our will. We've heard about modern wedding cakes made of cheese, jelly, profiteroles, sandwiches and digestive bis-cuits but the essential truth remains the same. A wedding cake represents abundance, fertility and hospitality and whether you cut it with a knife, a sabre or a cheeseparer, the symbolic moment when husband and wife cut the 'cake' is when they open up their newly minted marriage to family and friends. Today's wedding cake retains its iconic status but reflects the diversity of modern lives. It's so cool to see same-sex grooms or brides atop the cake. Not all marriages last forever but 99% of the time a marriage is made with the very best of intentions. Play your part.

(v: Catching the bouquet, Wearing white dresses, Will you marry me?)

Well put together

Is a fabulous, slightly counter-intuitive expression, for women who always seem to get it right. It means that the outfits are good, inspiringly arranged and either bang 'on trend' or foxily bohemian. It means that she knows how to sling together a certain bag with a certain high heel, and a particular print with a just-so fur stole. You wouldn't have necessarily thought of it but she has an innate originality, which means that she can do just that. She looks so great that you are happy to express your undiluted admiration for the fact that she wears it well.

(v: Animal prints, Elegance, Fur, Style, Tweed, Vintage)

Wellington boots

Although once associated with the British aristocracy, the wellington boot is now a must-have fashion accessory, sought after by both young and old from New York to Shanghai.

In 1817, Arthur Wellesley, 1st Duke of Wellington, instructed his shoemaker to make a simple modification of his stiff leather boot. What resulted was a hardwearing yet comfortable boot that could be worn both in battle and in the drawing room. According to Adam Edwards, author of *A Short History of the Wellington Boot* (2006), the wellington boot tells the tale of the rise and fall of empires, corporate piracy, fetish wear and transatlantic rivalry. The wellington boot has come to encapsulate the image of Britain's war heroes, voyagers, the royal family and even fashion models of the moment.

Frankly, it can look a little ridiculous wearing wellington boots to the opera. However, as long as you're within striking distance of a bit of grass then they are indeed sartorially acceptable. Kate Moss may grace the fields of Glastonbury in hers, but the wonderful quality of the wellington boot is that they can be embraced by all of us whatever our size. Whether we choose to wear them with jeans or a dress, the wellington boot is the essence of style, in that it's both comfortable and practical, so we'll never look like mutton dressed up as lamb.

Westwood, Dame Vivienne [icon]

'I think people should make an effort every single day to try to look special.'

Wet-wipes

Easily and cheaply acquired, they are probably hideously ecologically dodgy. However, from loo seats (although we promise you won't get pregnant sitting on one) to baby sick to dog-poo (and that's just the half of it), they are unbelievably and stupidly useful. If you have everything but the kitchen sink in your handbag, you may as well throw in a packet of wet-wipes, just because you can.

(v: Babies, Festivals, Toy boys)

What becomes of the broken-hearted?

Unless you are very unlucky, you will get over it.

(v: Age of bereavement, Agony)

What we learned from the war

How to build a bridge

Waterloo Bridge, fondly known as 'the ladies' bridge' was, in the main, built by women as part of the Second World War effort. During this period women worked in the construction industry, pitching in on everything from joinery, carpentry, welding and carrying cradles of molten metal, much of the undocumented war effort was dependent on them.

Not to waste anything

Don't throw things away. For instance the remains of a chicken carcass can be used to make risotto, soup or chicken curry. Buy fresh food; it's more versatile when it comes to cooking. As far as possible try to buy locally sourced products. The rule of thumb with convenience foods is that the more ingredients they contain, the worse they are for you. Keep packets of rice and pulses in your store cupboard to a sensible minimum and use them up. As a result of the austerity measures of the Forties and early Fifties, Britain was healthier than it had ever been.

<u>Dig for victory (victory gardens)</u>

Everybody's doing it – including the Obamas – and it's just about possible that Detroit, once the heart of industrial America, may be able to save itself from disintegration by turning itself into a gardening community. If you have a window ledge, a tiny front or back garden, a patio or a deer park you can start digging. Buy packets of seeds and follow the instructions. Grow tomatoes, potatoes, lettuces, straw-berries and herbs. If you have enough space, plant apple and pear trees.

(v: Cooking, Make do and mend, Pre-threaded needles)

Where's my fucking pony?

All of us from time to time have an over-developed sense of entitlement.

(v: Riding)

White

Originally inspired by Queen Elizabeth the Queen Mother, who wore white when she mourned her mother on a visit to Paris in 1937, Coco Chanel loved a touch of white at her collar. She knew that it throws light up to the face; making almost everyone look as if they are in a picture painted by Vermeer.

Linen sheets. Pure white walls brighten up your life. Just keep it all as fresh as a daisy.

(v: Beds, Wearing white dresses, Wedding cakes)

Whither feminism?

Where did feminism go and why has it become such a dirty word? Presumably it has overridden its jokey 'wimmin' satirical soubriquet by now. Shouldn't our deep, complex and poignant history be a key element in the educational curriculum for young women (and men) in the twenty-first century?

If the whole issue was really about good healthcare, equal pay and the right to vote, surely we need to pay more than a little respect to those who led the way – such as Florence Nightingale, Marie Stopes and the Pankhursts. And what about 'books as bombs'? Authors such as Simone de Beauvoir, Betty Friedan, Germaine Greer, Kate Millett and Andrea Dworkin drove the public debate about gender and were often pilloried and reviled in their attempt to do so. There is a long list of people we need to thank, so please let's not forget what they stood for, who they stood up to, and how much we owe them.

(v: Hilary Mantel, Principles)

Wifey

Inspired by the Marquis of Bath, this pet name is deployed by young female celebrities (Cara Delevigne, Rihanna) for their BF. Fun girl-to-girl endearment but smacks slightly of condescension to the real thing.

(v: Totes amaze: abbreviations and neologisms)

Wild

'I'm not dangerous, I'm deadly.'

– ANITA PALLENBERG

Wild nights

'Wild nights – Wild nights!
Were I with thee
Wild nights should be
Our luxury!
Futile – the winds –
To a Heart in port –
Done with the Compass –
Done with the Chart!
Rowing in Eden –
Ah – the Sea!
Might I but moor – tonight –
In thee!'
– '*Wild nights – Wild nights*', EMILY DICKINSON

Wild swimming

'A form of positive existentialism, a sensual well-meaning love for life in which one is immersed in the present.'
– *Wild Swim*, KATE REW

(v: Adventure, Flow, Water)

Will you marry me?

This is the twenty-first century. It's okay to ask.
(v: Engagement, Wearing white dresses, Wedding cakes)

Wine

There's a lot of snobbery talked about wine. You may be someone who knows your Fleurie from your Rioja, or just a 'one above' house type of girl, but a glass of wine marks the moment you award yourself a unit of pleasure. Sheer joy.
(v: Ballooning waist, Benders, Emotional overdrinking)

Winter

'Unseen buds, infinite, hidden well,
Under the snow and ice, under the darkness, in every
   square or cubic inch.'
– 'Unseen Buds', WALT WHITMAN

'When daffodils begin to peer,
With heigh! the doxy over the dale,
Why, then comes in the sweet o' the year;
For the red blood reigns in the winter's pale.'
– *The Winter's Tale*, IV. iii., WILLIAM SHAKESPEARE

Who doesn't love the first chill of winter combined with a bright blue sky or the joy of waking up to a snowbound winter world or the mystery of making a magic spell to celebrate the winter solstice? On the other hand, whose heart doesn't sink at the thought of waking up, still exhausted, in the darkness, and feel their spirits lowering when the street lights come on at 4 p.m.? Winter, quite literally, can feel like our darkest hour and seems at times to be never-ending but don't forget that it's just a matter of time before the first crocuses come pushing up through the earth. Winter is when the world renews itself again – and you are included in that.
(v: Blues, Magic spells, SAD, Suicide)

Wisdom

'Wisdom is the daughter of experience.'
– LEONARDO DA VINCI

(v: Libraries)

Witch-hunts

The persecution of women through accusations of witch-craft has a dark history in the western world. But while women may no longer be drowned in barrels in fast-flowing rivers or burnt at the stake, witch-hunts are still alive and well. The focus hasn't changed much. Generally a woman perceived as not taking a traditional route in terms of career, marriage or children can come under scrutiny and then find herself the subject of an obscene level of criticism. So next time you see a woman being hounded through the press, don't leap to conclusions, research the facts and, perhaps more importantly, the way the facts are presented and think again. If necessary, offer support via the web or any other means at your disposal.

(v: Violence against women)

Wolf-whistling

Being wolf-whistled at in the street can feel boring and undermining but in the new age of pornification, it has taken on an almost Sixties, retro *Carry On* feel. Of all the sexist assaults, wolf-whistling has begun to be the least offensive and you may well miss it much more than you imagine once it finally stops.

(v: It's a gift, Saucy seaside postcard)

Women's movement

The seven demands of the movement were . . .

1. Equal pay.
2. Equal education and job opportunities.
3. Free 24-hour nurseries.
4. Free contraception and abortion on demand.

5. Financial and legal independence.
6. An end to discrimination against lesbians and a woman's right to define her sexuality.
7. Freedom from intimidation by the threat or use of violence and an end to male aggression and dominance.

Workwear
(v: Suits, Vintage, Well put together)

(The) Worst has already happened
Often the thing you fear most has already happened to you.

Wrath
'Don't let the sun go down on your wrath.'
– EPHESIANS 4:26

'You are allowed quite a lot of late Sundowns.'
– ANTONIA FRASER

Wrinkles
Some people hate their wrinkles and some people love them. Depending on your perspective, they are either the mark of your experience and the map of your life or they are the signifier of impending middle age and all the indignities that come with it. We recommend that you focus on the former.
(v: Facial exercises, Skin)

Xenophobia
We are all multicultural now.

XXXs
Spread them reasonably liberally but wisely.

Yoga
You've read enough about the benefits of yoga to last a lifetime, and maybe the next one too. Suffice to say it is 'a good thing', it comes in a variety of forms and there is probably a yoga studio (reasonably) near you, but don't forget yoga is a series of meditations not a quick-fix exercise routine.
(v: Ballooning weight, Waist)

You decide
We all give advice and most of us seek advice and there is plenty of advice, whether you want it or not, in the pages of this book. But only you can decide.
(v: Accepting advice)

You're the bomb!

A fantastic Trinidadian expression which means that you are it, you make it happen, you are where it starts and finishes. 'You're the bomb'.

(v: Bien dans ta peau, Necessary vanity, Secret confidence)

You're only young twice

Stop procrastinating. Stop making endless lists. Or telling people at dinner parties how you're going to write a novel/ move to New York/start that lavender farm. We've heard it all before. And it's boring – though we say it with love. You're the only grown-up in the room now. Just give it a go. You only have to do it once. If you hate it, well, then you have your answer, but you might just surprise yourself and those around you.

Zoology

'Life can only be understood backwards; but it must be lived forwards.'

– SØREN KIERKEGAARD

(v: David Attenborough)

❧

Bibliography

Acocella, Joan, *New Yorker*, 17 November 2008, 'The Child Trap: The rise of overparenting'

Adewunmi, Bim, *Guardian*, June 2011, 'Faith-based fashion takes off online: Clothes designed for women who want to dress modestly are a growing phenomenon'

Andre, Rae, *Positive Solitude: A Practical Program for Mastering Loneliness and Achieving Self-Fulfillment* (Harper Perennial, 1992)

Athill, Diana, *Life Class: The Selected Memoirs of Diana Athill* (Granta, 2010)

Behrendt, Greg and Liz Tuccillo, *He's Just Not That Into You: The No-Excuses Truth to Understanding Guys* (Harper Element, 2005)

Bernstein, Elizabeth, *Wall Street Journal*, 14 August 2012, 'Are We All Braggarts Now? Boasting Epidemic Goes Viral; Crowing Boosts Self Esteem but It's Annoying'

Bond, Michael, *New Scientist*, 23 February 2009, 'When you should trust your gut'

de Botton, Alain, *Status Anxiety* (Penguin, 2005)

Bunting, Madeleine, *Guardian*, April 2011, 'Nigella Lawson and the great burkini cover-up: Was Nigella

Lawson's beach burkini a defence against the Australian sun, or a subversive political statement?'

Burchill, Julie, *Guardian*, 9 September 2000, 'Relax? Don't do it'

Burkeman, Oliver, *Guardian*, 15 August 2012, 'I'd never boast about it, but I'm a master of the new art of underbragging'

Campbell, Joseph, *The Hero with a Thousand Faces* (Fontana, 1993)

Cosslett, Rhiannon Lucy, *Guardian*, 8 January 2013, 'Slut-shaming shames us all'

Csikszentmihalyi, Mihaly, *Flow: The Psychology of Optimal Experience* (Harper Perennial, 2008)

Day, Elizabeth, *Observer*, 11 August 2012, 'Bye bye, Kardashians: Olympic athletes give women new, strong role models: Skinny models, actresses and reality TV stars are no match for our powerful female athletes. Now, after London 2012, all women can value their bodies and play to their strengths'

Didion, Joan, *The Year of Magical Thinking* (Fourth Estate, 2006)

Dreger, Alice, *The New York Times*, 21 August 2009, 'Where's the Rulebook for Sex Verification?'

Dolgoff, Stephanie, *My Formerly Hot Life: Dispatches From Just the Other Side of Young* (Ballantine Books, 2010)

Duggan Emily and Shannon Firth, 19 August 2012, 'Games winners inspire women to take up sport: Legacy hopes borne out by poll',

Ephron, Nora, *I Feel Bad About My Neck: And Other Thoughts on Being a Woman* (Black Swan, 2008)

Firestone, Lisa, *Psychology Today*, 2 April 2012, 'The Abuse of Overparenting: We're all guilty of over-protective acts that hurt our children'

Fraser, Giles, *Guardian*, 12 December 2011, 'Occupy's starfish power regenerates protest: The Occupy movement's absence of leaders that so baffles the establishment is what makes it a catalyst for lasting change'

Gibbs, Nancy, *Time*, 20 November 2009, 'The Growing Backlash Against Overparenting'

Gluck, Marion and Vicki Edgson, *It Must Be My Hormones* (Michael Joseph, 2010)

Grouse, Anouchka, *No More Silly Love Songs: A Realist's Guide to Romance* (Portobello Books, 2011)

Hamzelou, Jessica, *New Scientist*, 1 December 2009, 'The loneliness of three degrees of separation'

Hoggard, Liz, *How to Be Happy: Lessons From Making Slough Happy* (Ebury/BBC Books, 2005)

Israel, Betsy, *Bachelor Girl: The Secret History of Single Women in the 20th Century* (William Morrow, 2002)

Kennedy, Sister Stanislaus, *Moments of Stillness* (Transworld Ireland, 2009)

Meston, Cindy and David Buss, *Why Women Have Sex: Understanding Sexual Motivation from Adventure to Revenge (and Everything in Between)* (Bodley Head, 2010)

Moore, Thomas, *Care of the Soul: How to Add Depth and Meaning to Your Everyday Life* (Piatkus Books, 1992)

Monro, Kate, *The First Time: True Tales of Virginity Lost & Found (Including my Own)* (Icon Books, 2011)

Moore, Suzanne, *Guardian*, 15 January 2011, 'It's time to get angry: all this polite and smiley feminism is getting us nowhere'

Moran, Caitlin, *How To Be a Woman* (Ebury, 2011)

O'Connell, John and Jessica Cargill-Thompson, *The Midlife Manual* (Short Books, 2010)

Patterson, Christina, *Independent*, 10 April 2009, 'Martin Amis the Gynocrat'

Perel, Esther, *Mating in Captivity: Sex, Lies, and Domestic Bliss* (Hodder & Stoughton, 2007)

Pine, Karen J. and Simonne Gnessen, *Sheconomics* (Headline, 2009)

Robson, Julia, *The National*, 27 June 2010, 'Return of androgyny gives women more fashion options,'

Ross, Tim, *Daily Telegraph*, 9 December 2010, 'One in five women is childless by the age of 45'.

Ruddock, Jill Shaw, *The Second Half of Your Life* (Vermilion, 2011)

Scanlon, Jennifer, *Bad Girls Go Everywhere: The Life of Helen Gurley Brown* (Oxford University Press, 2009)

Seligman, Martin E.P., PhD, *Authentic Happiness: Using the New Positive Psychology to Realise Your Potential for Lasting Fulfilment* (Nicholas Brealey Publishing, 2003)

Shalit, Wendy, *A Return to Modesty* (Pocket Books, 2000)

Shilling, Jane, *The Stranger in the Mirror: A Memoir of Middle Age* (Chatto & Windus, 2011)

Strauss, Neil, *The Game* (Canongate Books, 2007)

Tarrant, Shira, *Bitch Magazine*, May 2009, 'The Great Cover-Up: Can High Necklines Cure Low Morals?'

Tweedie, Jill, *Letters from A Fainthearted Feminist* (Robson, 1998)

Vernon, Mark, *The Philosophy of Friendship* (Palgrave Macmillan, 2006)

Watson, Shane, *How to Meet A Man After Forty And Other Midlife Dilemmas Solved* (Penguin, 2009)

Watters, Ethan, *Urban Tribes: Are Friends the New Family?* (Bloomsbury, 2004)

Wolf, Naomi, *The Beauty Myth: How Images of Beauty Are Used Against Women* (Vintage, 2007)

Wolpert, Lewis, *You're Looking Very Well: The Surprising Nature of Getting Old* (Faber & Faber, 2011)

Some entries in the book are inspired by features and reviews that have appeared in the *Evening Standard*, *Observer*, *Independent* and *Red* magazine – LH

Credits

p.93 *I Capture the Castle*, Dodie Smith, 1949. Reprinted by kind permission of The Random House Group Ltd and Laurence Fitch Ltd

p.97 *Lassie Come Home*, Eric Knight (Cassell, Orion Publishing Group, 1942)

p.110 'Never Again Would Birds' Song be the Same', *The Poetry of Robert Frost*, Robert Frost (Vintage Classics, 2001). Reprinted by kind permission of The Random House Group Ltd

p.125 *One Flew Over the Cuckoo's Nest*, Ken Kesey (Penguin (new edition), 2005)

p.151–2 India Knight, *The Sunday Times*, NI Syndication

p.162 & 188 *The Pursuit of Love*, Nancy Mitford (Penguin, 2010) By kind permission of Rogers, Coleridge and White

p.188 *One Art*, Elizabeth Bishop (Chatto & Windus, 1994) Reprinted by permission of The Random House Group Ltd

p.189 © Patrick Marber, *Closer* (Methuen Drama, Bloomsbury Publishing Plc., 1997)

p.203 *The Stranger in the Mirror*, Jane Shilling (Chatto & Windus, 2011). Reprinted by permission of The Random House Group Ltd

p.224–5 'Fashion, beauty and women's lives: the great debate', Emma John, 27 February 2011, the Guardian News & Media Ltd 2011

p.244 *The Power of Now*, Eckhart Tolle (Hodder & Stoughton, 2001)

p.252 *Anger in the Sky*, Susan Ertz (Hodder & Stoughton, 1943)

p.277 *The Turquoise Bee: The Love Songs of the 6th Dalai Lama*, Rick Fields (Harper Collins US, 1994)

p.282 *Status Anxiety*, Alain de Botton (Penguin, 2005)
p.294 *Outliers*, Malcolm Gladwell (Penguin, 2009)
p.324 *Wild Swim*, Kate Rew (Guardian Books, 2009)

Can't Live Without

Websites

www.absolutevintage.co.uk – a massive selection of vintage clothing

www.alcoholics-anonymous.org.uk – alcoholics anonymous

www.alittlebird.com – culture and style recommendations

www.ar457.com – argan oil cosmetics

www.argos.co.uk – arm weights

www.artisanparfumeur.com – the scent of decadence

www.avenue32.co.uk – luxury shopping online

www.batistehair.co.uk – dry shampoo

www.biotherm.co.uk – Skindrink serum

www.bookgroup.info – local reading groups

www.bravissimo.com – bras for bigger boobs

www.bumbleandbumble.com – hair fixers

www.byterry.com – make-up for grown-ups

www.camper.com – wide-fit shoes and boots

www.canoethewye.co.uk – on the river

www.caudalie.com – Caudalie Vinoperfect complexion correction

www.citylit.ac.uk – night school

uk.clarins.com – face powder that defeats shine

www.clarisonic.com – facebrush

www.coco-de-mer.com – saucy knickers etc.

www.counselling-directory.org.uk – professional support for any problem

www.cremedelamer.co.uk – super lip balm

www.cutlerandgross.com – very classy shades

www.darphin.com – French skincare

www.dauntbooks.co.uk – books

www.divorcesolicitors.com – family lawyers specialising in divorce, adoption and domestic abuse

www.thedispensary.net – frocks from Notting Hill boutique

www.drhauschka.co.uk – quince and rose day creams. Perfect for young girls

www.drifters.co.uk – narrowboat drifters

www.dyptyqueparis.com – candles and scent

www.elizabetharden.co.uk – night cream

www.environ.co.za – alpha-hydroxy acid creams

www.esteelauder.co.uk – Advanced Night Repair, what it says on the tin

www.estherderm.com/en – lotions and potions from France

www.evafraser.com – facial fitness

www.evelom.com – hot cloth cleanser

www.famousdave.co.uk – fake tan

www.figleaves.com – swimwear and shape wear

www.firebox.com – solar charger for phones

www.fitflop.com – wellness footwear

www.uk.freecycle.org – 'freecyling' for unwanted possessions

www.gaggiagelatiera.co.uk – ice-cream maker

www.georgiafoster.com – hypnotherapy for emotional overdrinking

www.gerrysummerjewellery.com – fruity cocktail rings at all prices www.getsomeheadspace.com – tips on meditation

www.greatwriting.co.uk – creative writing forum

www.harissalon.com – hair and beauty

www.uk.havaianas.co.uk – the original flip flop

www.healgel.co.uk – advanced skin rescue gel

www.hermes.com – unisex scent

www.ila-spa.com – organic skincare for sensitive skin

www.imedeen.co.uk – vitamins for skin

www.jaeger.co.uk – gorgeous boutique clothing and
    accessories

www.johnlewis.com – black-out blinds

www.kiehls.co.uk – Creme with Silk Groom, perfect for
    long hair

www.korres.com – scented Greek skincare

www.landmarktrust.org.uk – rental properties for weekend
    breaks

www.languagecourses.co.uk – learn a language

www.laprarie.com – posh perfection

www.lasenza.co.uk – tit-tape or 'stick and show roll'

www.lauraleejewellery.com – trinkets, treasures and
    talismans

www.the-little-things-in-life.co.uk – vintage wedding
    jewellery

uk.lizearle.com – top cleanser

www.lkbennett.com – clothing

www.londonsmiling.com – fantastic dental practice

www.luluguinness.com – 1950s-style handbags

www.lumie.com – mood-brightening lights

www.mamamio.com – all over body buff care

www.margaretdabbs.co.uk – goddess of feet

www.mariobadescu.com – sorts out tricky skin

www.themayfairpractice.com – doctor for discreet botox

www.miicosmetics.com – the best face base in the business

www.millerharris.com – niche scent

www.mooncup.co.uk – periods without pollution

www.moroccanoil.com – serious hair nourishment

www.myswitzerland.com – train holidays

www.nationaltrustcottages.co.uk – rental properties for weekend breaks

www.neilson.co.uk – sailing courses and adventure

www.neomorganics.com – luxury candles and scent diffusers

www.nespresso.com – espresso machine

www.netaporter.com – designer clothing and accessories

www.nowness.com – all things fashion, culture, art and gastronomy

www.outerreefsurfschool.com – surfing

www.perriconemd.com – cosmeceuticals

www.philipkingsley.co.uk – swim cap hair protection

www.pinelodgeexmoor.co.uk – riding holidays and cottages in Exmoor National Park

www.powerplate.com – Virgin gyms and elsewhere

www.the-print-warehouse.co.uk – embossed business cards

www.quirkyalone.net – discussion site for cool singles

www.rapidlash.com – eyelash miracle grow

www.rawfirepits.co.uk – portable fireplaces

www.salomon.com/uk – hiking shoes

www.scholl.com – party feet

www.theschooloflife.com – talks, gigs, secular sermons

www.sipsmith.com – Hammersmith gin

www.southbankcentre.co.uk – free music events

www.spacenk.co.uk – skincare and make-up from around the world www.spasecretsmagazine.com – everything mind, body and soul

www.stripwaxbar.com – waxing

www.suedevittbeauty.com – no-fuss eye pencils

www.surfdome.com – for adventure

www.sustrans.org – cycling

www.sweatybetty.com – sportswear and fitness classes for women

www.ted.com – download brainy 20-minute talks

www.tendskin.com – stops razer/wax burn

www.thelmandlouise.com – women's travel site

www.toast.co.uk – clothing and shoes

www.triyoga.co.uk – yoga and meditation

www.tweezerman.com – precision plucking

www.universalaunts.co.uk – parties, escorting children, help

www.violetvintagejewellery.com – beautiful and accessible vintage jewellery

www.viviscal.co.uk – healthy hair growth

www.volunteering.org.uk – volunteering

www.theweek.co.uk – the week's news in one hour

www.weleda.co.uk – homeopathic ointments

www.thewhitecompany.com – bedding

www.thewhiteleyclinic.co.uk – help with vein problems

www.wildswim.com – wild swimming

www.thewinesociety.com – wine tasting

www.yapp.co.uk – family run wine specialists

www.ysl.com – bright eyes

www.yuroll.com – jade face roller

Books

According to Queenie, Beryl Bainbridge (Little, Brown & Company, 2001)

A Legacy, Sybille Bedford (Penguin, 2005)

Angel, Elizabeth Taylor (Virago, 2006)

Ariel, Sylvia Plath (Faber & Faber, 1968)

Armadale, Wilkie Collins (Penguin, 2004)

The Bachelors, Muriel Spark (Penguin, 1963)

Bad Blood: A Memoir, Lorna Sage (Fourth Estate, 2001)

By Grand Central Station I Sat Down and Wept, Elizabeth Smart (Flamingo, 1992)

Castle Rackrent, Maria Edgeworth (Oxford Paperbacks, 2008)

Cold Comfort Farm, Stella Gibbons (Penguin, 2006)

Collected Poems of Emily Dickinson (Barnes and Noble, 2003)

The Fountainhead, Ayn Rand (Penguin, 2007)

The Haunting of Hill House, Shirley Jackson (Penguin, 2009)

The Heat of the Day, Elizabeth Bowen (Penguin, 1987)

The House of Mirth, Edith Wharton (Penguin, 1979)

I Capture the Castle, Dodie Smith (Vintage, 2008)

The King's General, Daphne du Maurier (Virago, 2004)

The Lover, Marguerite Duras (Flamingo, 1994)

Orlando, Virginia Woolf (Wordsworth, 1995)

The Passion of New Eve, Angela Carter (Virago, 1982)

Persuasion, Jane Austen (Penguin, 2006)

The Pursuit of Love, Nancy Mitford (Penguin, 1999)

The Rover, Aphra Behn (Nick Hern Books, 1999)

Under a Glass Bell, Anaïs Nin (Ohio University Press), 1995

Villette, Charlotte Brontë (Penguin, 2004)

Music

'All I Want', Joni Mitchell (*Blue*, 1972)

'Band of Gold', Freda Payne (1970)

'Blue Valentine', Tom Waits (*Blue Valentine*, 1978)

'Clean Up Woman', Betty Wright (*I Love the Way You Love*, 1972)

'Cry Me A River', Julie London (1955)

'Diamonds Are a Girl's Best Friend', Marilyn Monroe (*Gentlemen Prefer Blondes* soundtrack, 1953)

'Fake Plastic Trees', Radiohead (*The Bends*, 1995)

'Gloria', Patti Smith (*Horses*, 1975)

'I'd Rather Go Blind', Etta James (*Her Best*, 1968)

'I'll Take You There', The Staple Singers (*Be Altitude: Respect Yourself*, 1972)

'Is That All There Is?', Peggy Lee (1969)

'I Think I'm a Mother', PJ Harvey (*To Bring You My Love*, 1995)

'Jolene', Dolly Parton (*Jolene*, 1974)

'Keys to Your Heart', The 101'ers (*5 Star Rock & Roll Petrol*, 1976)

'Love is a Losing Game', Amy Winehouse (*Back to Black*, 2006)

'Milord', Edith Piaf (1959)

'Mrs Robinson', The Lemonheads (*It's a Shame About Ray*, 1992)

'My Funny Valentine', Chet Baker (1952)

'Piece of My Heart', Big Brother and the Holding Company (*Cheap Thrills*, 1968)

'Roadhouse Girl', Ray LaMontagne (*One Lonesome Saddle*, 2002)

'She Bangs the Drums', The Stone Roses (*The Stone Roses*, 1989)

'Someone to Love', The Great Society (1990)

'Strange Fruit', Billie Holiday (1939)

'Too Darn Hot', Ella Fitzgerald (*Ella Fitzgerald Sings the Cole Porter Songbook*, 1956)

Film

Alice Doesn't Live Here Anymore (dir: Martin Scorsese, 1974)

All About Eve (dir: Joseph L.Mankiewicz, 1950)

All About My Mother (dir: Pedro Almodóvar, 1999)

Annie Hall (dir: Woody Allen, 1977)

A Streetcar Named Desire (dir: Eliza Kazan, 1951)

The Bitter Tea of General Yen (dir: Frank Capra, 1933)

Black Narcissus (dir: Michael Powell & Emeric Pressburger, 1947)

Body Heat (dir: Lawrence Kasdan, 1981)

Bridesmaids (dir: Paul Feig, 2011)

Chinatown (dir: Roman Polanski, 1974)

The Devil Wears Prada (dir: David Frankel, 2006)

Double Indemnity (dir: Billy Wilder, 1944)

Fishtank (dir: Andrea Arnold, 2009)

Gone With the Wind (dir: Victor Fleming, 1939)

The Graduate (dir: Mike Nichols, 1967)

La Dolce Vita (dir: Federico Fellini, 1960)

The Last Picture Show (dir: Peter Bogdanovich, 1971)

Lolita (dir: Adrian Lyne, 1997)

Lost in Translation (dir: Sophia Coppola, 2003)

Thelma & Louise (dir: Ridley Scott, 1991)

To Kill a Mockingbird (dir: Robert Mulligan, 1962)

Vertigo (dir: Alfred Hitchcock, 1958)

Whatever Happened to Baby Jane? (dir: Robert Aldrich, 1962)

Who's Afraid of Virginia Woolf? (dir: Mike Nichols, 1966)

The Year of Living Dangerously (dir: Peter Weir, 1982)

Heartfelt thanks to:

First and foremost our publishers: Amanda Harris, Elisabeth Schmitz, Sarah Maclachlan.

Alexander Cochran and the fantastic team at Conville & Walsh, Tim Burke on Libraries, Bridget Connolly for making a working life possible, DBC Pierre on Magical Thinking, Simon Fellowes for the title, David Huggins, fellow embryo, Misha Glenny (you know why), Johnnie Fiori on Manifesting a Man, Gerard Kite for life support, Carolyn Holder on Perfect Mayonnaise, Louise Allen-Jones and Alice Keens-Soper for laughing in the right places, Alexander, Emelia and Louis Maltby for so much, Harland and Jane Miller for being themselves, Caroline Muir on Embroidery, Leonie Profit for Facial Acupuncture, Sasha Speed and all at Coutts and Co. on 'Money matters', Johnnie Shand Kydd for photography, Nic Cheetham and John Mitchinson on Benders, Brandi Stiles on Handstand Revolution, Nigel Langford and Harriet Vyner for Saturday morning calls, last but truly first Simon Finch and remembering Kate Courtenay, Caroline Hardy and Katie Pearson who left the party far too early.

– CBC

Simone Noakes for verbal brilliance; Damian Barr, Peter Da Silva, Helen Ward, Jean Egbunike, Geraldine Rudge, Lauren Shanley, Dale Russell, for case studies and encouragement. Eve Lom, Sue Devitt, Marcia Kilgore and Terry de Gunzberg for grown-up beauty advice. Hari Salem for blow-drying genius. Clare Park for photography. Georgia Foster for emotional overdrinking strategies. Uchenna Okoye of London Smiling for brilliant dental tips. Dr Mark Whitely (aka Dr Leg) for vein care. Margaret Dabbs for all things feet. Dr Marion Gluck for bio-identical hormone research. Andy Puddicombe for meditation. Joanna Hall for sharing her urban walking technique. Not forgetting Paddy Renouf for expert cocktail guidance. And Kate Mosse for believing in the project.

– LH

The Greys, for everything, always, Sister Kate, for copious amounts of out bailing and hilarity. Idina Pirie, for her friendship and inspiration with our beloved Min, Muff and Harry for letting me always run away to the farm, Sean the Taxi for keeping me on the road, Lucinda Chambers, the good fairy at the end of the garden, Hector Christie for seeing another way, and Kate Chancellor for the next good idea!

– SJL

Special thanks also to Jo Jones and Preeya Varsani at John Frieda for the fantastic hair serum, to Jaeger for the beautiful and generous accessories, to Louise Nason at Melt in Notting Hill for the divine chocolate, and to Ruthe Wainman at Thelma & Louise for the vouchers, all of which were used for our Dangerous Women gift.